MASTERING THE
INFORMATION AGE

■ ■ ■ ■

MASTERING THE INFORMATION AGE

A Course in Working Smarter, Thinking Better, and Learning Faster

MICHAEL J. MCCARTHY

JEREMY P. TARCHER, INC.
Los Angeles

Library of Congress Cataloging-in-Publication Data

McCarthy, Michael J. (Michael John), 1939–
    Mastering the information age : a course in working smarter,
thinking better, and learning faster / Michael J. McCarthy.
        p.   cm.
    ISBN 0-87477-537-X : $22.95 — ISBN 0-87477-575-2 (pbk.) : $12.95
    1. Learning.   2. Study, Method of.   3. Mental discipline—
Problems, exercises, etc.   4. Information retrieval—Problems,
exercises, etc.   I. Title.
LB1060.M37   1990   90-39573
371.3'028'1—dc20   CIP

Jeremy P. Tarcher, Inc.
5858 Wilshire Blvd., Suite 200
Los Angeles, CA 90036

Distributed by St. Martin's Press, New York

Design by Gary Hespenheide
Illustrations by STRADE, Denver, Colo.: Jim Golden

Manufactured in the United States of America
10 9 8 7 6 5 4 3 2 1

First Edition

■ ■ ■ ■

I dedicate this book to two women: To my mother Mary Louise McCarthy, who started me off with a lively curiosity about life and an insatiable hunger for learning. And to my beloved wife and best friend, Kathryn McCarthy, whose encouragement, inspiration, love, and support have made me who I have become.

■ ■ ■ ■

CONTENTS

■ ■ ■ ■

ACKNOWLEDGMENTS

In a general sense, my heartfelt gratitude goes to the many friends and teachers who have stimulated my thinking and contributed to my personal growth throughout the years. Thank you for being there.

In more specific terms, I wish to acknowledge my father Don McCarthy, a journalist and author, who taught me the power of words; my publisher Jeremy P. Tarcher for recognizing the gap that this book fills; my unrelenting editor, Rick Benzel, who contributed greatly to this book in many ways, and Paul Murphy, managing editor, for his expertise in putting the book together. In addition, I would like to thank Don Hawkins of AT&T, author Alfred Glossbrenner and Kathy Mulvey of DIALOG Information Services for their suggestions on Chapter 8; Dr. Jeffery Thompson for his guidance on neurophysiology; Mary Snyder for her help and support; Jim Golden of Strade (Denver), the artist whose creative genius produced the illustrations for this book; all of the students from my seminars who have taught me so much; and my friend Chester Stern for his incessant prodding and encouragement. The publisher also wishes to thank Richard Greene for his suggestions and time spent on Chapter 8.

Finally, it is with the utmost appreciation that I acknowledge Jack Forem, a writer I greatly respect and admire, for his collaboration on the final manuscript. Jack's monumental contribution of original ideas, skillful writing, and perceptive insights lifted *Mastering the Information Age* to its present level of excellence.

■ ■ ■ ■

INTRODUCTION

It is probably not necessary for a modern Paul Revere to gallop through the streets shouting "The Information Age is coming, the Information Age is coming." I am sure there is hardly a person among us who has not felt increasingly overwhelmed by the deluge of information being generated today.

In my own life, as a lawyer and businessman, I became acutely aware of the Information Age because of its profound impact in my work. I was faced with a daily flood on my desk—both at home and at work—of papers, memos, reports, journals, briefs, letters, contracts, and so on. From time to time I felt certain I was going to go under, if not drown, in the sea of information around me.

However, a number of years ago I began to hear about the emerging field of accelerated learning, particularly the work of Georgi Lozanov, a Bulgarian medical doctor and psychologist turned educator. Working with students learning foreign languages, Dr. Lozanov had developed numerous new techniques to help them increase their learning speed and ability to remember. His pioneering work was popularized in the United States in a book called *Superlearning*, by Sheila Ostrander and Lynn Schroeder.

As I considered my own dilemma of information overload, I began to explore how accelerated learning techniques as well as other new research in psychology and neuroscience could help me. Over time, I read the leading books in these fields, by such experts as Tony Buzan, Edward De Bono, Karl Albrecht, Peter Russell, Jacquelyn Wonder, Eric Jensen, Howard Gardner, and others. I took several training courses and received certifications in whole-brain learning, speed reading, and neurolinguistic programming.

Little by little, I began to implement these new skills and strategies in dealing with my own information load, and I found the results dramatic and impressive. Within a short time a system emerged that allowed me to manage information rather than letting it manage me.

In 1987 I founded a consulting company called McCarthy Learning Institute and developed Champion Speed Learning Systems and Active Reading techniques, which subsequently have been taught to thousands of people across the United States. My clients included working professionals, executives, business and salespeople, students, and ordinary individuals interested in learning how to improve their productivity, reading speed, and effectiveness. As the demand for workshops in this area mushroomed, it dawned on me that practically everyone in today's society could benefit from a concise course that would combine the diverse skills I have read about, learned, or personally developed to deal with information overload.

Mastering the Information Age is that course. In this book, I have distilled the most important and useful principles and techniques from hundreds in the fields of learning, reading, thinking, and memory.

Some of the ideas and techniques in this book may be familiar to you, or you may recognize them as plain common sense. Others will be new to you and perhaps difficult to believe until you try them. But the beauty of this book is how powerful the sum total of the ideas can be in helping to transform you into a smarter, more productive, efficient, organized, and *successful* person. Once implemented these ideas can become a new lifestyle that will promote your ability to become a faster worker, better learner, and more intelligent person. My experience has shown me that, with practice, anyone can become a Master of the Information Age, regardless of age or educational background.

THE OBJECTIVES

Mastering the Information Age incorporates three objectives, each as vital and necessary as the next. These include developing:

1. broad-based personal skills in learning, working, and thinking better;
2. specific information management skills; and
3. effective communication and presentation skills.

Following is a brief overview of how this book addresses these goals.

Goal Number One:
Developing Broad-Based Personal Skills
The first part of this book, chapters 1 through 6, explores the first aspect of becoming a Master: developing your personal skills to handle any work or study situation that involves information. Becoming a Master requires a broad-based foundation that allows you to function effectively regardless of the task at hand.

In Chapter 1, we will start by examining more precisely what the Information Age means and why it challenges us. We will then define what a Master is and why most people have not learned to be one. Being aware of these issues and basic definitions will allow you to see what becoming a Master entails and why it is important for your future to make every effort to become one.

Chapter 2 examines an essential element of this process: learning how to identify and transform negative beliefs about your abilities and intelligence into positive beliefs that support your learning and thinking. Many people are not Masters, and perhaps may never be, simply because they limit their own abilities with self-defeating attitudes.

Chapters 3 and 4 examine the fascinating concept of peak performance as it relates to learning and intelligence. You will see how using relaxation, nutrition, exercise, and even setting up the right external environment all contribute to putting you into a special "learning state" in which you can work or study with maximum effectiveness. You will also learn about the value of sharpening your senses and using your intuition in dealing with information. Included in these chapters are dozens of practical tips on improving your work or study habits.

Chapter 5 focuses on how you can enhance your memory

through a four-step program. You will also learn a variety of simple devices that can alleviate memory overload when it is more useful, as it often is, to record information rather than commit it to memory.

Chapter 6 teaches you how to think better and analyze information for accuracy and logic, both crucial skills in today's complex information world.

Goal Number Two:
Developing Specific Information-Management Skills

Much information comes to us in printed form. Chapters 7 through 10 focus on how you can learn to improve your ability to manage this flood of information, whether it comes to you unsought, or you go looking for it in your professional or personal research projects.

Chapter 7 presents the concept of defining your "information target zone" so that you will not waste time sorting through useless or irrelevant material. You will learn the steps for previewing reading materials to help you understand better and identify more precisely what information in a book, article, memo, or other source truly meets your needs.

Chapters 8 and 9 will teach you several powerful reading techniques that can enable you to increase your speed of information gathering. By practicing the exercises in these chapters, you will *at least double or triple your reading speed*.

Chapter 10 is aimed at familiarizing you with the many new information sources at your disposal when you need to find information not readily available. Many people experience "research anxiety," and are consequently nervous, if not terrified, about using libraries, online databases, CD-ROM, and other valuable sources of information that can simplify life.

Goal Number Three:
Developing Effective Communication Skills

A vital aspect of being a Master is knowing how to transmit information to others. The last chapter of this book is therefore aimed at helping you communicate information with clarity and power, in both writing and speaking.

HOW TO USE THIS BOOK

Mastering the Information Age is organized into a carefully planned sequence of explanations and exercises, just as a course might be. If you follow it step by step you will find yourself growing steadily in your skills, and you will gain new confidence in the value of applying them to your daily life.

As you go through each section and chapter, you will also be able to implement immediately what you are learning. For example, after you read about the importance of establishing a learning environment, you may wish to improve your office or workspace at home following the suggestions in that section.

Here are a few other suggestions on how to gain the most from the time you spend with this book.

Participate

Most importantly, this book requires your *active participation*. As I said, it is really a course book. It differs from most books in that you will be asked to do more than passively take in the words. Really *using* this book assumes your active involvement. It is filled with quotes, techniques, and tools to allow you to change old habits and develop new skills, but the degree of your success depends in large part upon your willingness to become involved in the mastery process.

You may have heard of or even used "interactive" computer programs. These are programs for learning a new skill such as a language or a computer program itself. The computer presents you with some information and gives you an instruction or asks you a question. You respond, and then the computer responds to you. By interacting with the computer—answering questions, performing operations, *doing* something—the learner learns much more than by simply absorbing and trying to memorize information.

This book is designed as an interactive experience. To get the most out of it you must put yourself into it!

The book contains many exercises called Learning Activators. These are included to teach you in a direct way by involving you in a personal learning experience. In order to get full benefit from the Learning Activators, you will need to pause in your progress through the book and spend some time thinking and writing. This is absolutely vital if you are to derive maximum results from this book.

A physical exercise routine written down on paper will not get you in shape, no matter how many times you read it over. A diet plan won't take off any weight unless you follow it. Likewise, understanding the principles of peak intelligence and Active Reading must be accompanied by action on your part, or nothing will change.

Make a commitment to yourself: Complete all the Learning Activators with full and honest participation.

Give Up Your Self-Limiting Beliefs and Habits

No matter how successful you are, unless you are a very unusual person you have some bad habits that hold you back from greater success. These may be habits of negative thinking, notions such as "I don't learn new things easily," "I read slowly," or "I have a terrible memory." You may have a habit of procrastination, of inefficient reading, or of being easily distracted.

These and other self-defeating, self-sabotaging habits of thought and action can be replaced by more productive behavior. In Chapter 2 you will find a number of exercises to help you transform such limiting behaviors into more positive and productive ones. But you have to be willing to change, and you have to translate your desire into concrete action.

A frequent barrier to taking action is our reluctance to leave our established "comfort zone," that familiar place where there are no challenges. Challenges often create tension and the discomfort of something new. There is safety in the status quo, where the comfort zone surrounds us like the warm atmosphere of home.

The trouble with this approach to life is that nothing new ever happens in the comfort zone; it is "business as usual" and does not stimulate our brain or free us from the boundaries of our present level of experience. If you are to grow, you need to step outside the boundaries of your comfort zone, into the region of new experience where learning takes place.

Please Write in Your Book

Since this is a workbook to be used and not just read, you will need to write in it. If you are one of those people who can't bear to mess up a book with underlining and other writing, here is your chance to take a first step beyond your comfort zone.

Please approach this book with pens, pencils, colored markers, paper clips, sticky notes, and any other methods of marking you might devise. Underline, write notes in the margins, put a paper clip on a page that's important to you. These simple techniques personalize the book for you and allow you to pick it up any time in the future and quickly find the places that were most useful or important to you.

Of course, these instructions do not apply if you are borrowing this book from the library. If this is a library book, please be considerate of others and do not write in it. Copy the exercise pages on a duplicating machine, or use a separate writing journal of your own.

Decide What You Want from This Book

It is useful for you to take a few minutes to define your purpose and write down what you want to accomplish from reading this book.

If this is *your* book, you can write in the blank spaces provided below. Or you can start a journal and write your goals there. Either way, you will derive much more from the book if you set objectives for yourself.

1. What is your purpose in reading this book? Write down brief points, or elaborate as much as you like. You might take the following questions into consideration. A few examples are given to get you going.

- What do you want to learn?
    (Examples: Learn to locate information faster; overcome limiting beliefs about my ability to learn)
- What new skills would you like to acquire?
    (Examples: Read faster; enhance my memory; visualize success)

- What changes do you want to make in your relationship to the Information Age?
  (Example: Feel more in control)
- How much faster would you like to be able to read?
  (Go for it! What would you really like?)

YOUR RESPONSES:

2. What questions do you have about the process of becoming an Information Age Master? For example:

- How can I improve my thinking skills?
- What are the possibilities and limits of my intelligence?
- What are the mechanics of memory?
- How much time will I have to spend in order to double my reading speed?

YOUR QUESTIONS:

3. What do you anticipate will be the answers to the questions you just posed? Based on what you know, try answering them now. Then as you read this book, come back to this page and compare what you are learning to what you wrote. Write your answers in the space below. Don't be afraid to be wrong. This is not a test, it is a way for you to engage your brain in the active process of getting what you want from this book.

YOUR ANSWERS:

Mastering the Information Age can transform your life. If you implement most of the ideas in this book, you will find that your performance at work or study will substantially improve and your personal day-to-day satisfaction will increase. Even if you incorporate only 50 percent of the suggestions, the benefits you will gain will place you many steps ahead of most people in your personal quest for excellence. At the very least, this book will give you a new confidence in yourself and in your ability to meet the challenges of the future, whether you are a working professional or a student.

We cannot build a dam to stop the flood of changes around us. In a world in which, according to economist and management expert Peter Drucker, "knowledge has already become the primary industry," a world in which brain power has replaced muscle power as the essential passport to success, only those people will survive and flourish who have the tools to convert the flood of information and raw data into useful, coherent knowledge.

As I see it, you have only two choices: You can stay as you are and be overwhelmed by the tidal wave of change. Or you can begin to make the improvements suggested in this book to help you stay ahead and succeed. *Mastering the Information Age* invites you to be on the leading edge of progress.

Michael J. McCarthy
September 1990
Hotchkiss, Colorado

■ ■ ■ ■

C H A P T E R   1

Become a Master

You can't escape from the Information Age. Ready or not, you are right in the thick of it. Futurists such as Alvin Toffler, author of *Future Shock*, and John Naisbitt, author of *Megatrends*, have long predicted that information would soon overwhelm us. They were right. For most of us, information overload is now a reality.

If you are a working professional, you undoubtedly face a daily barrage of letters, memos, soft and hard computer copy, electronic mail, newsletters, articles in trade and professional publications, and entire books you need to read just to keep up with your job. If you are a student, you have stacks of required reading—textbooks, articles, journals, and so on—to wade through just to pass your courses. Whatever your situation, the amount of information you have to sort through and assimilate increases exponentially if you want to excel. Clearly, staying current with information has become one of the essential ingredients of professional or academic success.

Even on a purely personal level, you probably have a similar problem with information overload. If you are like most people,

To buy books would be a good thing if we also could buy the time to read them.

Arthur Schopenhauer

I feel like I'm drowning. Every night, I'm carrying home loads of things to read but I'm too exhausted. I keep clipping things and Xeroxing them and planning to read them eventually, but I just end up throwing it all away and feeling guilty.

Ghita Levine
Associate director of
news and information
Johns Hopkins University

there are piles of unread newspapers, books, and magazines in almost every room of your house. You constantly vow to get around to reading them when you "have some extra time," but invariably you end up throwing them out so they can be replaced by more current material (which you also don't read). This unending cycle makes you feel that you will never have a chance to really pursue subjects that interest you, or to acquire new knowledge that helps keep you up to date with life.

■ ■ ■ ■

THE NEW DISEASE: INFORMATION ANXIETY

Modern man is like the mythological Sisyphus, who was doomed to spend his life pushing a heavy rock up Mount Olympus only to have it roll back down every time he was about to reach the top.

Today our rock is information. No matter how valiantly we try to keep up, the weight of information continues to overwhelm us. Perhaps you feel like the executive who said to me recently, "The deluge never stops. By the end of a day I feel I just don't want to read another word or talk to another person."

Author Richard Saul Wurman has coined a phrase that evokes a feeling we all share: *information anxiety*, which he defines as "the ever-widening gap between what we understand and what we think we should understand. Information anxiety is the black hole between data and knowledge."

Information anxiety is the new disease of our time. Its symptoms include: feelings of frustration, such as when we look at the in-basket on our desk overstuffed with papers and memos; feelings of being continually behind, such as when we go to a newsstand and see hundreds of current magazines and newspapers that we could never find time to read; and feelings of ignorance, such as when we go to a library and see dozens of recently published books that we will never peruse. Information anxiety is a kind of stupor, a feeling that we simply can't keep up, can't read fast enough, don't know how to locate the information we need, don't have time to sort through or think about all the data surrounding us.

Unfortunately, the causes of this disease aren't going to go away. All indications and predictions are that the information glut is going to get worse . . . and worse. The Information Age has only just begun.

FOUR IMPLICATIONS

The Information Age is profoundly transforming our world. Just as the Industrial Revolution changed the face of the land and the nature of the workplace—replacing farms, woodlands, and meadows with cities, factories, and office buildings—the Information Age is bringing an equally comprehensive, radical, and even more rapid metamorphosis to the way we work and live. These changes mean that each of us faces many challenges. Consider the following four.

Continuing Information Explosion

For thousands of years, information was a simple matter. It was transmitted from person to person, generation to generation, through verbal communication. The sources of knowledge were usually within a person's own community. Everything one needed to know—about planting, herding, building, healing—was received from one's peers or from the elders and sages of the clan. Knowledge was refined at a gradual pace, if at all, and anything a person learned remained current throughout his or her lifetime. In short, life was uncomplicated and changed little from decade to decade.

The "big bang" of information was a single event: the invention of the printing press by Gutenberg in 1457. This momentous change in technology sparked a tremendous acceleration in the amount and kind of knowledge accessible to humankind. Suddenly information became available from far beyond the boundaries of one's local community. Furthermore, each new bit of information triggered a new generation of facts, ideas, and opinions that were then added into an ever-growing data pool.

This wealth of information caused rapid changes in the stock of human knowledge. Within one generation after Gutenberg, keeping up with information became much more com-

The coming of the printing press must have seemed as if it would turn the world upside down in the way it spread and, above all, democratized knowledge. Provided you could pay and read, what was on the shelves in the new bookshops was yours for the taking. The speed with which printing presses and their operators fanned out across Europe is extraordinary. From the single Mainz press of 1457, it took only twenty-three years to establish presses in 110 towns: 50 in Italy, 30 in Germany, 9 in France, 8 in Spain, 8 in Holland, 4 in England, and so on.

James Burke

INFORMATION
14TH CENTURY

INFORMATION
TODAY

The pace of progress will accelerate so that even engineers and technical managers will find it necessary to recycle back through school after no more than ten years. In particular fast-moving technologies skills will become obsolete every five years or so.

Marvin Cetron
Owen Davies

plicated; within a few generations the increase became exponential. If the amount of information humanity possessed in the 14th century would fit into a wheelbarrow, by comparison what is known today could barely be squeezed into the Grand Canyon. Consider these facts.

- More new information has been produced in the last 30 years than in the previous 5,000.
- In the mid-14th century the Sorbonne library in Paris, the largest in Europe, contained about 1,300 books. Today there are several libraries that each contain *8 million* volumes!
- Every day, scientists and researchers put the finishing touches on 7,000 new scientific papers.
- Nearly 50,000 books are published in the United States every year, and approximately 10,000 periodicals.
- Eighty-five percent of the information in the National Institutes of Health computers is upgraded in five years.
- Americans are bombarded by about 50,000 advertisements per year, or about 140 per day.
- A typical weekday edition of the *New York Times* contains more information than the average person in the 16th century would encounter in *an entire lifetime*!
- The amount of available information now doubles every five years. By the turn of the century—only a few years away—the doubling time will be every 20 months.

Stop a moment and think about this frightening truth. Five years from today there will be twice as much known in your field as there is today. If you work in one of the fastest-growing fields, such as computers or scientific research, the doubling time is even shorter.

Experts estimate that at the current rate of knowledge expansion, a student who graduates from college today and does not update his information will find that within 15 years, 90 percent of what he learned in school will have become obsolete. The good old days, when a college degree would earn you most of the knowledge and skills you would need for your entire career, are gone forever.

The information explosion has been further complicated by the progress of Western civilization to the age of high technology. The printed word has become only one of numerous media for conveying information. We now have computers, telephones, video, compact disc, and other electronic data delivery systems. Today, the combination of electronics, fiber optics, and satellite communications has made virtually instantaneous information transmission commonplace. It is now possible, for example, to transmit the entire contents of the *Encyclopedia Britannica* in two seconds! One 5¼-inch compact disc can store an entire 250,000-page encyclopedia and still have room left over.

This increase in the sources, quantity, and speed of transmission of information has created the predicament of our Information Age: too much information coming at us, and too little time to deal with it.

Changes in the Economy and Workplace

The second change the Information Age brings is a major change in our economy. We have entered an era in which brain power has replaced muscle power as the force behind economic life. Already in the United States and many other countries the majority of careers and occupations revolve around some form of information processing. Education, the media, banking and finance, insurance, all businesses dealing with computer technology, communication, data processing, lawyers, accountants, writers, consultants, and many others all deal primarily with information.

This growing shift in the economy toward knowledge-based careers means that many jobs will become obsolete, going the way of the blacksmith and the telegraph operator. Other jobs will change rapidly, compelling people to master new skills and new knowledge. An ever-widening gap will separate those who have the requisite mental skills to meet the demands of a brain-intensive economy from those who do not. These changes are occurring so swiftly that the United States Congress has declared the 1990s to be the "Decade of the Brain," just one indication of the importance learning and clear thinking must play in our lives.

Even though these technological advances originally sought to control information and bring order to the office, in many instances they have done just the opposite. The electronic office promised to reduce paper work and lessen work loads, but it has, in fact, generated more information that must still be printed and—even more challenging—be assimilated. Since computers entered office systems, paper utilization has increased six-fold.

Peter D. Moore

I just graduated and already I'm way behind.

Anonymous

15

We are now in the third stage of the industrial revolution. The first involved machines which extended human muscle; the second used machines to extend the human nervous system (radio, television, telephones); the third is now utilizing machines which extend the human mind—computers.

About half of all service workers (43 percent of the labor force by 2000) will be involved in collecting, analyzing, synthesizing, structuring, storing, or retrieving information. . . . By 1995, 80 percent of all management will be "knowledge workers."

Marvin Cetron
Owen Davies

Knowledge is the currency of exchange in the Information Age. As John Kenneth Galbraith explains:

Money is what fueled the industrial society. But in the informational society, the fuel, the power, is knowledge. One has now come to see a new class structure divided by those who have information and those who must function out of ignorance. This new class has its power not from money, not from land, but from knowledge.

With so much of the global economy based on knowledge and so much new information coming from scientific and technological research every day, power will be in the hands of those who possess or can provide knowledge to others. Knowledge is what allows people to act, to make decisions, in business and in personal health and well-being. People who do not understand how things work—whether it be financial markets, medical procedures, or fuel injection engines—or who cannot locate the data they need, will be at the mercy of others. Only those who have correct, current knowledge will be in control of their own lives and destinies.

New Definition of Information

The third challenge we face is that information is now so omnipresent and complex that instead of informing us, it frequently overwhelms us. Information today comes in many packages. Consider the following categories of information with which we are involved.

■ Basic facts about science, literature, history, and so on, that we learn in school—usually from books—and need to remember throughout our lives.
■ New data about developments in science, technology, medicine, politics, and other areas that continually change the way we live and demand our understanding. We learn most of these through newspapers, magazines, and television.
■ Facts about our job that we learn through professional training, workshops, courses, or specialized journals.
■ Names and facts about places we visit and people we meet.

■ Data relating to our personal situation (such as health, diet, buying a home, personal finances) that we learn from newspapers, brochures, friends, books, and so on.

There is also a new and vital kind of information that has greatly compounded our information overload. Thanks to electronic technology, we can now gather enormous amounts of data quickly and chart, graph, and manipulate it in a variety of ways in order to arrive at a sense of current *trends*. This capability has given rise to a new profession, known as futurists. We are inundated with information not only about the past and the present, but about the future as well.

For example, investors both large and small now depend on predictions about anticipated trends in the international financial markets. Population growth and geographical shifts are routinely forecast and used by marketing specialists. Scientists and researchers alike are making predictions about the environment and problems of global warming, endangered species, rain forest destruction, food production that depends on chemicals, and so on. The success of books such as *Megatrends* and *Megatrends 2000* reveals the general public's desire to understand the future.

All this information and all of these sources heavily tax our thinking and memory skills. The information explosion has created so much data that, in reality, almost anything we learn is only a small piece of a gigantic puzzle. It is practically impossible to *know* something, because there is so much information about each topic. Even when we know lots of facts, it can still be difficult to understand an issue and make a decision. This contributes to our sense of anxiety.

Information has become so complex, we are often distrustful of it. We have learned that anything we know today can change tomorrow. What may be true this week, this month, or this year can easily become false within a short period of time. Moreover, we have also learned that whatever we read or hear has been selected and "massaged" by other people and is therefore colored by many different factors, such as prejudices, points of view, or simply the time or space available to present the information. These factors also make it difficult, if not impossible, to know what to believe.

We have for the first time an economy based on a key resource [information] that is not only renewable, but self-generating. Running out of it is not a problem, but drowning in it is.

John Naisbitt

There's a compelling reason to master information and news. Clearly there will be better job and financial opportunities. Other high stakes will be missed by people if they don't master and connect information.

Everette Dennis

No doubt the 21st century will bring even more complexity to what we know as information. You as an individual will need to be ever more capable of envisioning your future and contemplating what you may need to learn or do to keep pace with the trends that affect your life.

Converting Information into Knowledge: The Information Equation

The fourth challenge we face is knowing exactly how to use information in our daily lives. The tremendous proliferation of data can overload us and exhaust us, or it can give us profit and wisdom. Like gasoline or money, information is a form of energy that takes on power when it is put to use.

A library filled with books is nothing without the other end of the information equation, which is *you*. Your job is to convert information into *knowledge*—knowledge that you can utilize for your personal and professional enrichment and for the benefit of the planet as a whole.

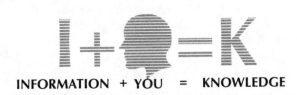

INFORMATION + YOU = KNOWLEDGE

While information consists primarily of data and facts, knowledge is something far more profound. Knowledge is information that has been thought about, that has been experienced and integrated. Knowledge has to do with meaning and understanding.

The dictionary defines information as a collection of "unorganized or unrelated facts or data," and knowledge as "the sum of information conserved by civilization." Thus we see a progressive refinement from facts and data, to information, and finally to knowledge.

How accurately this image depicts today's world! There is a great deal of data and myriad facts; there is plenty of information, but knowledge is harder to come by. Indeed, the challenge of the Information Age can be defined as *creating knowledge*

out of information, getting to the essence of information, making sense of it, making it meaningful and useful as an individual.

The process of converting huge amounts of information into useful, meaningful knowledge requires time and thought. "You can mass-produce raw data and incredible quantities of facts and figures," writes Theodore Roszak; but, as he adds,

> you cannot mass-produce knowledge, which is created by individual minds, drawing on individual experience, separating the significant from the irrelevant, making value judgments.

Unfortunately, the pace of modern life leaves most of us little time to think.

WANTED: SKILLS FOR THE 21st CENTURY

Why is it that most of us have not already learned to deal with these challenges, to effectively manage the information around us? The major reason is that our education and culture have not given us the mental skills and attitudes required to deal with the rapidly changing nature of life today. Most of us have received a 19th-century education, consisting mostly of the three Rs: readin', 'ritin', and 'rithmetic. This is woefully inadequate for the complexities of the Information Age.

The visionary writer H. G. Wells once said that "Human history becomes more and more a race between education and catastrophe." Wells died nearly fifty years ago; he could not have known how true his words would become.

12. Do you need to keep up with the latest information in your field?
13. Do you want to remember more of what you read?
14. Do you feel stressed by the information demands of your occupation or schoolwork?
15. Does your mind tend to wander when you read?
16. Does a modem-connected online database computer hookup intimidate you?
17. Do you sometimes need to actively seek additional information to support a decision or complete a project?
18. Would you like to improve your ability to communicate information?
19. Do you feel a need to use more of your creativity?
20. Would you like to think more clearly?

If you answered YES to at least five of these questions, you are probably suffering from information overload.

The original root of the word "information" is the Latin word informare, *which means to fashion, shape, or create, to give form to. Information is an idea that has been given a form, such as the spoken or written word. It is a means of representing an image or thought so that it can be communicated from one mind to another.*

Rather than worrying about all the information afloat in the world, we must ask ourselves what matters to us, what do we want to know. It's having ideas and learning to deal with issues that is important, not accumulating lots and lots of data.

Theodore Roszak

I loved learning, it was school I hated. I used to cut school to go learn something.

Eric Jensen

Before we examine the reasons education has not equipped us for the Information Age, I would like to say that this analysis is not meant as an indictment of the dedicated educators who struggle against great odds—including inadequate federal, state, and local education budgets, antiquated buildings and equipment, and undermotivated students.

The underlying problem is that as a nation we do not place a high priority on education. We routinely pay executives six- and seven-figure salaries and give athletes a million dollars a year to throw a ball through a hoop, but the people who teach our children have to support their families on mediocre salaries. In consequence we fail to attract to education many of our best minds, who realize they can make a better living in other fields. Many of our social problems, including the much-publicized illiteracy of our youth, stem at least in part from this under-valuing of education and educators.

When we change this and apply more of our attention and resources to learning, we can make the educational process exciting, effective, and productive. When we show respect for our teachers and compensate them adequately for their knowledge and skill, we can ensure that the future of our planet will be in competent hands.

It is in this spirit that I propose to look at how the way many of us were taught has left us ill prepared for the challenges of the Information Age. If you have completed your education, take heart: It is never too late to learn new habits and skills. If you are currently a student, this analysis can prompt you to begin making changes now.

Emphasis on Facts Rather Than on Understanding or Knowledge

Most of us were conditioned to equate learning with the memorization of facts. Success in school generally meant being able to regurgitate at test time a set of facts we learned in class or from a standardized textbook.

This kind of "knowledge" is narrow and superficial. Knowing the difference between clear-cut "right" and "wrong" answers does little to help us in our complex, multidimensional lives. In the real world, decisions are seldom based on a simple "right answer" but rather on analyzing vast amounts of information and choosing from among many alternatives a single direction that we think will create positive results. No wonder many people feel overwhelmed when life presents them with problems that cannot be solved by reading one book or choosing (a), (b), or (c) from a list.

As a result of this emphasis on memorizing facts, our schools have not taught us to use our brain at its true capacity to create knowledge. The capabilities of that magnificent instrument have not only been underdeveloped, but many feel that our education has actually been harmful to our ability to think and analyze. "If we had deliberately planned to fetter our brains," Jean Houston wrote about our schools in *The Possible Human*, "we couldn't have done better." Today we know that the brain is enormously flexible and capable of exceptional learning and understanding, if we are taught the right skills.

Failure to Encourage Independent Thinking

Our education has often trained us to accept blindly what we were taught. We were seldom encouraged to question the validity of the information or ideas presented to us. We were not taught to think clearly and critically, to evaluate the logic or accuracy of information, or to distinguish between useful and nonessential data. We were rarely asked to contemplate the relevance of information to our own lives. We assumed, "If you learn it in school, it must be true."

What happens when people take this assumption out into the world and believe that something must be true if one expert says so, or if they see it on the television news? Where would we be if people like Copernicus, Newton, and Einstein had not questioned the truth of the "reality" they were taught? Where will we be if we do not develop more independent thinkers in every profession to guide us into the next century?

The Information Age requires that we move beyond trust and acceptance to independent thinking. With so many conflicting sources of information available, it is essential that we develop a critical eye and learn how to probe the accuracy, meaning, and relevance of each new bit of information we encounter.

I am entirely certain that twenty years from now we will look back at education as it is practiced in most schools today and wonder that we could have tolerated anything so primitive.

John W. Gardner

Out of my general world-pattern-trend studies there now comes strong evidence that nothing is going to be quite so surprising and abrupt in the future history of man as the forward evolution in the educational process.

R. Buckminster Fuller

We've got a lemon factory and we're turning out 80–85 percent lemons.

Albert Shanker, on the American school system

21

I roamed the countryside searching for answers to things I did not understand. Why thunder lasts longer than that which causes it, and why immediately on its creation the lightning becomes visible to the eye while thunder requires time to travel. How the various circles of water form around the spot which has been struck by a stone and why a bird sustains itself in the air. These questions and other strange phenomena engaged my thought throughout my life.

Leonardo da Vinci

The intellectual equipment needed for the job of the future is an ability to define problems, quickly assimilate relevant data, conceptualize and reorganize the information, make deductive and inductive leaps with it, ask hard questions about it, discuss findings with colleagues, work collaboratively to find solutions and then convince others.

Robert B. Reich

Emphasis on Academic Skills Rather Than Life Skills

Depending on our goals, most of us assumed that our education would end after high school, college, or graduate school, and then we would begin "real life." But as many critics of the educational system have pointed out, the skills needed for success in school—memorization, test-taking, the ability to "psyche out" what the teacher wanted—have little in common with the skills needed for success in life. Not only did education fail to provide us with the thinking skills needed for learning; in many cases it did not provide the skills needed for successful living, such as self-discipline, time management, ability to prioritize tasks, and a lifelong love of learning.

The fast pace of progress requires an ongoing process of learning throughout life. Those who recognize this truth and attend seminars and continuing education courses or go back to school for new degrees or new knowledge, do better at keeping up with change than those who stop learning when their formal education ends. Regardless of whether you go back to school, no doubt you are discovering, as the Information Age unfolds, that the business of life *is* learning.

Use of Standard Curriculum and Teaching Methods Rather Than Addressing Individual Learning Styles

Education has also failed to devote enough time and attention to developing the special intelligence of each student. Because most psychologists mistakenly believed that intellectual capacities are fixed at birth, our schools rarely made an effort to develop a student's maximum learning ability and personal intelligence. All attention was given to the subject matter, and virtually no attention to the learner himself.

Recent research in neurophysiology and cognitive psychology suggests that we each have a much greater learning potential than we ordinarily exhibit, and that there are many kinds of intelligence, not just one. In his book *The Triarchic Mind*, Robert Sternberg of Yale University distinguishes three aspects of intelligence.

1. *Analytic*, which helps us grasp and retain information and think clearly and critically.

2. *Synthetic*, which gives us the power to come up with new ideas and new solutions to problems. Another name for this is creativity.
3. *Practical*, which corresponds to "street smarts" or the ability to put ideas into practice, to translate thought into action.

Another angle on multiple intelligences comes from "split-brain" research, which has shown that the two halves of our brain operate differently. The "left brain" responds to information presented sequentially and logically and focuses on words and details. The "right brain" sees the whole picture and not just parts; it is more visual and creative. Thus, people who are more analytical, logical, or verbal learn in different ways from those who are artistic, sensory, or intuitive.

Instead of recognizing and addressing these different types of intelligence and learning styles, our schools present a standard curriculum to all students, using standard instructional methods for everyone and judging everyone by standardized tests. The material is presented, but is it *learned*?

The answer is no. Generally only the 25 to 35 percent of students who are naturally more verbal, analytical, and mathematical do well on standardized tests. Little or nothing is done to help other types of learners grasp the material. The "good" students are rewarded and appreciated, but the others are not and consequently lose self-esteem and self-confidence. They begin to believe they are "slow learners," or worse.

Lack of self-esteem is one of the most commonly recognized problems in American education today, and yet it is often the schools themselves that have crushed our confidence, by making us believe we cannot learn, or by forcing us to use a thinking style not suited to our abilities and then punishing us for not learning well.

A Belief That Learning Must Be Difficult

Our educational system seems to operate under the belief that in order to get knowledge, you have to work hard and suffer. The typical sterile classroom does not support the belief that learning can be fun and easy. Yet learning is one of the most joyful and natural aspects of being human. Just watch little

In a world that is constantly changing, there is no one subject or set of subjects that will serve you for the foreseeable future, let alone for the rest of your life. The most important skill to acquire now is learning how to learn.

John Naisbitt

There is no end to education. It is not that you read a book, pass an examination, and finish with education. The whole of life, from the moment you are born to the moment you die, is a process of learning.

J. Krishnamurti

People are going to be most creative and productive when they're doing something they're really interested in. So having fun isn't an outrageous idea at all. It's a very sensible one.

John Sculley
President of Apple
Computers

children learning something new: They exude curiosity and excitement. Research shows that students who learn in a relaxed, pleasant atmosphere, without pressure, utilizing methods that bring fun into the process of learning, learn faster and better than students in the typically pressured and overserious environment of most of our schools.

Failure to Provide Training in Technology

One final reason that education has failed to prepare us for the Information Age is that it often did not train us to use the technology that is so central to contemporary information processing. Educators cannot be blamed for this, because technological advancement has been so rapid that when most adults today went to school, the technology did not even exist!

Knowledge of these tools is indispensable to success in school and in one's personal and professional life. Those whose resistance or fear of technology prevents them from using computers, databases, and other high-tech devices will hold themselves back from full and successful participation in the Information Age.

BECOMING A MASTER

Taken together, the explosion of information and the serious inadequacies of our educational system have combined to keep us unprepared for the challenges of life in the Information Age. As a result, most of us have enormous information GAPS— that is, we do not have the skills necessary to keep up with the constant demand to Gather, Access, Process, and Share information. Here's what I mean.

GATHERING. Gathering information involves using our senses and learning faculties to pick up and absorb information of all kinds, primarily by reading and listening. Most of us read far too slowly, have undependable concentration, suffer from inefficient learning and study habits, and manage our time poorly.

ACCESSING. Information accessing means knowing where and how to get information when we need it. New information

All of us, you, your children, your neighbors and their children are everyday geniuses, even though the fact is unnoticed and unremembered by everyone. That's probably because school hasn't encouraged us to notice what's hidden inside us waiting for the right environment to express itself.

Peter Kline

What usually happens in the educational process is that the faculties are dulled, overloaded, stuffed and paralyzed so that by the time most people are mature they have lost their innate capabilities.

R. Buckminster Fuller

The illiterate of the future are not those who can't read or write, but those who cannot learn, unlearn, and relearn.

Alvin Toffler

sources (such as newsletters and online databases) and new technology (computers, modems, CD-ROM) are continually arising, but most of us have a gap either in knowing about these sources, knowing how to use them, or knowing which are the best ones. We also need to learn how to narrow our focus to the specific information we need so that we don't waste time on inappropriate methods and sources.

PROCESSING. Information processing comprises those thinking skills that contribute to turning voluminous amounts of information into the knowledge we need in order to make personal and professional decisions, solve problems, ascertain trends, and so on.

SHARING. Information sharing is knowing how to communicate the information we have. It includes writing effective reports, memos, and papers; conducting successful meetings; and making clear, concise, and convincing presentations.

Despite these information gaps, the education or training you received in the past does not have to limit you in the present or in the future. You don't need to live in a state of perpetual information anxiety or abandon your quest for knowledge and success.

Instead, you can become a Master of the Information Age. The techniques you will encounter in these pages can more than compensate for the background or training you may lack. By helping you to control the flow of information, they will liberate you from the oppressive feeling of information anxiety. Instead of viewing the vast amount of information available today as an enemy, something to be feared and avoided, you will learn to see it as a friendly ally that can support you and help you respond to the challenges ahead in your career and personal life.

What it comes down to is that modern society discriminates against the right hemisphere.

Roger Sperry

G. A. P. S.
GATHERING/ACCESSING/PROCESSING/SHARING

ELEMENTS OF MASTERY

Let's take a moment to examine this term *Master*. A Master of information is someone who:

- knows where and how to find the information he needs, in an accurate and up-to-date form.

Five daily newspapers arrive in my California driveway. The New York Times *and the* Wall Street Journal *are supplemented by three local papers. . . . As for magazines, I read, or at least skim,* Business Week, Forbes, The Economist, INC., Industry Week, Fortune. *Other subscriptions include* Sales and Marketing Management, Modern Health Care, Progressive Grocer, High Tech Business, *and* Sloan Management Review *from MIT. . . . I religiously read* Business Tokyo, Asia Week, *and* Far Eastern Economic Review. *I glance at* Newsweek *and* Time *. . . but I devour* The New Republic, Policy Review, Foreign Affairs, The Washington Monthly, *and* Public Interest. *. . . How about books? . . . a dozen or more each month. . . .*

Tom Peters

- knows how to extract the *essence* of information and does not spend a lot of time on details and superfluous material.
- knows how to research information using the latest research tools and technology. He knows what technology is available (CD-ROM, online databases, etc.) and understands how and for what purposes he can use it.
- is a superior reader. She reads quickly and understands what she reads. Rather than passively taking in words, she reads actively, thinking about the material and what she wants to learn from it before, during, and after a reading session.
- is a good listener, giving full, thoughtful attention to a speaker so that he understands and remembers what is said.
- knows how she learns best (reading, asking questions, taking a course) and uses that method as much as possible.
- knows how much time to devote to gathering information, and when to stop gathering and begin to evaluate what he has.
- realizes that it is not possible to know everything, and chooses to learn what is particularly germane to her personal and professional life.
- knows how to use the public library or a university research library, where he has access to more information than he could possibly ever use.
- distinguishes between information that is worth keeping in memory, and information that can be looked up when needed.
- knows how to judge between useful and useless information.
- has a wide range of information sources that consistently bring her into touch with new ideas and points of view.
- takes an active role in relation to information: asks questions, makes conscious connections and

associations to previous knowledge, questions information that doesn't fit with what he already knows, thinks critically, and decides what is important to his concerns.

■ is adept at interpersonal communication and relational skills.

■ knows how to deliver information efficiently and clearly to other people, either in writing or in speaking, whether to one person or a group.

Is this a description of you? If not, it will be—if you learn the principles and techniques in these pages.

Books in a large university library system: 2,000,000.

Books in an average large city library: 1,000,000. Average number of books in a chain bookstore: 30,000.

Books in an average neighborhood branch library: 20,000.

Lois Horowitz

RESOURCES

Education

Bloom, Alan. *The Closing of the American Mind.* (New York: Simon & Schuster, 1987). A look at how higher education has negatively affected the intellectual fiber of our society.

Jensen, Eric. *Super-Teaching.* (Del Mar, CA: Turning Point, 1988). An important how-to book for teachers.

Information

Harman, Willis. *Global Mind Change: The Promise of the Last Years of the Twentieth Century.* (Indianapolis: Knowledge Systems, 1988). The author, president of the Institute of Noetic Sciences, postulates that we are in the midst of one of the most drastic shifts in history through a global change in consciousness.

Wurman, Richard Saul. *Information Anxiety.* (New York: Doubleday, 1988). Outlining the history of information, this work identifies the contemporary malady of information anxiety.

Organizations

SALT (Society for Accelerated Learning Teachers), 2740 Richmond Avenue, Des Moines, IA 50317.

National Association of Humanistic Education, 211 Bennett Circle, Carolloton, GA 30017.

Turning Point, Box 2551, Del Mar, CA 92014. Seminars and products to boost teaching and learning capabilities.

■ ■ ■ ■

CHAPTER 2

BELIEVE IN YOUR SUCCESS

In this chapter, you will learn how your attitudes and beliefs about yourself strongly govern your level of performance. I will introduce you to research on the leading edge of science demonstrating how your thoughts and feelings directly affect your body and mind, and therefore profoundly influence all your actions. The exercises in the early part of the chapter will help you evaluate your own personal beliefs about success and becoming a Master. The remainder of the chapter contains several techniques to help you transform any limiting beliefs that you might have into attitudes that support your self-confidence and natural intelligence.

■ ■ ■ ■

In the past decade, the emergence of new information about nutrition, exercise, and health has prompted many people to adopt a new lifestyle. Many of us have improved our diet, added more exercise to our daily routine, and learned that our physical well-being starts with positive attitudes and feelings. We have learned that we can have control over our lives, that we can do a lot to change for the better.

What many people have missed, however, is another gift of the information explosion: a vastly increased understanding about how the brain works and how enormous our human potential actually is. Scientists, psychologists, educators, and other researchers have been continually discovering new facts about how we think, remember, and learn, and about the power of the human mind. Dr. Glenn Dorman, director of the Institutes for the Achievement of Human Growth in Philadelphia, has an exciting way of summing up how great our mental capacity really is: "All humans are born with a greater potential than Leonardo da Vinci ever used."

In the numerous seminars I have given on the subject of mastering the Information Age, however, it has become increasingly clear that many people have a diminished view of their intelligence, learning abilities, and performance potential. Their higher possibilities are often buried beneath numerous conscious or unconscious limiting beliefs that undermine their self-esteem and self-confidence. Unfortunately, these negative attitudes become self-fulfilling prophecies, as most people achieve only those small goals they think they can reach.

Mastering the Information Age begins with recognizing the fact that you have the power to govern your beliefs and attitudes. The effectiveness of every technique in this book originates with your belief in your ability to change. Examining your own attitudes and learning how to dissolve limiting beliefs and inculcate positive ones is therefore a necessary first step if you want to succeed. Even if you generally feel positive about yourself, this chapter can help you achieve a higher level of self-esteem and confidence in your capabilities.

While this sort of psychological exploration might seem ancillary in a book on learning and information management, the fact is that all change requires a willingness to take control of one's thoughts and actions. Many people fail not because they lack intelligence or capability, but because they *believe* they do not have the talent or brain power to do what they dream of doing.

The birth of excellence begins with the awareness that our beliefs are a choice.

Anthony Robbins

29

There is nothing either good or bad but thinking makes it so.

Shakespeare

Man is what he believes.

Anton Checkov

The capabilities of the human mind are enormous. There is usually no inherent reason you cannot accomplish whatever goal you set for yourself. Evolution has provided the human species with the most sophisticated mental equipment on the planet to learn, to think, and to create. Yet most people limit their potential with negative beliefs about themselves. They seldom explore their hidden reserves of intellect and creativity, or challenge themselves to reach deep into their natural powers. Rather than leading their brain, they follow the path of least resistance.

Exercising successful leadership for your brain is in many ways similar to leading a successful company. Like a complex business, your brain has many divisions and departments with their own unique functions, working together to produce various products and services. To make its operations successful, you need to utilize the same kinds of management skills suggested in numerous books available on managing a business, such as *The One-Minute Manager* and *In Search of Excellence*.

You must understand how to create clear goals and how to motivate your company—i.e., yourself—to achieve them. You need to learn how to foster high morale and inspire productivity and constructive action. You need to know how to take control when problems arise that block your path to success.

In short, you are the chief executive officer of your brain. As CEO, you are ultimately responsible for the functioning of its many departments and divisions and are in charge of "quality control" for all its "products," such as thought, decisions, and beliefs. This is the most important principle in this book: *You are in charge. You have the ability to master your own destiny.*

THE POWER OF BELIEFS

A belief is a thought or idea that we accept as true. It can be an opinion, a fact, a doctrine, a guiding principle, a passion, or a faith in someone or something. We can have a belief in our doctor or teacher, in the value of regular exercise, in our ability to climb Mount Everest or to sail west from Spain without falling off the end of the earth.

A belief can be subconscious as well as conscious. There

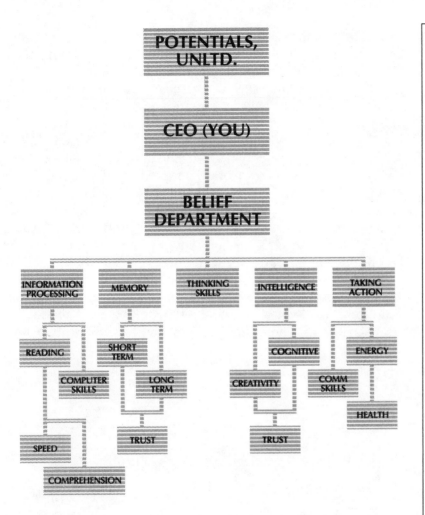

The Ties That Bind

In India, baby elephants are trained by tying them by the leg to a tree with a light rope. When they grow up, if a similar string is tied around their leg they will never break it, even though they now have the strength to pull the tree right out of the ground! Their "belief system" says that strings keep them bound.

We bind ourselves with our own strings. But unlike the elephants, we can choose to untie them. Whatever negative beliefs you may have, *you can choose to change them*. If your beliefs are not producing positive results in your life, you can choose to develop other ones. Just because your training and experience have given you a certain set of beliefs does not mean you have to live with them indefinitely. You can consciously decide to develop whatever new beliefs you need to meet challenges at work or in your personal life.

In short, you created the patterns that now exist. Your future experiences will either reinforce those patterns or mold them to a different model.

are hundreds of things we take for granted about life, things we've never thought about but accept as givens. For example, most of us have a belief, largely subconscious, in the truth of almost anything we see or hear in the media. Even if we sometimes question the validity of that belief consciously, our subconscious belief is often so strong that we automatically think, "What do *I* know?" or "That's what so-and-so says."

Although we may think our beliefs represent the truth, they are only our interpretations of the world. The problem is, however, that what we believe becomes our view of how things

Few people are capable of expressing with equanimity opinions which differ from the prejudices of their social environment. Most people are even incapable of forming such opinions.

Albert Einstein

are. We therefore end up reflecting our beliefs back onto the world and ourselves. We take them to be sacred and immutable and let them govern our perceptions and thoughts.

Suppose you are asked to give a speech or make a presentation. If you don't believe you are a good speaker, you will lack self-confidence. "I've always been a lousy speaker," you say to yourself. "Why should this time be any different?"

Feeling incompetent and believing in a poor outcome, you will not be motivated to draw on the best of your abilities. Why bother to organize your points carefully, think up good examples, find a few jokes to lighten the atmosphere, or prepare a powerful conclusion, since you already know the presentation will be boring? Therefore you will go into the meeting room prepared to prove your negative estimation true.

On the other hand, if you believe in your abilities, you will feel confident and act from a position of strength. Enthusiastic and motivated, you will take the time to prepare a good talk, to weave in ancedotes and humor. You too will go into the

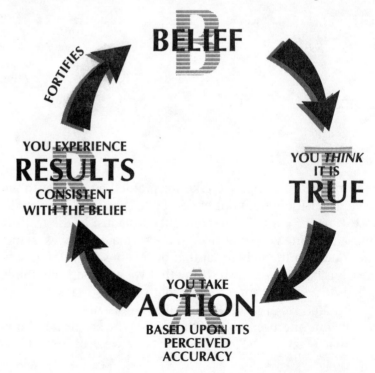

room ready to prove the truth of your beliefs.

The same relationship between beliefs and action exists in everything you do. Whether it's taking a test, writing a memo, reaching a sales goal, or understanding a complex book, your attitude plays a significant role in determining your success.

The chart depicts in graphic form how beliefs and actions sustain each other in a continuous cycle.

Breaking the Belief Barriers

For centuries, wise men and women have recognized the crucial role beliefs play in our happiness and success. "As a man thinketh in his heart, so is he," the Bible tells us. In every sphere of life, from health to love, relationships to learning ability, what we believe largely determines how we feel, how we think, and how well we perform.

The power of beliefs has become even more apparent in the past decade from research in many diverse fields. To begin, here are two striking illustrations of that power from sports.

Throughout the first half of the 20th century, athletes and trainers believed that the human body simply could not run a mile in less than four minutes. It was seen as an absolute barrier that could never be crossed. In May 1954, Roger Bannister, a British medical student, ran a mile in 3:59.4, thereby breaking both the "barrier" and the belief in the impossibility of the four-minute mile. In June another runner, John Landy, ran a mile in 3:58. In August Bannister and Landy competed in a thrilling race, in which both men broke the four-minute barrier. Since then, hundreds of runners have crossed the finish line in under four minutes. The impossibility was only in the mind.

Another supposedly impassable barrier was the human ability to lift 500 pounds. Along with a number of top athletes, the Soviet weightlifter Vasily Alexeev had lifted 499 pounds repeatedly but could not lift 500. However, his trainers believed he could do it. They put 501.5 pounds on his bar but rigged the scales so that he *thought* he was lifting 499 pounds. He lifted the bar successfully. When they showed him what he had done, he was then able to knowingly lift 500 pounds. Once that barrier was broken and people believed it was possible, many weightlifters have since surpassed this weight.

If you believe you can or you believe you can't, you're right.

Henry Ford

I always felt that my greatest asset was not my physical ability, it was my mental ability.

Bruce Jenner

As long as you can envision the fact that you can do something, you can do it— as long as you really believe it 100 percent.

Arnold Schwarzenegger

Your emotions affect every cell in your body. Mind and body, mental and physical, are intertwined.

Thomas Tutko, cofounder,
Institute of Athletic
Motivation

To a very large extent men and women are a product of how they define themselves. As a result of a combination of innate ideas and the intimate influences of the culture and environment we grow up in, we come to have beliefs about the nature of being human. These beliefs penetrate to a very deep level of our psychosomatic systems, our minds and brains, our nervous systems, our endocrine systems, and even our blood and sinews. We act, speak, and think according to these deeply held beliefs and belief systems.

Jeremy W. Hayward

In these cases and in countless others, belief was translated into physical capabilities. What people *thought* they could do influenced—indeed, *determined*—what they were able to do. What they thought was impossible, they couldn't do. What they believed they could accomplish, they did.

Educational researchers have found that a teacher's beliefs about a child's abilities can actually determine how well the child performs. Several studies divided children of equal aptitude into two groups. Teachers were told that one group had high IQs and should do well and that the other children were merely average. Invariably the group that was expected to excel did excel; the other group did poorly.

The medical profession is also beginning to understand and harness the power of belief. More and more instances are being documented of individuals who undergo "spontaneous remissions" from cancer and other life-threatening diseases. (A "spontaneous remission" is simply a case where a patient gets better but the doctor doesn't know why.) Researchers have found that one of the common factors in such cases is a strong will to live coupled with the patient's *belief* that he or she will actually become well.

Medicine has also carefully investigated the "placebo effect" and found additional compelling evidence of the power of belief. A placebo is an inert sugar pill with no medicinal properties. The patient is generally told that he or she is receiving a drug that will have the desired effect, such as relief of pain or healing of a specific illness or disorder. Believing that the effect will be forthcoming, the patient then transforms that belief into tangible, measurable biochemical processes that create healing.

There have been hundreds of well-documented studies of the effects of placebos. In one, patients with bleeding ulcers were divided into two groups. The first group was told they were being given a powerful new drug that would undoubtedly relieve their symptoms. Sure enough, 70 percent experienced significant improvement. The second group was told they would be given a new experimental drug about which little was known. This time only 25 percent got relief from their symptoms. Both groups received the same "medicine"—a placebo.

Many doctors have come to look upon positive beliefs as a genuine therapeutic agent, capable of altering the body's chemistry and mobilizing its defenses against disease. As Norman Cousins wrote in *Anatomy of an Illness*, "Drugs are not always necessary. Belief in recovery always is."

A Neurological View of Beliefs

Your brain consists of about 15 billion nerve cells, called neurons. Each neuron makes between 5,000 and 50,000 contacts with its neighbors, through electrochemical signals sent across the interconnecting axons and dendrites between them.

Considering that each of the 15 billion neurons makes this many connections, the number of interconnections that can take place is more than astronomical. The National Academy of Sciences estimates that "A single human brain has a greater number of possible connections among its nerve cells than the total number of atomic particles in the universe."

Most neuroscientists (specialists in the brain) now believe that all learning involves either the establishment of new neuronal networks or the connection of new input to existing networks. As our experience changes from moment to moment, the electrochemical patterns in the brain change as well. At any one moment, literally hundreds of billions of impulses are producing incalculably intricate waves of activity. This is happening in your brain now as you read this sentence. The British neuroscientist Sir Charles Sherrington poetically described this activity as "an enchanted loom where millions of flashing shuttles weave a dissolving pattern, always a meaningful pattern though never an abiding one . . . as if the Milky Way had entered upon some cosmic dance."

One of the most common theories regarding the brain's inner workings has seen it as a switching system, a sort of enormous telephone network in which, at any moment, countless billions of cells are connected in a complex information exchange. However, the patterns of neuronal connections are not permanently etched in the brain. Scientists now believe that once the neuronal networks are formed, they are not like the indelible grooves etched into a phonograph record. Rather, they seem to operate much like the changeable electromagnetic

Like a celestial chaperon, the placebo leads us through the uncharted passageways of mind and gives us a greater sense of infinity than if we were to spend all our days with our eyes hypnotically glued to the giant telescope at Mt. Palomar. What we see ultimately is that the placebo isn't really necessary and that the mind can carry out its difficult and wondrous missions unprompted by little pills. The placebo is only a tangible object made essential in an age that feels uncomfortable with intangibles, an age that prefers to think that every inner effect must have an outer cause. Since it has size and shape and can be hand-held, the placebo satisfies the contemporary craving for visible mechanisms and visible answers. . . . The placebo, then, is an emissary between the will to live and the body.

Norman Cousins

patterns on a computer disk that can be repeatedly and end-lessly modified.

When you learn something, a neuronal network is created in the brain. Repetition of that information or experience can strengthen the network. When you have an experience differ-ent from but *related to* the original network, the brain auto-matically "rewrites" the file to take the new input into account. The original network is thus replaced by a new, more inclusive set of pathways.

The importance of this should be obvious. Whatever you are today, whatever you know or don't know, is *modifiable*. Your skills and knowledge, your beliefs about your capabil-ities—none of this is etched in stone. It is completely open to transformation. That transformation is up to you.

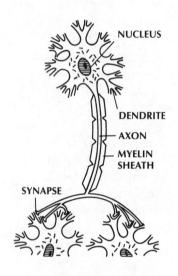

NUCLEUS

DENDRITE

AXON

MYELIN SHEATH

SYNAPSE

THE MIND-BODY CONNECTION

The awareness that mental beliefs affect the physical body can be traced to one of the great scientific advances of the 20th century: the consistent and undeniable proof that mind and body are intimately connected. "Every change in the mental-emotional state, conscious or unconscious," writes Dr. Elmer Green of the Menninger Clinic, "is accompanied by an appro-priate change in the physiological state." This connection is so immediate that some researchers, following Dr. Candace Pert of the National Institutes of Health (NIH), now speak of a "bodymind."

The evidence behind this lies in the fascinating and im-portant research done in the past ten years, much of it at NIH, which has shown that a group of at least 50 to 60 chemicals convey messages from the brain to the entire body. The most well-known of these are the endorphins, the body's natural pain-killers. These messenger molecules were previously known as neurotransmitters because they were believed to be produced and to be active only in the brain, facilitating communication among neurons. However, it is now known that they travel throughout the body communicating to every organ and lit-erally every cell.

What do they communicate? Indeed, everything: thoughts, feelings, beliefs, attitudes, moods, concepts. When we have a thought or feeling, that mental phenomenon gets translated within a split second into cascades of chemicals reaching every part of our body.

A classic example of this is the person walking across the grass who sees a coiled shape and thinks, "Snake!" This message of fear goes straight to the limbic system in the brain. There, the hypothalamus, acting as the manager of emotions, relays the message through the communication network of the spinal cord, and a chain reaction of physiological processes begins. The heart rate increases, breathing becomes rapid, blood pressure rises. Blood, carrying oxygen, is diverted from the brain to the muscles, giving the ability for "fight or flight." The endocrine system fills the blood with increased adrenaline, glucose, and other chemicals needed to support greatly increased physical activity. Of course, there is no snake, only a garden hose. But this imagined danger, this *thought*, is sufficient cause for the whole system to mobilize its forces.

In the same way, every thought has its physiological counterpart. Specific thoughts and feelings correspond to specific chemical combinations. A sad or angry thought means that our heart, lungs, liver, and kidneys experience that sadness or anger biochemically. Happy, optimistic, positive thoughts also are communicated to all parts of our body.

A belief, then, is more than just an idea. It is a psychophysiological whole, an interlocking system of thought, brain chemistry, and bodily response. Although you cannot see the biochemistry of the brain, you can see that people with high self-esteem and confidence, who believe in their abilities and their purpose in life, stand, move, speak with energy and vibrancy. Depressed people, people with low self-esteem who don't believe in themselves, often have poor posture, move slowly, talk slowly, even learn slowly.

Scientists can now trace the transformation of thoughts into matter by using a PET (positron emission tomography) scanner to visually monitor the activity of the brain. Whenever a particular portion of the brain is active, the blood flow to that area increases. When glucose is tagged with a radioactive isotope and injected into the blood, it can be observed as it is carried to those sites in the brain where most activity is going on. The PET scanner produces pictures of the brain, which change as the concentration of marker glucose molecules changes, as the brain thinks in different ways.

To think is to practice brain chemistry.

Dr. Deepak Chopra

Scientists have found that each distinct event in the mind, such as a strong memory, a sensation of pain, or a visual image, triggers a unique chemical pattern in the brain. The configuration is different for every thought. But, as Dr. Deepak Chopra comments, "If one could extend the portrait to be full-length, there is no doubt that the whole body changes at the same time, thanks to the cascades of neuro-transmitters and related messenger molecules."

In short, your brain converts thinking (beliefs) into your body and its actions. If you believe, "I can do it!" your brain tells your body to gear up with the energy you need for success. If you believe, "I'm not good enough," your brain tells your body, "Forget it. Don't even bother to try."

TAKING CONTROL: TECHNIQUES TO TRANSFORM NEGATIVE BELIEFS

With this larger perspective on the power of your beliefs, you should now be ready to begin identifying and defusing your limiting beliefs in order to create new, powerful, positive ones that can guide you toward becoming a Master. Let's begin by taking an inventory of those beliefs about yourself that influence your ability to learn and to meet the challenges of the Information Age.

■ ■ ■ ■

LEARNING ACTIVATOR #1
BELIEF INVENTORY

Part I
In this Activator you will examine your personal beliefs. Your purpose will be to discover what beliefs you have about yourself that are helpful and good, and what negative beliefs may be holding you back. Once

you know what beliefs are limiting you, you will learn several methods to overcome them.

To begin, try to discover what specific beliefs might be barriers for you. As examples, here are some limiting beliefs that students in my seminars have cited.

I have a bad memory.

I don't have time to read.

I always do poorly in math (languages, etc.).

I'm not smart enough.

Being intelligent isn't attractive.

If I try I will probably fail.

I'm too old to learn something new.

The mind is its own place and in itself can make a heaven of hell, a hell of heaven.

John Milton

To help yourself begin identifying some of your personal limiting beliefs, take a moment to think of a time when you experienced failure in a learning situation or felt you were unable to accomplish a task. Put yourself in that situation again. At that time, what were you saying to yourself and others around you? Were you saying things like, "I'm not smart enough," "This is too hard for me," or "I can't figure out how to do this"? What were your feelings: anger, frustration, guilt, doubt? What pictures came up in your mind? Perhaps you experienced your limiting beliefs as fears, such as "I'm afraid of trying this," or "I'm afraid of failing."

Write down as many limiting beliefs or fears as you can. You may experience them as feelings, statements, or actual mental images of a time when you failed at something. Translate your feelings and images into words as best you can.

Limiting beliefs and fears I have about learning or being intelligent are:

Reprogramming the unconscious beliefs that block fuller awareness of our creative/intuitive capabilities depends upon a key characteristic of the mind, namely that it responds to what is vividly imagined as though it were real experience.

Willis Harman, Ph.D.

Part II

Now take a moment to list some of those positive qualities that you believe honestly express your talents and capabilities in terms of learning and intelligence. For those of you who are a little shy about this (most of us find it easier to recognize and list our weaknesses and failings than our strengths), here are a few possibilities.

I am a fast reader.

I absorb new information quickly.

I love to learn around other people.

I enjoy the challenge of acquiring new knowledge.

I know how to quickly find information I need.

Now it's your turn. Some of the ways I feel positive about my intelligence are:

If you absolutely cannot find any positive beliefs about yourself, this chapter will help you develop some. For now, do not force yourself; either list a few qualities you think you might have, or simply move on to the next section.

▪ ▪ ▪ ▪

CREATING POSITIVE OPPOSITES

Now that you have identified some of the beliefs that hold you back, let's explore one powerful technique to transform them into positive opposites that will support your success. The following anecdote explains how it is done.

A young man named Jeff, who believed he had a bad memory, came to one of my seminars. In grade school and high school, Jeff had no trouble understanding the material he was studying, but whenever he had to take a test he would forget what he had learned. Although Jeff became successful in a sales career, he continued to be haunted by the belief that he had a bad memory. The older he got, the more the belief controlled his behavior. It seemed that the only thing Jeff could always remember was that he had a "bad memory."

In my seminar on developing reading skills, I invited Jeff to join me in front of the room and asked him to write five things that he had learned from what he had just read. He froze. I then asked him to teach me what it was like to be inside his body and not be able to remember.

"First of all," he said, "you have to get a knot in your stomach that spreads all the way through your chest." I did that. He then told me to imagine a large iceberg in my head. I asked him if he heard any internal voices. He responded that there was one that said, "You can't remember anything." I started that monologue in my head, too.

In an effort to match Jeff's posture, I also hunched my shoulders, stiffened my neck, and looked vacantly down toward the floor. I held my head stationary and shifted my eyes around without seeing anything. Soon, I was in front of the class looking just like Jeff, telling myself I couldn't remember. I found I could not remember five things I had just read, either! In imitating the physical and mental characteristics of a person in the midst of a "bad memory" attack, I too achieved the state of a bad memory.

The next step was to reverse the process: to change what Jeff was seeing, hearing, and feeling inside in order to change his ability to remember. To start this procedure it is necessary to find the "positive opposite" of each limiting physical and mental component.

I handed Jeff a marking pen and invited him to stand in front of the board. First, I asked him to change his internal dialogue by saying to himself, "I have excellent recall." Then I asked him to imagine a relaxing light expanding from his stomach to his chest. I told him to picture a warm beach scene, look at the ceiling, and let the material that he had read appear in his mind. He smiled and in a few moments wrote the five points on the board.

This story is one example of much anecdotal evidence showing that eliminating limiting beliefs begins by defining a

It's only a thought, and a thought can be changed.

Louise May

We are what we imagine ourselves to be.

Kurt Vonnegut, Jr.

new belief that is opposite to the one you hold. When you have identified a belief that is holding you back, it is necessary to create an alternative belief that is more positive, since your mind cannot change without a new pattern to supplant what is currently there. The following Activator will help you identify a positive opposite for a limiting belief you previously identified.

▪ ▪ ▪ ▪

LEARNING ACTIVATOR #2
CREATING A POSITIVE OPPOSITE

From the list you made in the last Activator, pick one of the limiting beliefs or fears that you would most like to change. As you look at your list, one particular belief will probably stand out over the others. If so, choose that one.

A limiting belief or fear I have about learning or being intelligent that I want to change is:

Now, think about a recurring situation in your personal or professional life, such as taking a test, reading a report or a memo, writing a paper, or listening to someone speak. Imagine the entire situation as fully as you can in your mind's eye, including sounds, body posture, and so on. When you have brought a full image into your mind, think of the limiting belief you wrote out above, and imagine that your mind's "belief department" begins to broadcast that message into the learning situation you are envisioning. Write what you experience when this belief or fear shows up in your behavior.

My posture is:

I experience the following physical sensations:

I can hear these internal messages:

I can see:

Other relevant aspects of my experience are:

Now identify the positive opposite of the belief or fear you wrote above. What would be an opposite belief that would support the emergence of your peak intelligence? Write it down. The positive opposite of my limiting belief or fear is:

Look at this positive statement and imagine a person who is experiencing the power of that belief. What would that person feel, see, and say? What positive internal dialogue would you expect the person to hear? Describe that person's experience.

His or her posture is:

He or she experiences the following physical sensations:

The internal "audiotapes" sound like:

The internal "videotapes" look like:

The outside world looks like:

Other relevant aspects are:

■ ■ ■ ■

MAKING THE CHANGE: THE QUICK-CHANGE TECHNIQUE

An essential element of learning how to change your beliefs is the understanding that *you cannot hold opposite beliefs simultaneously.* You can have the internal messages and external physical appearance of either a negative or positive belief, but you can't have both simultaneously. For instance, try to tell yourself that you have a good memory and a bad memory at the same time. Or try to match the physical demeanor of a person who is confidently working or studying at his maximum level and at the same time one who is sure he is dim-witted.

You can jump back and forth in your mind between the opposites, but you cannot *experience* them both at once. This is like the familiar figure that appears to be a vase and then suddenly two faces looking at each other, and then again a vase. Sometimes your brain sees one, sometimes the other, but never does it see both simultaneously. Look at the following illustrations and notice how your brain can shift between the alternative interpretations.

The choice of operating according to the limiting belief or the positive belief is up to you. You must first know that it is possible to choose, and then you have to know how to implement the image you want. The belief replacement technique I will teach you as a catalyst for change I call the *quick-change technique*.

■ ■ ■ ■

LEARNING ACTIVATOR #3
THE QUICK-CHANGE TECHNIQUE

Use the limiting belief you chose for the last Activator. Act as if you are experiencing that limiting belief in a learning situation now. Before you begin, relax for a minute. Close your eyes and take a couple of deep, slow breaths.

1. Take a moment to reexperience what you want to change. Heighten your awareness of the negative belief and how it affects your attitudes and actions by imagining it vividly in your mind. As you do this, be aware of your feelings and notice your posture. Actually see and hear the messages that your brain's belief department is playing.
2. Acknowledge that you want to change to a positive attitude. This is best done by saying out loud to yourself, "I want to change and I will change." In doing so, you put your brain's belief department on notice that something new is coming.
3. Remain in the mental state you want to replace, and begin to envision an image, small and in the distance, of what you would be like if you had all aspects of the positive opposite.
4. This step is a pivotal moment in which you are establishing a balance. At this point you are *experiencing* the limiting state, and *imagining* yourself poised in the distance with complete mastery of the positive opposite. Allow the limiting state to loosen its hold on you as you prepare for the next step. Imagine the positive opposite gaining energy as it gets ready to replace the limiting state. Experience the tension between the two.
5. In a flash (less than ½ second) bring the positive state in to replace the negative state. Immediately change your physical demeanor—not just in your imagination!—to reflect your new attitude as you embrace the positive opposite. Sit straighter, breathe more deeply, smile: whatever is appropriate to your new belief.

It all depends on how we look at things, and not how they are in themselves.

Carl G. Jung

Brains aren't designed to get results; they go in directions. If you know how the brain works you can set your own directions. If you don't, then someone else will.

Richard Bandler

6. Experience the new videotapes and audiotapes of the positive opposite. (You wrote down what you thought they would be in the previous Activator.) Pay attention to the new feelings and to the replacement posture. Feel what this change will mean for your life.
7. Repeat the series of steps 1–6 two or three times, briefly opening your eyes between each series. You will notice that it becomes more difficult to put yourself in the original negative state because the replacement state is becoming your new reality.
8. Once you have completed this exercise, *immediately take action*. Make a physical move toward engaging in action with your new belief.

■ ■ ■ ■

You will find the quick-change technique an effective tool the next time you are having difficulty in a learning situation or any other circumstance. As you continue to use it, it will become less mechanical and you will be able to execute it quickly and smoothly in any situation. Clearly, although the technique is called "quick change," lifetime habits do not change in seconds. You will need to use this technique over time and come back to it again and again if you find yourself slipping back into familiar destructive patterns.

What you have just done derives from the methodology known as neurolinguistic programming (NLP). It is modeled after a technique developed by Richard Bandler, cofounder of NLP, which he called the Swish Pattern in his book *Using Your Brain for a Change*. NLP is a relatively new discipline that has produced a series of techniques to affect personal change by using language to program the mind.

AFFIRMATIONS

Another effective device to influence your beliefs is the process of using affirmations. Affirmations are positive statements you communicate to yourself aloud or in writing several times a day. The goal of affirmations is to help you create beliefs and behavior that will enhance your capabilities by ensuring that your internal mental dialogues are positive.

Identifying the positive opposite of your limiting beliefs is an easy way to begin generating affirmations to support your specific needs. The following affirmations have been created by reversing some sample limiting beliefs. You can use them as examples when you create your own affirmations. For a little fun, and to bring home to you the desired effect of using affirmations, try the following experiment as you read the pairs of statements below out loud:

1. Read the limiting belief statement with the lethargic tone of voice and physical demeanor of a person who believes the truth of the statement.
2. Read the positive affirmation with the excitement and vigor of a convincingly impassioned actor or actress.
3. As you read each pair, notice how different you feel as you read the negative and then the positive statement.

Change your thoughts and you change your world.

Norman Vincent Peale

Remember, happiness doesn't depend upon who you are or what you have, it depends solely upon what you think.

Dale Carnegie

"I have a bad memory."
MY MEMORY IS EXCELLENT.

"Intelligent people are boring."
INTELLIGENT PEOPLE ARE INTERESTING.

"I don't have time to read."
I HAVE PLENTY OF TIME TO READ.

"Studying is a waste of time."
STUDYING IS BENEFICIAL TO ME.

"I can't remember much."
I REMEMBER EVERYTHING THAT IS OF VALUE TO ME.

"If I try I will probably fail."
I AM CERTAIN TO SUCCEED.

▪ ▪ ▪ ▪

LEARNING ACTIVATOR #4
CREATING AFFIRMATIONS

Pick a limiting belief from those you listed in Learning Activator #1 that you would like to change. Write it below.

Now write the positive opposite of the limiting belief.

The act of writing down the positive opposite sends a new message to your brain. Take a moment to read it to yourself, look at it, and feel what it is like to say the positive opposite.

The best way to create an affirmation is by personalizing the positive message in the form of an affirmative statement written in the present tense. In other words, speak as if the statement is true *now* rather than in the future. Don't say, "I will learn to communicate better"; say, "I am an excellent communicator." To make the affirmation personal, use the following examples as a guide.

I, _____, believe that learning is easy.
I, _____, remember everything I want to.
I, _____, have plenty of time to read.

My personal affirmation is:

Once you have formulated your affirmation, repeat it to yourself from time to time throughout the day. I also suggest that you write it at least twenty times a day to help make it more real to you. You can also print it on a three-by-five card or a larger sheet of paper and place it in a conspicuous place in your home and workplace.

▪ ▪ ▪ ▪

Don't limit yourself to one affirmation. Create them from several of your limiting beliefs, and focus on the ones most significant at any given time. The more often your "belief department" receives the supportive message embedded in your affirmations, the easier it will become to liberate and realize your full potential.

EXAMINE YOUR BELIEFS WITH RATIONAL THINKING

One other important and effective means of eliminating negative beliefs is a method advocated by the British philosopher and mathematician Bertrand Russell. Russell's plan entails carefully examining your belief system to determine whether your beliefs are rational or irrational.

Rational beliefs are those consistent with your carefully thought-out understanding of how things are. Irrational beliefs are essentially automatic reactions based on childhood conditioning. For example, you may have developed the irrational belief that "successful people only succeed by manipulating others." This belief may have squelched your own ambition and capability for success. After all, you don't want to consider yourself someone who steps on others!

If you consider this belief calmly and rationally, you will see that although the statement may be true of some people, countless others certainly succeed without meeting this negative requirement. The result is that you can stop sabotaging your progress; you can allow yourself to become successful and still maintain your self-respect.

The first step in this method, then, is a careful examination of your values and belief system. What do you believe about yourself and your capabilities? Where did these beliefs come from: parents, peers, teachers? Are these beliefs true? Are they helpful? If you think they have been true of you in the past, do you want to continue in the same pattern, or create new beliefs more consistent with your capabilities and goals? Then, as Russell suggests:

> Let your conscious beliefs be so vivid and emphatic that they make an impression upon your unconscious strong enough to cope with the impressions made . . . when you were an infant.

One change always leaves the way open for the establishment of others.

Niccolo Machiavelli

Look into the irrationality closely with a determination not to respect it and not to let it dominate you. When it thrusts foolish thoughts or feelings [limiting beliefs] into your consciousness, pull them up by the roots, examine them, and reject them.

The American psychologist Albert Ellis has used a similar approach in a system called rational-emotive therapy (RET). RET is a method that emphasizes our ability to govern our feelings and actions by clarifying our thinking. In his many books, Ellis teaches that "by rationally and realistically organizing and disciplining his or her thinking, a human being can live the most self-fulfilling, creative, and emotionally satisfying life."

A substantial part of RET involves examining the language of one's thinking for what Ellis calls irrational beliefs. For example, when a client says, "I *must* work harder at my job," the RET therapist would suggest that he really means, "*It would prove better* if I worked harder at my job." Or, if a person feels, "I *never* can read fast enough," a more truthful appraisal might be, "I *have often not been able* to read as much as I want in the time I have had available—but that doesn't mean I couldn't learn to read faster." Again, "It would be a *disaster* if I lost my job," probably translates into "It would be *inconvenient* if I lost my job at this time, but it might lead to something better."

This approach defuses much of the emotional intensity generated by words like "must," "should," "never," "disaster," and enables the individual to see the situation more clearly and with a broader perspective. From there, solutions can more readily be found.

THE BELIEF BEHIND SUCCESS

The fruit of transforming negative beliefs into more constructive ones through positive opposites and affirmations is not only a new psychological perspective, but also increased success. This is because, as we have discussed, your beliefs are at the root of your actions.

Whatever method you use, if you work conscientiously and consistently at eliminating your limiting beliefs and encouraging the growth of more positive beliefs, and then follow through with dynamic actions, you will find that all enterprises meet with greater success and that you grow in happiness.

You have no doubt heard it said that "Nothing succeeds like success." In the context of beliefs, nothing can create a positive belief as quickly as the experience of success. Every success you have restructures the neuronal networks in your brain and strengthens the positive habits and attitudes in your unconscious belief system. You will soon fill your brain archives with records of success.

Then, whenever new experiences and challenges present themselves and you request your brain's belief department to make an evaluation, instead of receiving messages like "No way" or "I can't handle that," you will receive messages of confidence: "That's easy. I can do that." Using these techniques and insights, you can spark a new momentum in your life and put yourself on the way to becoming a Master of the Information Age.

At this point, take a moment to review the purpose statement at the beginning of the chapter. Have you accomplished the purpose? Do you feel that your beliefs and attitudes promote your success? Have you mastered the techniques that can help you weaken and eliminate your limiting beliefs? Have you assimilated all the important material? If you don't feel you've gotten it all, take some time to review the sections you haven't fully mastered before going on to Chapter 3.

RESOURCES

The brain

Changeux, Jean-Pierre. *Neuronal Man: The Biology of Man.* (New York: Pantheon Books, 1985). A provocative inquiry into the biology of the mind by a famous French neurobiologist.

Hooper, Judith and Dick Teresi. *The Three-Pound Universe.* (New York: Dell Publishing, 1986). A highly readable book providing a well-documented tour of the human brain.

Restak, M.D., Richard. *The Brain.* (New York: Bantam Books, 1984). A comprehensive book based on the PBS series of the same name; includes information on the PET scanner device.

Mind/body

Cousins, Norman. *Head First.* (New York: E. P. Dutton, 1989). The author of *Anatomy of an Illness* presents the growing scientific evidence that positive emotions can heal the body.

Dychtwald, Ken. *Bodymind.* (Los Angeles: Jeremy P. Tarcher, 1977). One of the first books to cover the interrelationship of mind and body.

Franklin, Jon. *Molecules of the Mind: The Brave New Science of Molecular Psychology.* (New York: Dell Publishing, 1987). A discussion of how the mind is affected by chemicals produced within and without the body. Based on a Pulitzer Prize-winning set of articles by the author.

Garfield, Charles A. *Peak Performance: Mental Training Techniques of the World's Greatest Athletes.* (Los Angeles: Jeremy P. Tarcher, 1984). An abundance of practical exercises to relax, visualize, and foster peak performance. Presented in terms of sports, but applicable to all endeavors.

Ornstein, Ph.D., Robert and David Sobel, M.D. *The Healing Brain.* (New York: Simon & Schuster, 1987). A neurobiologist and physician give examples of how the brain and body work in concert.

Positive thinking

Bandler, Richard. *Using Your Brain—for a Change.* (Moab, Utah: Real People Press, 1985). A compilation of a series of demonstrations by the author, cofounder of Neuro Linguistic Programming, in which modifying beliefs is a central theme.

Maltz, Maxwell. *Psycho-Cybernetics.* (New York: Simon & Schuster, 1968). How the power of belief and positive self-image can bring success.

Ray, Sondra. *I Deserve Love.* (Berkeley, CA: Celestial Arts Publishing, 1987). How to use affirmation to improve self-esteem and relationships. Techniques applicable to all aspects of life.

Robbins, Anthony. *Unlimited Power.* (New York: Fawcett Book Group, 1987). One of the best books on achieving success through developing peak performance levels by one of the leaders in the neurolinguistic programming field.

■■■ ■

CHAPTER 3

ENTER THE
LEARNING STATE

Ever since the renowned psychologist Abraham Maslow wrote
about "peak experiences" in the late 1960s, scientists and psychologists have been intrigued by the concept of a special frame
of mind that contributes to the highest levels of human performance. Today many researchers talk about the existence of
a "flow" state, a particular mental and physical condition that
allows us to cross the boundary from our usual level to truly
superior performance. Pioneer flow state researcher Mihaly
Csikszentmihalyi of the University of Chicago defines flow as
"a state of concentration that amounts to absolute absorption
in an activity . . . that marvelous feeling that you are in command of the present and performing at the peak of your ability."

Other researchers have called it peak performance, peak
intelligence, or "the zone." Whatever its name, psychologists
now recognize that there are many things people can intentionally do to help themselves function at this heightened level.
The next two chapters are about making use of these known
factors to develop your own flow state for mastering the Information Age.

The points we will cover in this chapter can be summarized in the following three principles and their action corollaries:

1. A relaxed and receptive mental state is crucial to becoming a Master. This frame of mind greatly enhances learning, concentration, thinking, memory, and action. Stress is detrimental to all aspects of information processing and productivity.

   Action corollary: *You can decrease stress and create a relaxed mental state at any time.*

2. The environment in which you work or study is a critical part of being a Master.

   Action corollary: *You can easily enrich your environment to facilitate learning, creative thinking, and optimum performance.*

3. Your physical condition is vital to peak mental performance and optimum functioning of your brain.

   Action corollary: *You can improve your physical condition by applying a few simple principles regarding proper diet and exercise.*

■ ■ ■ ■

No man can think clearly when his fists are clenched.

George Jean Nathan

STRESS: THE MASTER'S NUMBER ONE ENEMY

One major challenge we all face in the Information Age is stress. Between our responsibilities at work, lack of sufficient time, an overload of information, and various personal issues, hardly anyone can go through a day without facing a number of stressors.

However, stress is a Master's number-one enemy. It reduces our productivity and greatly diminishes our ability to be clear-minded, logical, insightful, and creative. As Karl Albrecht notes in his book *Brain Power*, when a person becomes stressed

> his or her higher level thinking processes, such as memory, logical reasoning, idea production, and decision making, tend to suffer. The nervous activation of the brain, combined with the increased flow of stress hormones, tends to cause whole portions of the brain to more or less shut down their activities. This biological fact means that complex mental tasks present much more diffi-

culty to a person when he or she is experiencing the tension of a pressure situation than when fully relaxed.

Medical research has found that stress creates approximately 1,000 chemical and physical changes in the body, including the production of stress hormones like adrenaline and cortisol. These chemicals speed up metabolism and generate the "fight or flight" response, which initially causes a surge of energy but eventually exhausts us if the stress continues.

In addition to the detrimental effect of stress on mental functioning, the medical profession now believes that from 75 to 90 percent of the physical ills that afflict us are due to stress. Stress is strongly implicated in premature aging, the destruction of brain cells, and the weakening of the immune system.

In simple terms, stress comes from an inability to deal with the pressures and demands of life. Sometimes the source of the stress is within us: we can't work or read fast enough, we're too tired, we don't have the right background to do a job, we're not good at communicating what we want, and so on. These inabilities create anxiety, frustration, worry, and other mental and physical expressions of stress. Other times, the origin of our stress is external: too much noise in our environment, constant interruptions, unrealistic demands and deadlines, too many phone calls and meetings, and so on.

In order to master the Information Age, you must learn to manage stress effectively. Part of this process is knowing how to change your perceptions about yourself and your ability to meet the challenges of the Information Age. This is why the techniques you learned in the previous chapter to change your beliefs and attitudes is so important. Learning to feel confident about yourself and approaching each day with a positive attitude can go a long way toward helping you cope with the stressors in your work and personal life.

The most important method of managing stress, however, is actually to reduce your reaction to it. This approach is a direct frontal attack on stress, and it involves learning one or more meditation or relaxation techniques to help you stay calm and focused. Extensive psychological and biomedical research over the past 20 years has shown that the most effective of

Brain Waves

Brain waves are measured by hooking the subject up to electrodes that serve as tiny microphones to pick up and amplify the subtle electrical activity taking place within the brain as neurons "talk" to each other across the synaptic gap.

Communication between neurons begins with an electrical impulse that travels down the axon. This electrical signal never takes place in only one neuron; signals occur in millions or hundreds of millions of neurons at once and create changing patterns of electromagnetic fields. These patterns are measurable. The most common device to measure brain-wave activity is the electroencephalograph (EEG). A more recent device is known as the Mind Mirror. The EEG generally registers the overall brain-wave pattern while the Mind Mirror measures the output of each hemisphere for each category of brain wave.

these techniques can greatly diminish the negative physical and emotional consequences of stress.

THE ALPHA LEARNING STATE

A calm, relaxed state of mind and body—the opposite of the stress response—is the optimum state for peak learning and intelligence. Giorgi Lozanov, the originator of accelerated learning, was one of the first to demonstrate that the intentional creation of a relaxed state resulted in enhanced learning capabilities. A major component of the success of his system, and of all subsequent learning acceleration programs, is getting oneself into a relaxed state of body and mind in which the brain produces steady alpha rhythms.

Types of Brain Waves

Alpha waves are one of four types of brain waves that correspond to different mental states. The four types are called alpha, beta, delta, and theta.

BETA. Beta waves occur when the mind is active and in a "seeking" mode. You might think this would be the best state for learning, particularly when you consider that in the beta state your brain is working at its fastest rate. However, research has demonstrated that a fast-moving brain is not necessarily a fast-learning brain. In this state, the brain is apparently too busy to focus and absorb or to process information effectively. Imagine trying to thread a sewing needle with both your hands moving around at high speed and you will begin to understand the principle.

Beta is the brain wave characteristic of harried moments, times when you are rushing around trying to get a hundred things done at once, dealing with phone calls one after another, attempting to read a stack of memos for a meeting or to fit six errands into half an hour. Usually, after the dust settles around this kind of activity, it becomes clear that you really accomplished less than you had hoped for.

Stress and beta waves are closely related. The daily stress brought on by the demands of work or school can cause your brain to race with anxiety and worry as you attempt to process huge amounts of material or make important decisions. This state is only marginally productive, whether in a learning situation or any other endeavor that requires effective action.

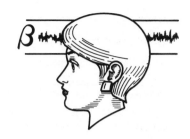

ALPHA. By contrast to the busy, sometimes frantic tempo of beta, alpha waves reflect a calm, relaxed mind and brain. They characterize a state of restful alertness that is conducive to receptivity and rapid assimilation of information. The physical state that generally corresponds to alpha—relaxation, a dissolving of muscular tension, and a slowing of the heart rate—has been found to aid memory and contribute to efficient thinking. In this state, learning happens effortlessly.

Alpha waves are also characteristic of meditation. It is the state in which we daydream and allow our imagination to flow freely.

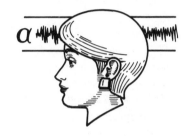

THETA. Theta brain waves occur during deep meditative states when a person experiences profound inner quietness. Writer Arthur Koestler called it "reverie"—a drowsy, twilight state midway between being awake and falling asleep. In his study of accelerated learning, British researcher Colin Rose says that "Thousands of artistic and literary inspirations and scientific inventions have been credited to this state, a sort of free-form thinking that puts you in touch with your subconscious." Theta also appears to be the state in which the body's immune system operates most efficiently.

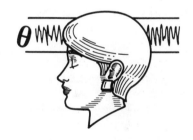

DELTA. Delta waves occur during deep, dreamless sleep.

Mastery of the Information Age depends on our ability to create and sustain for ourselves the alpha state that is so conducive to learning and productivity. In the next sections I will introduce you to four powerful methods to help you achieve a peak learning state characterized by a predominance of alpha rhythms:

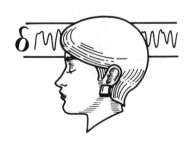

- a simple system of deep diaphragmatic breathing called alpha breathing;

- meditation and relaxation techniques;
- specific kinds of music and sounds; and
- "brain machines."

Alpha Breathing

Deep breathing is important for three reasons. First, your brain requires a large amount of oxygen to function at its peak level of intelligence. Even though it weighs only three pounds, a mere 2 to 3 percent of your total body weight, your brain uses *20 to 25 percent* of your oxygen intake. Deep breathing ensures that the brain's oxygen demand is satisfied.

Second, deep breathing is extremely useful for relaxation. In *Peak Performance*, author Charles A. Garfield said, "Of all the relaxation skills, diaphragmatic, or belly, breathing is the easiest to learn, providing almost immediate feedback through the attainment of a soothing sense of relaxation that you can often feel throughout your body." Diaphragmatic breathing is easy to learn because you already know how to do it. It is simply a matter of reeducating yourself in the natural way you breathed as a child.

Third, maintaining a steady natural breathing cycle is one of the most effective ways to establish a relaxed rhythm for your brain to follow. Our bodies have natural internal rhythms. These rhythms fall out of synchrony with each other when stress causes our breathing to become more rapid, our brain-wave state to remain locked in beta, our heart rate to increase, and all our organs to intensify their level of function. The farther we move from our natural relaxed rhythms, the more difficult it is for our brain to operate at peak intelligence.

Using alpha breathing, you can consciously control the depth and rhythm of your breathing to increase oxygen intake and produce the state of relaxation characterized by alpha brain waves.

Before you learn the technique of alpha breathing, you need to learn how to breathe from your diaphragm. Most people in our stressed society breathe shallowly, mostly in the chest. Natural deep breathing begins with the expansion of your lower abdomen, causing the diaphragm to move downward and draw air into the lungs, and then ends in your chest.

Controlled deep breathing helps the body to transform the air we breathe into energy. The stream of energized air produced by properly executed and controlled deep breathing produces a current of inner energy which radiates throughout the entire body and can be channeled to the body areas that need it the most, on demand.

Nancy Zi

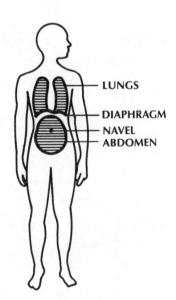

LUNGS

DIAPHRAGM
NAVEL
ABDOMEN

"Breathing with your abdomen" means that you use your abdominal area to move the diaphragm. You might experience the expansion and contraction of the abdominal air as bringing air into your *stomach*, but that is not the case. Look at the diagram in the margin and imagine that you have squeezed the bulb on the eyedropper by contracting your stomach, so that all the air has been expelled from the dropper tube. In order to bring air in (inhale), you need to expand your abdominal muscles and release the bulb.

Let's try this now. In order to facilitate learning, I have broken the process of diaphragmatic breathing into a series of steps. This may make it feel strange and mechanical at first, but the process is actually continuous, smooth, and natural, as you will experience once you incorporate it as your normal way to breathe.

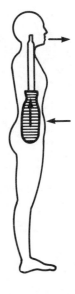

1. Place your right hand over your navel and your left hand on your upper abdomen just below your rib cage. Relax all of your abdominal muscles. Begin with an inhalation that causes your right hand to move slightly outward. Your hand should move as a result of the inhalation, not from forcing it with your stomach muscles.
2. As you complete your in-breath by filling your lungs, your chest will expand, causing your left hand to move outward and upward. Again, the movement should result solely from your inhalation, not from pushing with your stomach muscles.
3. Exhale by reversing steps 1 and 2. Make certain you relax on the exhalation and let the air naturally flow out without forcing it.

As we free our breath (through diaphragmatic breathing) we relax our emotions and let go of our body tensions.

Gay Hendricks

Take at least four seconds from the beginning of the inhalation to the end of the exhalation in each breathing cycle.

People who meditate often use regular, rhythmic breathing to help them achieve a relaxed state. A steady breathing cycle lasting four seconds or more will help you achieve a relaxed alpha state that supports your peak intelligence. The following simple two-minute exercise can be used to help you prepare for any learning task or regain a relaxed state when you are under stress. Try it now, and then continue to use it on a daily basis in the future.

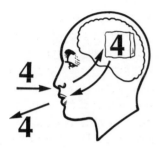

▪ ▪ ▪ ▪

LEARNING ACTIVATOR #5
ALPHA BREATHING

1. Using diaphragmatic breathing, inhale *through your nose* to the count of four (one second per count). While inhaling, imagine that oxygen is going directly to your brain.
2. Hold your breath for a count of four. As you hold your breath, imagine that the oxygen is cooling your brain.
3. Exhale *through your mouth* for a count of four. While exhaling, imagine that any tensions in your mind or body are being released into the atmosphere.
4. Without pausing after the exhalation, immediately repeat steps 1–3.
5. Complete steps 1–4 a total of four times.
6. Resume natural breathing.

Try this now and you will immediately notice the relaxing effect. Your relaxation will be even deeper if you perform alpha breathing with your eyes closed to avoid external distractions.

▪ ▪ ▪ ▪

While breathing is ordinarily an involuntary act that takes place without conscious direction, by occasionally monitoring it you can make adjustments to help you regain the rhythm of alpha breathing. The act of observing your breath has a naturally calming and focusing effect.

Monitor your breathing from time to time. Set up some "memory triggers" for yourself. For example, every time you get in your car, take a moment to monitor your breathing before you turn on the engine.

Meditation and Relaxation Techniques

Meditation techniques are a second way to achieve an alpha state. Meditation has existed for millennia. Yoga, Zen, transcendental meditation, centering prayer, and many other practices have as their goal a state of expanded awareness and deep inner peace known as Enlightenment. These ancient practices, rooted in spiritual traditions, produce a quiet, peaceful, alert mind and a deeply relaxed body.

These techniques have also been supplemented by modern methods such as the relaxation response, autogenic training, and various kinds of "guided" meditations, many available on cassette tape and involving visualization. Most of these 20th-century developments have no spiritual aspirations but merely strive for a relaxed state of mind and body.

Many of these practices are quite easy to do, and their results can be profoundly beneficial to peak performance of learning- and thinking-related tasks. The most extensively researched of the techniques is transcendental meditation (TM), which has been taught around the world for over 30 years. Over 350 published studies indicate that TM practice produces a state of rest and relaxation deeper than sleep, reduces anxiety and stress, alleviates insomnia, lowers high blood pressure, and strengthens the immune system. Its benefits over the long run appear to produce a slowing of the aging process; five-year TM meditators test out with a "biological age" averaging 12 years younger than their chronological age. An organization consisting of several thousand physicians (the American Association of Physicians Practicing the Transcendental Meditation Program) endorses TM for its stress-reduction and general health benefits.

Many of the benefits that meditators experience can be gained in other ways. The following Activator contains a technique that you can learn quickly and use in your daily life. Utilizing breathing and mental awareness, it is similar to some Zen and yoga practices. By helping you relax and dissolve tension, it will keep you from feeling stressed due to information overload. You can use this technique to alleviate anxiety before or after any learning or work situation.

We are sick with fascination for the useful tools of names and numbers, of symbols, signs, conceptions and ideas. Meditation is therefore the art of suspending verbal and symbolic thinking for a time, somewhat as a courteous audience will stop talking when a concert is about to begin.

Alan Watts

If we were to ask the brain how it would like to be treated, whether shaken at a random, irregular rate, or in a rhythmic, harmonious fashion, we can be sure that the brain, or for that matter the whole body, would prefer the latter.

Itzhak Bentov

■ ■ ■ ■
LEARNING ACTIVATOR #6
A SIMPLE MEDITATION TECHNIQUE

When Mozart was composing at the end of the eighteenth century, the city of Vienna was so quiet that fire alarms could be given verbally, by a shouting watchman mounted on top of St. Stefan's cathedral. . . . In twentieth-century society, the noise level is such that it keeps knocking our bodies out of tune and out of their natural rhythms. This ever-increasing assault of sound upon our ears, minds, and bodies adds to the stress load of civilized beings trying to live in a highly complex environment.

Steven Halpern

The purpose of this meditation exercise is to help you attain a state of deep rest and relaxation to quiet your mind. You will find it effective if practiced daily.

Begin by finding a relatively quiet place where you will be free from interruptions. Sit comfortably, in a chair, on a couch or bed, or wherever you can sit with your spine comfortably erect. Don't slouch or lie down—that would tend to put you to sleep.

Close your eyes.

After a few moments, begin to observe your ordinary breathing. Don't try to *do* anything. Breathe only through your nose. Place your attention on either.

the flow of breath at the tip of your nostrils, feeling the air flow quietly in and out; or

the rhythmic rise and fall of your chest or abdomen.

Either is fine, but decide which you will do and stay with that. When you find your attention wandering and other thoughts arising, simply bring your attention gently back to your breathing. Don't try to control your breathing if it starts to slow down or soften. This shows that you are relaxing. Your job is not to direct, just to quietly observe.

Continue in this way for 5 to 15 minutes. When you are finished, take some more time to come out slowly. Rub your hands together, stretch, and only then open your eyes.

■ ■ ■ ■

Meditation and relaxation techniques are easy to do and are effective. But, as with everything, you have to *do* them to get the results. I recommend that you learn at least one of these techniques and use it *regularly*, adding it into your daily routine for a few minutes before breakfast, when you come home from work, or both if you have the time. You cannot become an Information Master unless you have learned or developed some effective technique or strategy to reduce your level of stress.

Getting in Synch with Music
Another effective way to produce a relaxed peak learning state is to use certain types of music in the background. Modern-

day music therapists are rediscovering a truth known to ancient cultures: Music can affect our brain, body, and spirit.

The Greek mathematician and philosopher Pythagoras taught that music could harmonize our mental rhythms and put us more in tune with natural law. Plato and his pupil Aristotle also believed strongly in the power of music "to harmonize the soul and body."

The brain and body are extremely sensitive and responsive to sound, whether or not we are conscious of it. Sounds can and do excite or calm our emotions, raise or lower our blood pressure, and affect our respiration and brain cells. Pleasant sounds and music can induce a relaxed, receptive learning state characterized by alpha brain rhythms, while unpleasant sounds can have a harmful effect on both body and mind.

Today we live in noise-polluted environments, making it difficult to focus, to relax, and to concentrate. Think, for example, of how you feel when a loud noise startles you. Your heart races, you gasp for breath, and you tense up, knotting your stomach. Internally, your blood pressure rises, and stress-related chemicals such as adrenaline pour into your bloodstream. Unfortunately, research indicates that our bodies react according to this same general pattern (although not so dramatically) from common sounds like traffic noise, heavy machinery, and even the white noise of office equipment.

Sounds reach the brain following two pathways, one to the auditory center in the temporal lobe, the other to the brain stem, which controls the autonomic nervous system. The autonomic nervous system governs respiration, circulation, digestion, and glandular production. It is easy to speculate that the body's stress reaction to some sounds—as well as the soothing effect of other sounds—is caused by the sound impulses directly influencing this vital control center.

Another reason sounds have such a powerful effect on us is that they consist of waves, which interact with the wave patterns of our brains and bodies. All of nature is composed of rhythms and frequencies. Indeed, contemporary physics often speaks of the universe as a web of interconnecting wave patterns. All matter is in a constant state of rhythmic oscillation and pulsation.

Without music, life would be a mistake.

Friedrich Nietzsche

Just as certain selections of music will nourish your physical body and your emotional layer, so other musical works will bring greater health to your mind.

Hal A. Lingerman

The simplest single-celled organism oscillates to a number of different frequencies, at the atomic, molecular, sub-cellular, and cellular levels. Microscopic movies of these organisms are striking for the ceaseless, rhythmic pulsation that is revealed. In an organism as complex as a human being, the frequencies of oscillation and the interactions between those frequencies are multitudinous.

George Leonard

At the most basic level, every living thing is vibrating to specific frequencies. Outside us, we find the ordered rhythmic motion of stars and planets, the cycles of the moon, the ebb and flow of tides, the rhythm of the seasons. Within us, we have our daily circadian rhythms, the rise and fall of hormonal concentrations in the blood, the beating of the heart, the constant inflow and outflow of breath, and literally dozens of other internal rhythms. As one physicist phrased it, "We are finding that the universe is composed not of matter, but of music."

Research in various parts of the world, from India to Canada, Kansas, and Colorado, has demonstrated that a measurable and powerful effect can be produced on plant growth by playing music or broadcasting ultrasonic frequencies to the plants. In one study, plants that were "serenaded" had 72 percent more leaves and grew 20 percent taller than those that were not.

I mention this not just for curiosity's sake. The human nervous system is infinitely more sensitive than the simple nervous systems of plants. If plants experience such dramatic effects from sounds in their environment, we certainly do also. We can choose to use sounds to produce harmony in our being and liveliness in our brain.

One of the primary methods used by Georgi Lozanov to create and maintain a relaxed learning state in his classes was to play music from the Baroque period. (Baroque music flourished from about 1600 to 1750. Well-known Baroque composers include Bach, Handel, Vivaldi, and Corelli.) The slow movements of Baroque compositions, generally designated as "largo" or "adagio," have approximately 60 beats per minute. This is close to the rate of the human heartbeat in a relaxed state.

Multiple sources of similar vibration in the same environment tend to modify their frequencies so that they are in synchrony with each other. Lozanov found that the rhythm of the heart and breathing would tend to synchronize with the beat of the music. The brain would follow the relaxed frequency of the breathing and heartbeat to its own harmonic place of relaxation. This is called the "biological following response" and explains why you can shift your brain-wave state by regulating your breathing.

Not only will your brain fall into step with the internal cadence of your breathing and heart rate, it will also tend to match certain external frequencies, such as sound vibrations. This is why using appropriate music can be so effective: it puts you into a relaxed frame of mind that supports mastery.

Many teachers of accelerated learning who incorporate music in their classes have consistently found that it is useful not only for inducing a heightened learning state but also because it stimulates the nonverbal right hemisphere of the brain. Learning is far more integrated and powerful when both hemispheres are actively involved in the process. Creativity and problem-solving ability are also greatly enhanced.

With the growing awareness in society of the power of sound and the value of a relaxed, alert mental state, a number of modern composers have created music specifically designed to influence our mental activity and improve brain functioning. Some have incorporated the sounds of nature, such as dolphin or whale calls, bird songs, or ocean waves. These sounds may be electronically altered or used in their pure form.

In addition, in my research I have found many synthesized sounds to be effective in enhancing mental clarity, creativity, and focus. I believe that the proper use of music and other specific sound patterns is one of our most powerful and practical tools to positively influence learning capacity and actually increase intelligence.

I recommend that you play some appropriate music as background while reading or studying. If you are distracted by the music at first, turn the volume down until it is almost imperceptible. As you begin to get accustomed to it, slowly raise the volume with successive sessions until you find the level that best supports your learning.

In my seminars, I occasionally find musicians or music lovers who simply do not like to read with music on; their minds are so trained to listen to the music that it divides their attention and makes concentration difficult. If after trying music for some time you think you are in this category, feel free to work without it. But I encourage you to give the music a thorough trial first.

A list of some of the musical selections I recommend is included in the box on the next page.

Music is a readily available, highly effective tool that you can use to improve both your cognitive and physical abilities.

Arthur Winter, M.D.

Suggested Music for Study

Contemporary
A Journey Home—Georgia Kelly and Dusan Bogdanovic (Global Pacific)
Available Light—W. A. Mathieu (Windham Hill)
Breathe—Sky Canyon and Marcus Allen (Narada)
The Fairy Ring—Mike Rowland (Narada)
Fresh Impressions—Georgia Kelly and Dusan Bogdanovic (Global Pacific)
Glass Green—Tim Story (Windham Hill)
Imaginary Roads—William Ackerman (Windham Hill)
Waters of Life—Bob Kindler (Global Pacific)
Nightnoise—Billy Oskay and Micheal O'Douhnaill (Windham Hill)

Baroque
The slow movements of many Baroque compositions are excellent for helping the brain settle into a peak-learning mode. Several suggestions:

Brain-Mind Machines

Just as you would go to a local health club to use exercise machines and free weights and join aerobics classes or other forms of physical exercise, you can now find "brain gyms" with equipment to work out your mind. These "brain gyms" are leading-edge technology and still quite experimental, but they are becoming popular in several major cities across the United States. This newly emerging field is similar to the physical fitness boom of the '60s and '70s, although still far smaller in scope.

Sound and light machines, which utilize rhythmic tones and flickering lights to lead the brain toward an alpha state, are also available for purchase and home use. These machines are based on research into the "flicker phenomenon," identified about forty years ago by British neuroscientist W. Gray Walter.

Dr. Walter found that rhythmically flashing lights altered brain-wave activity and produced trancelike states of relaxation and vivid mental imagery. Subsequent research suggested that flicker effects at certain frequencies could enhance intellectual functioning and produce greater synchronization of the two brain hemispheres. Other researchers found that adding rhythmic auditory signals intensified the effects.

The sound and light machines now in use consist of goggles containing tiny light bulbs or LEDs, stereo headphones, and a console that permits the user to control the frequency and type of audiovisual stimulation. The most sophisticated of these devices include computers equipped with sound synthesizers using powerful microprocessors that permit a virtually infinite number of audiovisual experiences. Smaller systems are preprogrammed with an assortment of programs, but also allow the user to create and store a variety of personalized programs. The least expensive models allow preselected programs only.

As the Information Age creates more and more demand on the brain, a number of companies are making these "brain machines" available to employees. According to Michael Hutchison, author of *Megabrain* and publisher of a brain-machine newsletter called the *Megabrain Report*, these devices "represent a historic breakthrough in human development that will allow large numbers of humans to function consistently at levels of mental efficiency, creativity and intelligence that have in the past been attained, for the most part, only by the gifted few."

Nevertheless, as you consider using any of these devices or any new ones that appear on the market, I suggest that you use caution and investigate carefully. Your brain is a delicate instrument, and these devices are still in the experimental stage.

CREATING AN ENRICHED ENVIRONMENT FOR WORK AND LEARNING

Just as your brain state affects your ability to be a Master, so do your external surroundings strongly affect your ability to cross over the line to peak performance. Yet many people continue to operate in conditions that are destructive rather than supportive of their productivity. The conscious and subconscious messages you receive from your physical surroundings can stimulate or depress your learning and working abilities.

Peak intelligence emerges most easily in an enriched environment. The beneficial effect on the brain of an environment rich in stimuli was discovered first by Mark Rosenzweig and colleagues at the University of California at Berkeley. Beginning in the 1960s the Rosenzweig group raised rats in an environment enriched by "toys" such as ladders, wheels, and mazes. Alongside this group of privileged rats was a comparable group raised in an "impoverished" environment: a plain box. Both groups received the same food and water.

After only three months, the "enriched" rats performed better in various behavioral tasks and were healthier. When the brains of the two sets of rats were examined, some striking findings emerged. The cerebral cortex (the seat of higher intelligence) of the enriched rats weighed 4 percent more than the cortexes of the impoverished rats. The environmental stimulation had caused brain cell growth to occur.

This experiment was replicated in the early 1970s by Dr. William Greenough, chairman of the program in neuroscience and behavioral biology at the University of Illinois. Creating what he called "the rat equivalent of Disneyland," he also found an increase in brain size and weight in the more fortunate

BACH
Aria from The Goldberg Variations
Largo from Harpsichord Concerto in F Minor
Adagio from Concerto in D Minor for Two Violins

CORELLI
Largo from Concerto no. 7 in D Minor, op. 5
Any largo movement from 12 Concerti Grossi, op. 6

HANDEL
Any largo movement from 12 Concerti Grossi, op. 6
Largo from Concerto no. 1 in B-flat Major, op. 3

VIVALDI
Largo from "Winter," from The Four Seasons
Largo from Concerto in D Major for Guitar and Strings
Largo from Concerto in C Major for Mandolin, Strings, and Harpsichord

For an expanded list, see Superlearning by Lynn Schroeder and Sheila Ostrander.

rats, as compared to the control group living in a more barren, less stimulating environment. The weight increase was a result of the growth of new dendrites, the part of the brain cell that connects to other cells.

There is now increasing evidence to support the importance of enriched environments for human beings. For example, children who are removed from environments where they are undernourished or deprived of intellectual and sensory stimulation show significant growth in mental and emotional faculties when moved to improved surroundings. Perhaps even more dramatically, research shows that elderly people who move to nursing homes, where stimulation and challenge are at a minimum, experience a rapid loss of mental function. These studies point to the importance of the environment for developing and maintaining a high level of mental acuity and creative intelligence.

Both at home and at your workplace, you can modify your environment to support your work. Here are some suggestions.

ESTABLISH A LEARNING CENTER. Designate a specific place as your "learning center." Having one place set aside where you study or work in a concentrated manner helps get your brain in the habit of getting down to the business of information processing whenever you are there.

PREPARE A GOOD LIGHT SOURCE. Always make sure you have enough light for reading. Natural light or full-spectrum light is best for your eyes. However, do not use too much light, and do not have the light focused in such a way that the page is bright and the surroundings relatively dark. Light should be diffused so that it comes from several different sources and does not create a glare on the page. Avoid high-intensity "reading" lamps, since they do not provide diffused light. Usually you will know if your light is adequate by how you feel. If your eyes feel strained, the lighting may need adjustment.

GET A COMFORTABLE CHAIR. How you sit to read or study can influence how alert you are and how quickly you become tired. You will find that your reading speed, comprehension, and

Once we are destined to live out our lives in the prison of our mind, our duty is to furnish it well.

Peter Ustinov

clarity of thought will be increased just by sitting in an appropriate posture and placing your book in the optimum relationship to your eyes.

Your chair should help you sit in a posture that is comfortable but not *too* comfortable. As a general rule, your mind
responds to a slouched or horizontal position with a brain-
wave state below alpha (i.e., in the direction of sleep). An erect
posture transmits a message of alertness to your brain and also
permits your breathing to be more full and complete.

KEEP IT COOL. The best temperature for the brain is about 65
degrees Fahrenheit. This is the temperature that will promote
maximum clarity of mind. It is cooler than most people commonly set their thermostats. If it feels cold, try wearing a sweater
rather than turning up the heat.

PLAY SOME MUSIC. As we discussed earlier, music is a powerful
learning aid. I suggest that you play some of the recommended
selections while reading or studying.

KEEP YOUR SURROUNDINGS BRIGHT AND PLEASANT. In addition
to sufficient light and comfortable temperature, the surroundings should be pleasant and have an uplifting quality. Subdued
pastel colors, beautiful paintings or posters, a window with a
view of nature, all uplift our mood. Choose artwork that is
relaxing, however; avoid busy scenes that remind your brain
of noise and crowds. It is also good to have plenty of fresh air,
with cross-ventilation to keep the air flowing.

HAVE POSITIVE MESSAGES VISIBLE. Write out your own affirmations on pieces of colored paper or 3 × 5 cards and display
them in your learning space. (Refer to chapter 2 to refresh your
memory on how to create affirmations.) The positive messages
will remind you of your true capabilities and will foster the
emergence of your peak intelligence. Some of the affirmations
I post around the room during my seminars include:

LEARNING IS FUN AND EASY.

I EXPECT SUCCESS.

Do You Need Help Organizing Your Workspace?

Are clutter and disorgani-
zation part of your Information Age problem? If
you feel you never have
enough space or have
trouble finding what you
need when you need it,
consider purchasing some
office furniture such as
wall units, organizers, and
stackable baskets. You
might consider hiring a
professional organizer to
consult with you to design
your workplace for maxi-
mum efficiency. This spe-
cialist can help you use
space most effectively, design better filing and storage systems, and steer you
to the best products for
your purposes. Many spe-
cialize in home offices.
Current fees range from
about $50 to $125 per
hour; if your needs are not
extensive the cost need
not be high.

The act of smelling something, anything, is remarkably like the act of thinking. Immediately at the moment of perception, you can feel the mind going to work, sending the odor around from place to place, setting off complex repertories through the brain, polling one center after another for signs of recognition, for old memories and old connections.

Dr. Lewis Thomas
President Emeritus
Sloan-Kettering
Cancer Center

I TRUST MY PEAK INTELLIGENCE.

I AM MASTER OF THE INFORMATION AGE.

EVERY PROBLEM IS AN OPPORTUNITY FOR GROWTH.

Using the walls of your office or workspace for verbal or visual statements that contain powerful positive messages (such as affirmations, favorite quotes, photos of personal heroes) can provide you with motivation and ongoing reminders of your own ability to function at high-performance levels.

Setting up an environment that supports peak performance takes some time and thought, but if done, it will serve you well. I believe that once you experience the advantages of working and studying in an ideal environment, you will find yourself drawn to re-create that situation in the future.

AROMATHERAPY: USING YOUR SENSE OF SMELL TO ENHANCE LEARNING

While today we simply enjoy certain scents and shun others, ancient cultures knew how to use scents to produce specific results. Practitioners of yoga, for example, have long used incense for its calming effect on the mind, and many religious ceremonies employ various scents, such as frankincense and myrrh, to encourage feelings of devotion.

The intentional use of scents to direct feelings, stimulate creative thinking, and heal body and mind goes back millennia. It formed an essential part of the Egyptian healing arts, and vials of aromatic oils have been found accompanying the mummified bodies of the Pharaohs. The ancient Greeks placed fragrant plants near the windows of their homes, in the belief that the scents had a healthy effect upon the occupants. Monks in medieval monasteries planted specific herbs near their infirmaries to help in the healing process.

These practices are part of the ancient knowledge of aromatherapy, the study of how aromatic plant oils (derived from herbs, flowers, and other plants) affect the body and mind. Many schools of Oriental medicine, including Ayurveda, the ancient Indian system of natural healing, still utilize the therapeutic properties of plants and their oils. Today, aromatherapy is taught in most French and English medical schools; some major American medical schools, such as Yale, Stanford, and the University of Cincinnati, have complete departments that study only the olfactory sense.

In general, when we encounter a pleasant odor we tend to relax and breathe more deeply; an unpleasant smell can immediately cause irritation, shortened breathing, and a general tensing of the whole body. Aromatherapists believe that scents can affect our feelings and behavior in subtle and specific ways, due to their innate molecular properties.

It is a scientific and medical fact that the sense of smell reaches more directly into our emotions than any other sense. Whereas the incoming information from all the other senses is first shuttled through the thalamus for redirection to various brain centers, the sense of smell is directly hooked into the limbic system, the part of the brain with primary responsibility for emotions.

You can use this knowledge—both ancient and modern—in a powerful way. The intimate natural connection that scent has with emotions can be put to work to improve your memory, learning, and creativity. You can use scents to help you relax, or to stimulate your brain.

Aromatherapists have specifically identified certain scents as influential in mental alertness and in relaxation.

Smell is a potent wizard that transports us across thousands of miles and all the years we have lived.

Helen Keller

Mental alertness	Relaxation
Peppermint	Rose
Basil	Chamomile
Lemon	Lavender
Cinnamon	Orange
Rosemary	Ylang-ylang

By combining these essential oils, aromatherapists have developed various blends designed to enhance learning, creativity, and relaxation. When I use these essential oil blends in my seminars, students typically report results consistent with the objective of the blend.

Many aroma oils are available commercially, along with various types of atomizers for diffusing the aroma into the air. Make certain that you get the true essential oil and not a chemical substitute. Oils are generally available in health-food stores, "New Age" bookstores, and by mail order.

Memories, imagination, old sentiments, and associations are more readily reached through the sense of smell than through any other channel.

Oliver Wendell Holmes

Here's one example of how to use the relationship between smell and memory to make you a better learner. Pick a scent you enjoy, and use it every time you are in a learning situation. When you are going to read letters, memoranda, reports, or books, begin those information-processing sessions by smelling your chosen scent. Eventually you will associate this scent with learning; simply smelling it will "remind" your brain that it is time to concentrate and learn.

You can set up separate associations for different tasks. Use one scent to associate with pleasure reading, one for work-related reading, and a third for writing reports or papers. Eventually the association will link the scent to a specific learning or working task and help to trigger your brain into the learning state.

You can even use scents to reprogram yourself to enjoy a task you don't enjoy doing. Associate it with a scent that you particularly like, and have that scent in the air just before and during the time you are working on the task. This may sound farfetched, but if you try it, you will find that it works.

THE BRAIN REGIMEN

Most of us give little thought to how our diet and physical condition affect our thinking. However, what you have learned so far in this book about the mind-body connection should be enough to convince you that top mental performance can only be gained when the body is functioning at its best. As Jean Houston wrote in *The Possible Human*, "You cannot have a successful and permanent extension of mental, psychological, and spiritual capacity without working toward an enhancement of physiological capacity."

Top athletes spend countless hours training for their performances. They employ not only physical routines and dietary regimens, but mental training as well. Whatever your profession, information management is surely a large part of your daily work. Your main tool is your brain. Think of yourself as an athlete, striving for your best, in training for mastering your information environment. This section will tell you what you need to know about your physical routine to keep your brain in top working order.

Foods and Brain Chemistry

According to Massachusetts Institute of Technology researcher Judith Wurtman, author of *Managing Your Mind and Mood Through Food*, "foods influence the production of chemicals in the brain that are directly involved in determining mood, mental energy, performance, and behavior." For example, certain foods increase mental alertness and can perk you up when you need a boost of brain energy to increase your productivity or to succeed at an information-processing task. Other foods are natural tranquilizers that can calm you down when you need to relax in order to maximize your focus and concentration. Knowing the effects of different foods is important to help you operate in peak performance mode.

Whether foods are energizing or relaxing is to a large degree a function of the particular chemicals they stimulate the brain to manufacture. Neurotransmitters—the chemicals that carry messages from neuron to neuron in the brain—appear to be responsible for our feeling calm or alert. Scientists have identified over fifty of these chemical compounds, each of which represents or conveys its own specific message.

The neurotransmitters *dopamine* and *norepinephrine* cause alertness and an energetic mental attitude. When the brain is producing these two chemicals, we have a tendency to think more quickly, feel more motivated and responsive, and be more mentally alert. On the other hand, *serotonin* is more calming and produces a less active brain. When the brain is actively producing serotonin, we are more relaxed and slowed down, better able to concentrate. Feelings of stress, tension, and anxiety are diminished.

Your brain produces these neurotransmitters from amino acids, the "building blocks" of proteins. In particular, two amino acids are important. *Tyrosine* is the principal ingredient in do-

Although there is a great deal of controversy among scientists about the effects of ingested food on the brain, no one denies that you can change your cognition and mood by what you eat.

Arthur Winter, M.D.
Ruth Winter

A Warning

There are many food supplements that contain the amino acids necessary to enhanced brain functioning, but I suggest caution in using them. Make certain you research the data on the source and concentration of the amino acids. In *Managing Your Mind and Mood Through Food*, Judith Wurtman says that to take amino acids "in their concentrated form, from a bottle, is to put yourself at risk for some potentially harmful side effects," such as changes in blood pressure from tyrosine and dizziness or extreme drowsiness from tryptophan. In fact, in early 1990 the U.S. Food and Drug Administration (FDA) ordered all tryptophan removed from the shelves of drugstores and health-food stores due to health problems resulting from its use.

In addition, as Dr. Richard Restak points out in his book *The Brain*, "Generally there is little evidence that mental performance in healthy people can be boosted by [amino acid] food supplements." In *fresh* foods, nature has provided these proteins in an easily assimilated form.

pamine and norepinephrine. It helps produce alertness and energy. *Tryptophan* is the essential constituent of serotonin, which generates a feeling of calmness and relaxation.

Dr. Wurtman's research, conducted at the MIT Clinical Research Center, concluded that it is possible to maintain control of alertness and relaxation by the following strategy.

For alertness: Eat a protein food alone or with carbohydrates. "You will find yourself responding more quickly and with greater accuracy to mental challenges," she writes. "You will be more alert, more motivated, more mentally energetic." Recommended protein foods include:

- Fish, chicken, and lean beef
- Low-fat or nonfat dairy products such as cottage cheese, yogurt, and milk
- Dried peas, beans (except kidney beans), and lentils
- Tofu
- Eggs
- Grains, seeds, and nuts

For relaxation: Eat a carbohydrate alone, without protein. You will feel less anxious and stressed, more calm and focused. Carbohydrate foods are in two categories, sugars (called simple carbohydrates) and starches (complex carbohydrates).

- Complex carbohydrates (starches): bread, including muffins, bagels, and rolls; pasta; potatoes; rice; other grains, such as corn, barley, and oatmeal.
- Simple carbohydrates (sugars): candy; cookies; pie; cake; and soft drinks.

Starches are turned into sugars by the body. When you eat starch, the pancreas produces insulin that allows the body to metabolize the starch into sugar. This then generates energy for the body to use. The slow metabolism process by which starches are converted to sugars allows the energy to be made available gradually.

On the other hand, eating sugar results in a large amount of insulin being produced immediately by the pancreas. This may create a feeling of increased energy in the short run but eventually creates a "rebound effect" of nervousness and anxiety. The moral of the story is: Go for the complex carbo-hydrates. Simple sugars are not a productive food for peak intelligence.

When you follow these simple rules, you can get results quickly. If you notice that you are becoming "hyper" or anxious, you can eat as little as one to two ounces of relaxation-producing carbohydrate foods, and within about half an hour you should begin to notice some calming effects. The same is true when you become sleepy or dull. Eating some protein—even just three or four ounces—will give you a mental boost within thirty minutes.

Most people eat a diet too heavy in fats. Although the American Heart Association recommends a diet consisting of 15 to 20 percent protein, 55 to 60 percent carbohydrates, and 20 to 25 percent fats, most Americans get 40 percent or more of their calories from fats. In addition to all the known hazards of fatty foods, such as linkages to heart disease, stroke, and certain kinds of cancer, fats are not a good brain food. Because they take a long time to break down, fats require that blood be diverted away from the brain to the stomach and intestines, resulting in a slowdown of mental processes, dullness, lethargy, or even sleep. Avoid them if you want to think clearly.

The blood supply to the brain can be further inhibited if cholesterol from fatty food accumulates in the arteries and restricts the normal blood flow. Because oxygen reaches the brain via the bloodstream, a diminished blood flow means less oxygen. A reduced oxygen supply to the brain has been clearly implicated in the aging process. It has also been found to reduce significantly the amount of serotonin, norepinephrine, and dopamine in the brain. For all these reasons (as well as the calories!) I recommend that you keep fat intake to a minimum.

Vitamins, Minerals, and the Brain

Certain vitamins and minerals are necessary for proper functioning of the brain. "A deficiency of any nutrient that is used by the brain can cause irritability, depression, and mental malfunctioning," says Dr. Brian Morgan of the Institute of Human Nutrition at Columbia University.

We particularly need the B-complex vitamins thiamine,

A Brain-Power Menu

Here is a recommendation for a true "power lunch" that uses these principles to increase your mental alertness for your afternoon tasks:

■ For the main dish, a salad or sandwich made from poultry (skinless), fish, lean meat, or eggs (maximum of 3–4 egg yolks per week)
■ Whole-wheat bread, roll, or pita bread
■ Low-fat yogurt or cottage cheese
■ Optional: fresh fruit or vegetables

This lunch will be digested quickly and will energize your brain for the afternoon. If you typically feel sleepy or sluggish after lunch while your system is struggling to digest a high-fat, high-sugar meal, try this and see the difference.

To get an idea of a complete dietary program designed for optimal brain functioning, refer to the "14 Day Brain Power Maintenance Diet" contained in *Brain Power* by Vernon H. Mark, M.D.

niacin, and B_{12}, as well as vitamins D and E. These vitamins are probably the most crucial for healthy functioning of the nerve cells and have been linked to memory and learning.

Vitamin B_1 (Thiamine). This vitamin is central to carbohydrate digestion. Carbohydrates break down into sugars such as glucose, which fuels the brain. Thus thiamine directly affects our intelligence. Good sources of thiamine include brewer's yeast, sunflower seeds, oats, wheat germ, salmon, and brown rice.

Vitamin B_3 (Niacin). Niacin is vital for strong mental functioning. It is abundant in chicken (light meat), swordfish, beef liver, peanuts and peanut butter, canned tuna, brown rice, and avocados.

Vitamin B_6 (Pyridoxine). This is used in the brain to help produce serotonin, the calming chemical. Deficiencies of serotonin can lead to depression. You can get vitamin B_6 from beef liver, bananas, chicken, sunflower seeds, lentils, and fish such as mackerel, halibut, and tuna.

Vitamin B_{12}. This vitamin is essential for proper functioning of the nervous system. It aids in the process of building the myelin sheath that carries the electrical impulse from the nucleus of the neuron along the axon. It also helps to form blood cells, which are needed to carry oxygen to the brain. A deficiency of B_{12} can result in moodiness, depression, confusion, and memory loss. By far the best natural source of the vitamin is beef liver; other sources include oysters, beef, lamb, yogurt, and other dairy products such as milk, cottage cheese, and Swiss cheese. B_{12} is not found in vegetables, so those on a strict vegetarian diet need to look to supplements for this important vitamin.

Vitamin D. This vitamin helps in the assimilation of calcium and magnesium, vital for mental alertness and the health of nerve cells. The body manufactures vitamin D from sunlight, and most milk products in the United States have vitamin D added. If you are allergic to milk and don't use milk products, you may need a vitamin D supplement.

Vitamin E. This vitamin increases cell oxygenation and helps the nerve cells better utilize the oxygen available. Good sources of vitamin E are whole wheat, other whole grains, and seeds.

Choline. A food substance some nutritionists consider a vitamin, choline seems to be important for good memory and may help to prevent memory loss. It is found in beef liver, soybeans, eggs, and brown rice.

Minerals are important in maintaining the metabolism of the body, thus insuring that the brain continually has the proper supply of oxygen, blood, and amino acids. Key minerals for the brain include iron, copper, zinc, iodine, calcium, potassium, magnesium, and selenium.

All these vitamins and minerals can be obtained from a healthy diet, including plenty of fresh fruit and vegetables. For many reasons, however—mineral-deficient soil, farmer-to-table time lag, strict vegetarian diet, prevalence of processed foods, tendency to eat junk food—some people feel they need vitamin and mineral supplements.

If you use a supplement, know your source and pay attention to the dosage. The FDA has established a standard for vitamin needs, called the Minimum Daily Requirement. Note the word "minimum." This is not the same as what might be needed for *optimal* brain functioning. It might be wise to consult a medical or nutrition expert to find out what supplements best fit your specific needs.

Alcohol, Caffeine, Tobacco, and the Brain

Alcohol. It has been known as a scientific fact for many years that alcohol destroys brain cells. It is also common sense that it slows you down and dulls your mind. According to the authors of the recent book *Positive Living and Health*, the effects of alcohol on the brain are quite predictable. "First it disables the intellect, hampering judgment, memory, and problem-solving abilities. Eventually it breaks down more fundamental functions, like balance and coordination."

Current research suggests that alcohol has a destructive effect on memory. Heavy users of alcohol often have severe memory disorders, and even moderate drinking may be detrimental. Dr. Vernon Mark, neurosurgeon and author of *Brain Power*, writes: "Poisoning by alcohol is the most common form of brain poisoning in our society."

Caffeine. Some nutrition authorities suggest that caffeine is safe to use as a stimulant to generate alertness and alleviate drowsiness. Caffeine does help produce an alert mental state. It can speed up reaction time and improve concentration and accuracy on simple tasks like typing or math computation.

On the other hand, caffeine is a powerful chemical that affects the central nervous system, the respiratory and circulatory systems, gastrointestinal secretion, and the metabolic rate. Medically it is considered a habit-forming drug, right alongside amphetamines, barbiturates, nicotine, and alcohol. Recent studies suggest that it may impair short-term memory.

In people who are sensitive to it, even 1 or 2 milligrams of caffeine can cause irritability and disturb sleep. (A typical cup of coffee contains 60 to 180 milligrams.) Although caffeine produces a state of arousal in the body, it actually decreases blood flow to the brain.

If you drink coffee, keep your daily dosage well under 500 milligrams. Similarly restrict your intake of caffeinated soft drinks, tea, diet pills, and analgesics containing caffeine. Larger amounts may entrap you in caffeinism, the medical term for caffeine addiction, which is characterized as "chronic low-level poisoning with symptoms that include sensory disturbances, nervousness, insomnia, and digestive distress."

Tobacco. Smokers claim that having a cigarette helps them think, but research shows that it just isn't so. Dr. George Spilich, chairman of the psychology department at Washington College in Maryland, found that although smokers were able to perform simple tasks successfully, they performed consistently worse than nonsmokers in tasks requiring understanding and problem solving.

Smoking can cause changes in the lungs that lower the amount of vital oxygen reaching the brain. Anything that decreases the flow of oxygen starves the brain of a vital "food" and impairs mental functioning; anything (such as exercise or deep breathing) that facilitates the flow of oxygen has a positive effect on all our information-processing faculties from sense perception to critical thinking and problem solving.

EXERCISE FOR YOUR BRAIN

Engaging in an active exercise program consistent with your age, health, and physical abilities is vital to proper mental functioning. Exercise brings more oxygen to the brain through improved blood circulation. As we have seen, this can strengthen memory and heighten your thinking and information-processing skills.

A recent study at Claremont College in California demonstrated that exercise can help keep your brain in shape as you age. Researchers Louise Clarkson-Smith and Alan Hartley found that active older adults performed better on cognitive and reaction-time tests as compared with a similar group of nonexercisers. In a survey of 120 men and women between 55 and 91, the active group made fewer errors in reasoning, remembered more, and reacted more quickly. They also excelled in vocabulary tests.

This is only one of a large number of studies appearing in recent years showing that the brain functioning of older adults can retain its strength and flexibility. Exercise is one effective way toward this goal.

Aerobic Exercise

Much is known about the value of aerobic exercise such as jogging, swimming, bicycling, and tennis. These activities have been shown to lower the heart rate, blood pressure, percentage of body fat, and the level of cholesterol in the blood, as well as reduce stress and tension markedly. An appropriate exercise program benefits the heart, lungs, and arteries. The main importance of aerobic exercise for developing peak intelligence and fostering peak performance is that the improved circulation and increased oxygen intake nourish the brain and nervous system. In short, exercise promotes the vitality and positivity needed to meet the Information Age with confidence.

Therapeutic Massage

Our mind and body are so closely connected that stress is felt in the entire organism. The art of massage is becoming increasingly accepted by health practitioners as a beneficial therapy to help reduce stress and enhance mental and physical function. Massage disciplines such as Swedish, Trager Work, Esalen, passive joint movement, acupressure, or deep tissue are available through a growing number of competent massage therapists. I strongly recommend the benefits of massage for helping you cope with the pressures of the Information Age.

6. Use your bed for *sleeping*, not for reading, talking on the phone, watching TV, etc.

7. Keep your bedroom environment quiet, dark, and comfortably cool (the ideal temperature is between 64 and 66 degrees F.).

8. Learn to tune out worries and anxieties at bedtime.

9. If you have chronic insomnia, see a physician or psychologist well-versed in sleep problems. (Not all of them are.) You might contact the American Sleep Disorders Association, 604 2nd St. SW, Rochester, Minnesota 55902 for information or a referral.

10. Don't use sedatives or sleeping pills; they actually disrupt natural sleep. Learn natural ways to relax—meditation, yoga, breathing exercises. Use natural relaxation helpers such as herbs.

The Importance of Rest

We rarely think about it, but one of the most vital factors needed for optimum mental functioning is adequate rest. The human nervous system works on a cycle of alternating rest and activity, and if we try to cheat by cutting down on rest, we simply cannot express our peak intelligence.

Research has shown, for example, that two nights of sleep deprivation results in an impairment of reading comprehension and decision-making ability. A recent study by J. A. Horne at Loughborough University in England demonstrated that just one night without sleep reduces our ability to do creative thinking. So be sure to get enough rest to support your activity.

During sleep, proteins and other chemicals in the brain used up during the day are replenished. If we fail to receive adequate rest, the repair and rejuvenation process is hampered, stress builds up, and our health suffers. The opposite effect is produced by giving the system *extra* rest, such as through a session of meditation or relaxation, or something as simple as a nap. A study at the University of Athens Medical School in Greece found that a 30-minute daily nap reduced the incidence of heart disease by 30 percent.

The fast pace of the Information Age demands full mental energy in the form of reading, concentration, thinking, decision making, and evaluating. Being a Master requires that you do everything possible to keep your brain healthy and fit, so that you can use your peak intelligence at every moment. Without eliminating stress and setting up a supportive environment to take in information and process it into knowledge, you will feel continually overloaded, tired, and on the losing side.

Because this chapter contains so many useful hints to help you become a Master of information, I urge you to take a moment now to reread the statement of purpose at the beginning of this chapter and reflect on whether you have accomplished the objectives. Do you appreciate your potential to work and learn at high levels, and have you absorbed the information, implemented the suggestions, and mastered the techniques offered to help make the "flow state" a more frequent reality in your life? If not, before you move on to chapter 4, take some time to go more deeply into the points you may have missed.

RESOURCES

Aromatherapy

Lavabre, Marcel. *Aromatherapy Workbook.* (Rochester, VT: Healing Arts Press, 1990). A well-researched book covering all aspects of aromatherapy.

Tisserand, Robert. *The Art of Aroma Therapy.* (New York: Inner Traditions, 1977). One of the earliest books on aromatherapy.

Aroma Vera, P.O. Box 3609, Culver City, CA 90231.

John Steeler, 3949 Longridge Avenue, Sherman Oaks, CA 91432.

Brain machines

Hutchinson, Michael. *Megabrain.* (New York: Ballantine Books, Inc., 1986). A look at machines that enhance brain function. You can also receive the author's newsletter, MegaBrain Report, by writing to MegaBrain Report, P.O. Box 2744, Sausalito, CA 94965.

Breathing

Ray, Sondra. *Celebration of Breath.* (Berkeley, CA: Celestial Arts Publishing, 1983). Breathing as a therapeutic tool. Includes a modality called rebirthing.

Zi, Nancy. *The Art of Breathing.* (New York: Bantam Books, 1986). An illustrated book with thirty exercises for improving performance and well-being through proper control of breathing.

Massage

Coleman, David, ed., *The Relaxed Body Book.* (Garden City, New York: Doubleday, 1986).

Meditation

Coleman, Daniel. *The Meditative Mind: The Varieties of Meditative Experiences.* (Los Angeles: Jeremy P. Tarcher, 1988). Provides an overview of the different types of Eastern and Western meditation practices.

Goldstein, Joseph and Jack Kornfeld. *Seeking the Heart of Wisdom.* (Boston: Shambala, 1987). Introduces the Vispassana mindful meditation practice.

Russel, Peter. *The TM Technique: A Skeptic's Guide.* (Boston: Routledge, 1977). Introduces the principles and benefits of transcendental meditation.

Music

Campbell, Don G. *Introduction to the Musical Brain.* (St. Louis, MO: MMB, 1983). Explains how the brain is involved in music. Includes several exercises.

Halpern, Steven and Louis Savary. *Sound Health.* (San Francisco: Harper & Row Pubs., 1985). How sound affects our health and how to make sounds more harmonious.

Katsh, Shelley and Carol Merle-Fishman. *The Music Within You.* (New York: Simon & Schuster, 1985). Two certified music therapists document how music can enhance well-being and performance. Includes exercises.

Nutrition

Mark, Vernon. *Brain Power*. (Boston: Houghton Mifflin, 1989). A neurosurgeon's program for maintaining and enhancing brain fitness.

Morgan, Brian and Roberta Morgan. *Brainfood*. (Los Angeles: Price Stern Sloan, 1987). How nutrition, including vitamin and mineral intake, affects mental processes.

Wurtman, Judith. *Managing Your Mind and Mood Through Food*. (New York: Harper & Row, 1986). Discusses the food-mind-mood connection. Suggestions on how to use food to regulate your psychological well-being.

Peak intelligence

Briton, Anthony. *Things You Never Learned in School*. (Los Angeles: Reality Publishing, 1988). Workbook filled with exercises that promote faster learning.

Dennison, Paul E. and Gail E. Dennison. *Brain Gym, Brain Gym for Teachers, Switching On*, and *Edu-K for Kids*. (EduKinesthetics, 1987). I recommend several books by these authors, who developed Educational Kinesiology.

Maslow, Abraham. *Toward a Psychology of Being*. (New York: Van Nostrand, 1986). The pioneering work on peak experience by the founder of the Human Potential movement and one of our most influential psychologists.

Ostrander, Sheila and Lynn Schroeder. *Superlearning*. (New York: Dell Publishing, 1979). The history and application of accelerated learning based on the work of its founder, Giorgi Lozonov.

Winter, Arthur and Ruth Winter. *Build Your Brain Power*. (New York: St. Martin's Press, 1986). Various strategies (including diet, exercise, music, memory skills, stress reduction, and visualization) to unfold the brain's potential. Many practical exercises.

Wonder, Jacquelyn and Pricilla Donavan. *Whole Brain Thinking*. (New York: Ballantine Books, 1985). Includes several techniques to achieve peak job performance by using both sides of the brain.

Wujec, Tom. *Pumping Ions: A Guide to Mental Exercises*. (New York: Doubleday, 1988). Exercises, problems, and brain teasers to stimulate creative thinking.

Sleep

Goldberg, Philip, and Daniel Kaufman. *Everybody's Guide to Natural Sleep*. (Los Angeles: Jeremy P. Tarcher, 1990). Comprehensive analysis of sleep problems, with suggestions on how to overcome them using natural methods.

Stress

Benson, Herbert and Miriam Z. Klipper. *Relaxation Response*. (New York: Avon Books, 1976). A critical work defining the body's response to stress and the methods of relaxation.

Seyler, Hans. *Stress Without Distress*. (New York: Signet, 1978). How to reduce stress.

■ ■ ■ ■

CHAPTER 4

Use Your Peak Intelligence

The knowledge you gained in chapter 3 can go a long way toward helping you cross the line into peak intelligence, but there is a lot more you can do. In this chapter we will continue our exploration of how to operate at peak performance levels as frequently as possible. We will focus on seven skills and strategies that can help you become a Master of information. As you learn these skills, you will find yourself reaching a level of effortless "flow" more often in your daily personal and professional life. You will learn how to:

1. use your whole brain and all your intelligences.
2. use visualization to target and achieve your goals.
3. develop your listening skills.
4. develop your intuition.
5. tap into your subliminal learning power.
6. use more of your experiences as learning opportunities.
7. develop powerful work habits and study skills.

**How the Development
of the Brain and Senses
Creates the "Whole Brain"**

To understand the unified and extensive nature of the "whole brain," let's look at the development of the brain from shortly after the point of conception. About two weeks after fertilization of the egg by the sperm, a tiny tube called the neural tube develops. This tube becomes the basis for the whole brain. Throughout the period in the womb, the neurons in the neural tube multiply at the staggering rate of 250,000 per minute.

From one end of the neural tube, the spinal cord emerges and begins to establish its labyrinth of nerve networks that connect the brain to all parts of the body. From the other end three little nodules emerge, which even-

You should come away from this chapter with a much deeper understanding of what it means to be a Master of information—and a much deeper sense of *yourself* as that master.

■ ■ ■ ■

If I asked you, "Where does learning take place?" where would you point? Probably to the top of your head, but that would be only partially correct. Your learning equipment extends far beyond the three pounds of matter in your head. Without its connection to the senses and the rest of the nervous system, your brain can accomplish very little.

In order for you to achieve your peak intelligence, it is necessary to expand your concept of where learning takes place to encompass what I call your "whole brain." A number of teachers of accelerated learning talk about "whole-brain learning," but they generally mean only the integration of the right and left brain hemispheres, whereas the term can mean much more than this, as you will see.

THE RIGHT AND LEFT BRAIN

In the 1960s Dr. Roger Sperry of the California Institute of Technology discovered that the two hemispheres of the brain perform different functions. His so-called split-brain research showed that each hemisphere specialized in different modes of thinking and perceiving. Since that time, hundreds of additional studies have been performed in the attempt to understand more fully what each hemisphere is responsible for. In our current state of knowledge, this is what we know:

The *right hemisphere* is the seat of creativity. It is nonverbal, imaginative, and holistic—that is, it perceives in terms of overall patterns and structures rather than parts. It is imaginative and has a good sense of space. It experiences concretely and emotionally and often makes decisions on intuitive hunches and feelings rather than logic. It is visual and also appreciates music and rhythm. It is the artist in us, the architect, the dreamer, the innovator.

The *left hemisphere* is responsible for analytic, rational, "scientific" thinking. It is the expert in language, the writer and speaker. It is methodical and tends to think in a sequential fashion, proceeding step by logical step rather than by intuition and feeling. It is also good at mathematics and at keeping track of time. The left hemisphere is the manager, the critical thinker, the accountant and budget maker, the procedures expert that lives in most of us.

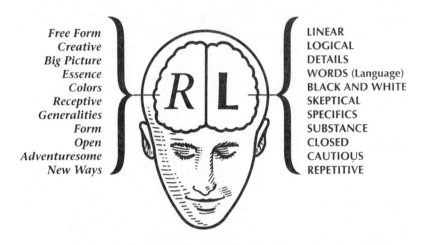

Free Form	LINEAR
Creative	LOGICAL
Big Picture	DETAILS
Essence	WORDS (Language)
Colors	BLACK AND WHITE
Receptive	SKEPTICAL
Generalities	SPECIFICS
Form	SUBSTANCE
Open	CLOSED
Adventuresome	CAUTIOUS
New Ways	REPETITIVE

tually develop into the three major divisions of the brain, the hindbrain (medulla, pons, and cerebellum), the midbrain (including the limbic system), and the forebrain (cerebral cortex). Early in the development process, the nascent brain sprouts buds that grow to become the eyes, ears, nose, and mouth.

Because of their common origin in the neural tube, all your senses in each part of your body connect to your brain through neural pathways. This interconnected network is a unit capable of taking in, sorting, storing, retrieving, and utilizing information. All parts of this holistic system are in communication with the others at all times, and the condition of each part affects all the other parts. This is your whole brain.

As research continues, it appears increasingly likely that the two sides of the brain do not work as distinct and separate departments somehow collaborating; the brain is more of a unified whole. Connected by the corpus callosum, a membrane made up of millions of neural fibers, the two hemispheres are in continuous communication. Even if the insights of future research require that the division of brain functions into hemispheres be replaced by a different understanding, what we have already learned remains meaningful: Our brain is capable of many diverse functions. In whatever part of it our rational, emotional, artistic, or verbal capabilities may be located or processed, those abilities can be developed beyond what our education has taught us.

One key to that development is to expand our sense of where learning takes place to include the whole brain. Our information-processing equipment doesn't end at the cerebral cortex. Indeed, complete learning involves the holistic activation of our entire learning apparatus. The five senses can be seen as extensions of the cortex. They are the brain's way of gathering information about the outside world. The eyes gather light waves, the ears gather sound waves, the somatic (feeling) system gathers sensations like heat, cold, and texture, and the nose and mouth gather molecules.

If you begin to view learning and performance as a synergistic function of your brain, your senses, and all parts of your body, you will see that in order to operate at peak levels, all aspects of the system need to be tuned up to maximum. The body must be fully healthy, the senses alive and alert, and the brain using its full potential. If you approach the Information Age with this expanded whole-brain concept, you will increase your capacity for mastery.

Think with the whole body.

Taisen Deshimaru

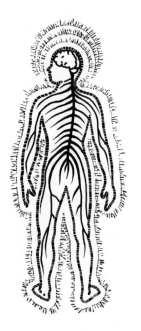

HEIGHTEN YOUR SENSORY AWARENESS

If knowledge begins with the gathering of information by the senses, to be a Master you need to use all your senses at a high level of refinement. Indeed, the quality of anything you produce is dependent on the quality of what goes into it. Computer people call this principle GIGO: garbage in, garbage out. A more ancient phrasing of the same principle says, "As you sow, so shall you reap." This is true of thinking and memory. It is also true of action, the end product of the learning process. The quality of our decisions and actions is the result of all the prior stages of information processing.

For example, think about the last lecture or seminar you attended. If you were tired, if you didn't care much about the topic, if your senses weren't tuned up to catch all the words or the graphics used by the speaker—then you simply did not understand it very well and you probably can't remember much of what was said.

Unfortunately, information overload and our high-pressure lifestyle often cause us to close off our senses. The stereotypical "closed" posture of an anxious, overstimulated person—hands covering the face, the body hunched up—indicates the body's protective mechanism against information bombardment. Think about how you feel when your desk is piled high with papers, your list of phone calls to return is two pages long, and it's

4:15. As anxiety mounts, your senses begin to shut down and you become increasingly unaware of your surroundings.

Yet, because our senses are truly our information gateways, it is vital that we keep these channels open and fully alive. One of the reasons we are overwhelmed by information is that we have dulled the sensory "tentacles" of our whole brain responsible for gathering and processing information. Enlivening our sensory input channels (making each extension of our brain more sensitive and alert) enables us to be more effective in processing information. It is like putting up a satellite dish to extend our TV signal-gathering power. In short, increasing the acuity of our individual senses makes us better information gatherers.

In addition, developing our individual senses and then consciously merging them with each other can open up new information pathways within the brain. As Jean Houston wrote in *The Possible Human*:

> Any single lensing is the enemy, restricting our freedom of choice, distorting both percept and concept. What I am urging . . . is the conscious development of awareness in all of our modes of knowing so that we may choose to use them freely and selectively.

Multisensory awareness can make us more masterful at the crucial stage where learning begins, and then throughout any learning experience. It is another way of applying our whole brain to learning and thus to mastery of the Information Age.

The rationale for using multiple senses in learning is as follows. Each sense has its own special ability to gather a unique piece of the information puzzle. These pieces are then transmitted to the specific target area in the brain for the particular sense. However, after initial processing, the information, in the form of electrochemical impulses, is broadcast through vast neural networks in the associational areas of the cortex for further processing. The associational areas comprise a majority—approximately 75 percent—of the cerebral cortex.

The end result is that sensory input from all of the senses is merged, sorted, and stored together. Incoming information is compared with existing information held in countless neuronal networks throughout the cortex. Hence, the more input

Our senses are indeed our doors and windows on this world, in a very real sense the key to the unlocking of meaning and the wellspring of creativity.

Jean Houston

from the different senses that the brain has to work with, the more thorough it can be in its processing.

The next time you are faced with information overload or a demanding learning situation, rather than unconsciously closing down your senses in response, consciously stay relaxed and open up your senses. Seek to become more alert. Use your eyes, ears, and touch to increase the level of detail you pick up. The additional input will help you to remember what you learned, deepen your perception and understanding of what you experienced, and enrich your thinking.

You can sharpen your individual senses as you would muscles or talents: by using them. The following exercise will help you strengthen your least-used senses as well as further develop your most dominant ones. It is aimed at enlivening your brain, just as relaxation techniques calm you down.

▪ ▪ ▪ ▪

LEARNING ACTIVATOR #7
SOS: SEPARATING OUT SENSES

Pick an object that you can hold in your hand. It can be a fruit, bottle, flower, pencil, cup, or anything else that you choose. Begin by taking a moment to relax. Then start to inspect the object in detail, *one sense at a time*. Try to ascertain everything you can with one sense before moving on to another. When you look at it, let your eyes pick up every detail of color, shape, shading. If it has a sound, listen to it carefully. Feel the texture, shape, and temperature. What is the range of tastes and smells? With each individual sense, discover what you can about the object. Again, direct your conscious attention *only* to the sense you have separated out. Because our visual sense tends to be so dominant, one way to facilitate perception through the other sensory channels is to close your eyes when you are not focusing on visual information.

Use this procedure regularly, like a meditation or relaxation exercise. You will begin to notice the acuity of each sense improve with frequent use of this Activator.

▪ ▪ ▪ ▪

All this sensory input, which begins in the brain, has its effect throughout the body.

Norman Cousins

The person who can combine frames of reference and draw connections between ostensibly unrelated points of view is likely to be the one who makes the creative breakthrough.

Denise Shekerjian

USE ALL YOUR INTELLIGENCES

The concept of whole-brain learning has also gained support from recent advances in cognitive psychology. Many researchers now believe that intelligence is not simply a matter of intellectual capacities, but that it has many different forms. Chapter 1 mentioned, for example, Robert Sternberg's "triarchic" theory, pointing to three kinds of intelligence. Noted Harvard University psychologist Howard Gardner suggests in his book *Frames of Mind* that there are at least seven distinct types of intelligence.

1. *Verbal-linguistic intelligence*, involving a sensitivity to the meaning, order, sounds, and rhythms of words and the functions and powers of language.
2. *Musical intelligence*, the ability to "hear" music in one's mind, to compose, and to think musically, especially in terms of melody and rhythm.
3. *Logical-mathematical intelligence*, the ability to use reasoning, ordering, and logical thought for problem solving, whether in mathematics and science or in the ordinary affairs of life.
4. *Visual-spatial intelligence*, including the ability to perceive accurately, to visualize, and to create artistic transformations of the visual world.
5. *Bodily-kinesthetic intelligence*, as exemplified in people like dancers and athletes who develop unusual mastery over the motions of the body.
6. *The personal intelligences*, including two aspects, the ability to access one's own inner feelings, and the ability to understand and be able to relate to other people.

Each of us favors one or two types of intelligence over the others. The words we use frequently reflect that favored mode. For example, a person who favors the visual system might use expressions like,

I see what you mean.

Do you get the picture?

Is that clear?

The seeing of objects involves many sources of information beyond those meeting the eye when we look at an object. It generally involves knowledge of the object derived from previous experience, and this experience is not limited to vision but may include the other senses: touch, taste, smell, hearing, and perhaps also temperature or pain.

R. L. Gregory

The more connections that can be made in the brain, the more integrated the experience is within memory.

Don Campbell

I never hit a shot, not even in practice, without having a very sharp, in-focus picture of it in my head. . . . First I 'see' the ball where I want it to finish, nice and white and sitting up high on the bright green grass. Then the scene quickly changes, and I 'see' the ball going there: its path, trajectory, and shape, even its behavior on landing. Then there is a sort of fade-out, and the next scene shows me making the kind of swing that will turn the previous images into reality.

Jack Nicklaus

A more auditory person might say,

> That sounds good to me.
> Can you hear what I'm saying?
> That rings true.

A more feeling (kinesthetic) person might say,

> How does that feel to you?
> Can you grasp the meaning?
> I think I have a handle on the information.

Do any of these expressions or groups of phrases seem especially comfortable and familiar to you? If so, that should give you a clue abut your own learning style.

Mastery of the Information Age is greatly facilitated by *knowing how you learn*. In order to determine this, begin to pay attention to your learning preferences; think about the seven intelligences above. Take advantage of your strongest intelligence, but don't rely on it entirely. The more channels you can use for learning, the better off you are. You may find that you can strengthen your weakest learning modes simply by paying attention to them.

USE VISUALIZATION FOR PEAK PERFORMANCE

Visualization is another ability of your whole brain that students and business people can take advantage of in many learning and work situations. It refers to *mentally* creating a state or situation—in pictures, sounds, feelings, and so on—that you desire to occur in physical reality. You might think of it as a disciplined exercise of imagination.

Visualization helps you to learn, remember, and create more effectively. By mentally creating images while you read, work, or study, you are better able to concentrate, consolidate information, and rehearse the steps needed to achieve your goals. Many memory improvement strategies are also based on the ability to visualize, since the technique helps you to process and associate information with knowledge you already possess.

Visualization techniques have been prescribed by popular self-help authors for decades. Because there was at first no scientific evidence for their effectiveness, many people did not take advantage of them. However, in the last decade, so many people have attributed their success to visualization, and so much research has been published around the world clearly demonstrating the power of visualization to transform the *physiology* as well as the mental state, that no one can now deny its validity and usefulness.

Many successful and creative people have developed their ability to visualize and actively use it to improve their concentration and performance. Top athletes like Jack Nicklaus, Arnold Schwarzenegger, Bruce Jenner, and Greg Louganis attribute their success to going over their performance visually many times, perfecting it in their imagination before undertaking it physically. Industrialists of the past and business leaders and entrepreneurs today use the power of visualization to mentally picture the product or create the outcome they desire before setting their enterprises in motion.

The effectiveness of visualization lies in the fact that the body treats the visualized images and thoughts as if they were the real thing. During visualization, neuromuscular templates are created—patterns of mind-body coordination that prepare us for whatever action we will eventually do. These neuronal networks or "neurological tracks" are just as they would be if the person actually *did* the actions.

Electromyographic studies (measurements of minute electrical activity in the muscles) have shown that when individuals visualize an action, their muscles undergo electrical activity corresponding exactly to the physical actions they are imagining. Psychologist Richard Suinn of Colorado State University used electromyographs to study the muscle response of a skier visualizing a race.

> Almost instantly, the recording needles stirred into action. Two muscle bursts appeared as the skier hit jumps. Additional muscle bursts duplicated the effort of crossing a rough section of the course, and the needles settled during the easy sections. . . . There was even a final burst of muscle activity after he had passed the finish line, a mystery to me until I remembered how hard it is to come to a skidding stop after racing downhill at more than forty miles an hour.

Before I put a sketch on paper, the whole idea is worked out mentally. In my mind I change the construction, make improvements, and even operate the device. Without ever having drawn a sketch I can give the measurements of all parts to workmen, and when completed all these parts will fit, just as certainly as though I had made the actual drawings. It is immaterial to me whether I run my machine in my mind or test it in my shop.

The inventions I have conceived in this way have always worked. In thirty years there has not been a single exception. My first electric motor, the vacuum wireless light, my turbine engine and many other devices have all been developed in exactly this way.

Nikola Tesla

The Chinese pianist Liu Chi Kung was imprisoned for seven years during the Cultural Revolution, during which time he had no access to a piano. When he returned to giving concerts again after he was released, his playing was better than ever. Asked how this was possible since he had not practiced for seven years, he replied: "I did practice, every day. I rehearsed every piece I had ever played, note by note, in my mind."

Bernie Zilbergeld, Ph.D.
Arnold Lazarus, Ph.D.

Research with other athletes has shown that visualization is often as effective and beneficial as physical practice. For example, psychologists tested student basketball players visualizing free-throw shooting. They found that players who spent three weeks not practicing but only visualizing the process—imagining shooting, mentally watching the ball go through the hoop, and correcting themselves when their shot "missed"—improved 23 percent, while the group that actually practiced improved 24 percent.

Many books have been published discussing the dominance of Russian and East European athletes in Olympic performances in recent decades. All agree that the main reason for their success is that in those countries as much attention is given to mental training as to physical training. Former Soviet sports psychologist Grigori Raiport wrote in his book, *Red Gold: Peak Performance Techniques of the Russian and East German Olympic Victors*, "A first grader in the Soviet Union gets more help [with mental training] then Olympic caliber athletes do here."

In the field of medicine, too, dramatic results are being seen when people use visualization to combat their diseases. Dozens of books by reputable physicians have documented hundreds of case histories where serious diseases such as cancer have been either cured or slowed down by visualization. Typically, a patient will visualize golden or white light healing the afflicted area, or perhaps will imagine the disease being attacked by bombs of love or devoured by birds. The variations are endless, but the results are consistent.

If you think you are not a "natural" visualizer, you are probably just too busy to note how frequently you actually do it. For example, how often do you worry about things that may never happen, clearly visualizing potential accidents or negative reactions that others might have? How often do you replay conversations and events in your mind, going over the details of a difficult or painful situation? This is visualization. You already know exactly how to do it.

To be a Master of the Information Age, you need to use this powerful faculty constructively, in two ways. First, use visualization to imagine *the final goal* or results you want to attain: the position and status you want to have, the completed report you need to write, the feeling you will have when you have delivered your presentation and are getting a standing ovation, and so on. How will it look and feel when you have achieved what you want? If you were the basketball free-thrower in the above experiment, you would see the ball fall through the hoop, hear the "swish" of the net, feel the elation in your body. This aspect, imagining the goal, is actually what you did in chapter 2 in Learning Activator #3.

Second, use visualization to imagine *the process* of achieving your goal. This entails going carefully and thoroughly through the sequence of steps you will need to take in order to bring the goal into being. If you are going to make a presentation, see yourself preparing your talk by gathering material and organizing it thoughtfully, then practicing your delivery, and finally giving the presentation with energy and confidence.

Here are some general rules on how to create visualizations that you can use to help you deal with real-life situations at work or in studying.

1. Always begin with a few minutes of alpha breathing or a relaxation technique of your choice. A relaxed state of mind and body is important for success, so be sure not to skip this step.
2. See as much detail as possible. See specific books and journals you will need to consult, and people you know you will want to talk to. When you first begin creating visualizations, your images may be somewhat vague and fleeting, but with practice they will become precise. The more precise you can make them, the more powerful they will be.
3. The most successful imaging utilizes every sense, so when you visualize it is important to include as many sensory details as you can. What do you hear (voices, music, environmental sounds)? Are there any associated smells (fragrances of a garden or perfume, smoke of a business meeting)?
4. Maintain control over your imagery. Don't allow yourself to drift off into your habitual negative self-suggestions. You may find this happening, especially if

Peak performers develop powerful mental images of the behavior that will lead to the desired results. They see in their mind's eye the result they want, and the actions leading to it. They rehearse. . . . They visualize, not as a substitute for a thorough preparation and hard work, but as an indispensable adjunct.

Dr. Charles A. Garfield

you've had lots of practice thinking about yourself in limiting ways. Keep coming back to the positive.

5. To strengthen the effect of the new imagery, you can make it brighter, more colorful, closer, larger, louder, sharper. If negative imagery comes up, you can weaken its effects by doing the opposite: fade the colors, make it smaller, dimmer, farther away from you, and so on.

The following exercise will help you gauge your visualization skills and allow you to begin immediately improving them.

■ ■ ■ ■

LEARNING ACTIVATOR #8
VISUALIZATION

Part I: Gauging Your Image-Making Skills
The first part of this Activator is designed to help you gauge your image-making capacity. As you go through it, close your eyes and allow the images to develop naturally and effortlessly, using every combination of your senses. Imagination works best in a relaxed alpha state, so before you begin this Activator, do a set of alpha breathing or other relaxation technique. Then perform the following:

1. Imagine yourself walking into your bedroom and see as many details as you can.
2. Imagine the face of a good friend and observe all of the facial features in detail.
3. Without looking, imagine what the cover of this book looks like.
4. Imagine that you are walking on the moon.
5. Imagine walking in a fragrant rose garden that overlooks the ocean.

What happened as you imaged each of these scenes? Which of your senses went into making up the pictures? Were the pictures vivid, weak, or nonexistent?

Part II: Developing Your Image-Making Skills
Here are some exercises for building your image-making skills. They are easy and can be done any time.

1. *Mental painting.* Look at an object, then close your eyes and imagine yourself painting or drawing it on a canvas. After your canvas is complete, open your eyes and compare your masterpiece with the original object.

2. *Create comparisons.* Play a mental game of comparing things you see with something else. For instance, a piece of string on the ground can be imagined as a river, a butterfly as an airplane, someone you are angry with as a Walt Disney character, your car as a spaceship, and so on. Practice thinking in visual metaphors. To keep this interesting, bring humor and exaggeration into the comparisons.

3. *See your phone conversations.* Whenever you are talking on the phone, imagine as clearly as possible the physical features of the person on the other end. Try this as an imagination-strengthening game *even if you have never seen the person before.* As he or she talks, let pictures develop that represent what is being said.

The words of language, as they are written or spoken, do not seem to play any role in my mechanism of thought. The physical entities which seem to serve as elements in thought are certain signs and more or less clear images.

Albert Einstein

Part III: Creating Your Own Visualization

Now you will put together all you have learned about visualization and apply it to your own life. Pick some goal you would like to achieve. This could be the completion of a report or paper, a promotion, a sale, a successful presentation, acceptance in an organization or a team—anything of importance to you.

First, as we discussed above, develop a clear multisensory image of the goal you wish to achieve. Then, *acting as if you couldn't fail,* write down the steps you would take to achieve that goal. Be as precise as possible.

Now, with your eyes closed, imagine each step occurring just the way you want it in order to be successful. With your mind and body, *feel* what each step feels like, *see* it, *hear* the sounds surrounding the actions and interactions. Doing this simulates the desired result and puts your brain in motion to accomplish your goal. Once you have taken all the steps to reach your goal, spend a few moments using as many senses as you can to experience the achievement.

Your visualization should be followed by action. Just seeing something will not make it happen—but when you do take action, you will find that in many ways the path seems to have been prepared. Your brain already knows what to do, and action produces to achievement.

■ ■ ■ ■

If you practice visualization each time you are assigned a project or have a report to prepare—or to achieve any of your personal goals—you will find that the technique will enhance your end product as well as simplify your process of getting there. If you have never used visualization before, I encourage you to try it more than once. With practice, it can become a regular part of your work or study habits that pays off in the long run.

DEVELOP YOUR LISTENING SKILLS

In the Information Age, communication is everything—it's how information becomes useful. Communication means essentially talking and listening to other human beings. Researchers estimate that we spend up to three-quarters of our waking hours in verbal communication. We listen to the radio, to audiotapes, to the voices from the TV screen, and, most importantly, to people close to us at home and at work. Yet research also indicates that most of us listen with an efficiency no better than 25 percent. That means we miss 75 percent, which stacks the odds against true understanding.

Unsuccessful, inefficient listening occurs when we are passive. We may hear the words, but we are not really giving our full conscious attention. Our minds are elsewhere, not fully focused on the person speaking. The inevitable consequences of passive listening include misunderstandings and miscommunications, confusion about instructions, and the loss of vital information.

On the other hand, effective listening is an *active* process, during which the mind interacts with both the speaker and the incoming information. Here are the basic principles of "active" listening.

Think about it. Don't just take in the information being presented. Interact with it in the following ways. Evaluate it by asking questions, such as: Does it make sense? Is it reasonable? What are the sources of this information? Is it believable? Why is the speaker telling me this? Analyze it by organizing the information into main points and trying to understand it step by step. Visualize it by converting the words into pictures as much as you can. The images will not only help you grasp and understand the points, they will also aid your memory. Associate it by connecting what is being said to your previous knowledge. Hook it into your mental data bank. Those connections will aid your understanding of the new material and will enrich the old material with new link-ups.

Our brain can process spoken language at about 500 words per minute; most people speak somewhere around 150 words per minute. You have plenty of time to think about what is being said without missing anything important.

Pay full attention. Often we only half-listen to others. We are busy with something else, or we are preparing our answer before we have really heard the other person. This prevents us from truly concentrating on the message and receiving all the information that is being communicated.

Use your heart as well as your head. Use your whole-brain skills—listen to the words, get the facts, but be empathic too. Pay attention to voice inflections and silences; listen "between the lines" for things left unspoken, such as how the person might be feeling about what he or she is telling you.

Use your head as well as your heart. If you tend to react emotionally or are an "empathizer" prone to getting caught up in another person's feelings, be sure also to think about what is being said. Listen to the logic of the sentences, the choice of words, the facts presented. This will help keep you from falling prey to emotional arguments that undermine your ability to think clearly.

Go for the essence. Try to grasp the core, the heart, of what the person is saying. The essence may be a feeling or a central idea, a key fact, or a main goal. Once you understand the essence, the details will make sense and you will know how to respond.

Give feedback. Use eye contact, nods, and smiles to let the speaker know you are paying attention. From time to time, rephrase what he or she has just told you: "As I understand it, what you're saying is . . ." This practice has several benefits. First, it helps you ascertain whether you are really getting what is being said, and it gives you the opportunity to correct anything you may have missed or misunderstood. Second, finding

The brain's calculations do not require our conscious effort, only our attention and our openness to let the information through. Although the brain absorbs universes of information, little is admitted into normal consciousness.

Marilyn Ferguson

words to express what you think you have learned will greatly enhance your retention of the information. Finally, your feedback lets the speaker know the message is getting across and encourages him or her to continue.

Watch the speaker. You can learn a lot from the speaker's body language, by watching for expressions, postures, or gestures. Nervousness and fidgeting may indicate that something is being withheld or is difficult to say; "blocking" gestures, such as crossing the arms or legs, may indicate defensiveness. Looking at the person who is talking might seem like a small matter, but often the information conveyed by body language is of equal value to the words used.

Ask questions. Questions serve two main functions. They can help draw out the speaker, urging him or her to continue talking and clarifying or expanding. They can also elicit information you need to help you understand fully what is being expressed. If you have no specific questions, you can elicit more information simply by saying, "Tell me more."

Keep quiet. While asking questions at appropriate moments can be helpful to both parties, most of the time it is better if you remain silent and listen, signaling your attention and interest with appropriate feedback. If you have something of your own to contribute, wait until the other speaker is finished. Try to avoid making judgments or coming to conclusions until you have heard the whole story.

Take notes. Many people miss out on valuable opportunities to learn or gather information because they fail to take notes when listening to a lecture or seminar presentation. Have pen and paper ready to write down details, ideas, and extrapolations that can be of benefit later. The process of note-taking gives you two additional modes of input (visual and kinesthetic) that can help you retain information longer and more concretely.

Above all, be the kind of listener you would like others to be. When you have something to say, either in your personal life or at work, you appreciate an attentive, caring listener. Give this gift to others.

Make use of these principles of active listening, and enjoy the tremendous benefit it will bring to your personal and professional life.

USING YOUR SUBCONSCIOUS

There is a whole world of information we take in parallel to our conscious thought processes that a Master can tap into. Research has shown conclusively that at any given time two channels of sensory information are delivered to our brain: conscious and subconscious. In a recent article, psychologist Daniel Goleman reviewed a large body of evidence suggesting that the unconscious mind "may understand and respond to meaning, form emotional responses, and guide most actions, largely independent of conscious awareness."

One reason for this, according to the latest theories of the nature of consciousness, is that our consciousness is by nature selective. Out of a huge number of impressions being picked up at any given time by our sensory systems, only a few reach our conscious awareness. All the rest, of which we remain unaware, are processed by the brain subconsciously.

Neurologically speaking, what is happening is this: Information is transmitted through the sensory pathways to specific brain receptor centers such as the visual cortex. Our *consciousness* of them, however, depends on the reticular activating system, a dense network of cells arising from the brain stem and spreading upward into the cortex, and this system can only work on a limited number of sense impressions at one time.

One of the earliest and most often quoted experiments demonstrating the separation of what we receive from what we are actually aware of was performed by pioneer researcher Benjamin Libet and his colleagues and was reported in *Science* magazine in 1967. Dr. Libet hooked subjects up to an instrument that measured minute electrical potentials in the brain, and then administered a stimulus at such a low level that the subjects could not consciously detect it. Even though the subjects reported that they were totally unaware of the stimulus, their brains responded to it.

According to George Miller, in his now-famous paper "The Magical Number Seven, Plus or Minus Two," originally published in *Psychological Review* in 1957, the human mind can only be consciously aware of seven (give or take two) items at a time. Miller stated, "There seems to be some limitation built into us either by learning or by the design of our nervous

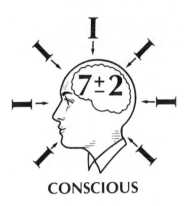

CONSCIOUS

SUBCONSCIOUS

The most complicated achievements of thought are possible without the assistance of consciousness.

Sigmund Freud

The conscious mind may be compared to a fountain playing in the sun and falling back into the great subterranean pool of subconscious from which it rises.

Sigmund Freud

system, a limit that keeps our channel capacities in this general range." On the other hand, the capacity for transferring information to the brain through subconscious channels seems to be way beyond the magical number seven.

Indeed, so much subconscious information processing takes place that one of the world's leading researchers in the field, Dr. Emmanuel Donchin, director of the Laboratory for Cognitive Psychophysiology at the University of Illinois, has speculated that "as much as ninety-nine percent of cognitive activity may be nonconscious."

Our daily lives are filled with examples of nonconscious information input. Literally thousands of bodily processes are monitored and adjusted by the brain in response to changing conditions in the environment, beyond the threshold of consciousness. Most of what we learn about our culture is absorbed subconsciously. Children begin speaking the language of their culture spontaneously; they pick up the words and even the grammatical structure of the language by the time they are two or three years old, without any conscious instruction or study.

Here's another example of the subconscious at work. How many times have you driven your car along a busy road and become deeply engrossed in thought? Later, your light of consciousness drifted back to the road and you realized that you had driven for miles on "automatic pilot." You had no conscious recollection of turning, slowing, passing, or any of the other driving maneuvers you must have performed. Your subconscious took over the wheel and safely negotiated the traffic on its own.

The significance of this for a Master of the Information Age is obvious: We can exploit our subconscious faculty extensively. In fact, the utilization of our subconscious learning abilities has been basic to the success of many accelerated learning programs. In addition to Georgi Lozanov, researchers throughout the world, such as Alfonso Caycedo in Colombia, Alfred Tomatis in France, Shinichi Suzuki in Japan, and Eric Jensen in America, have discovered that learning is facilitated when subconscious channels are employed.

■ ■ ■ ■

LEARNING ACTIVATOR #9
TUNE IN TO YOUR SUBCONSCIOUS SENSING

The purpose of this short Activator is to make you aware of the range of subconscious sensory input that your brain is picking up all the time. For instance, as you read this book your conscious attention is on the words and their meanings. You may also be vaguely aware of your hands holding the book, and maybe a thought or two apparently not related to the text. But until I mention it, you are probably not aware of your *toes*. Now you may notice that they are sending information to your brain—tight shoes, cramped, bent, cold, or numerous other messages.

Shift your conscious awareness to other parts of your body. What sensations are they picking up and sending to your brain? Is the air passing into your nose cold or warm? Is one nostril more open than the other? Allow your attention to expand to the noise coming in from your surroundings. Notice the smells in the air. What information is your peripheral vision receiving?

Until your conscious attention was directed to these sensory sources, they did not register in your awareness. Nonetheless they were being communicated to your brain.

■ ■ ■ ■

The power of intuitive understanding will protect you from harm until the end of your days.

Lao Tzu

A Master of the Information Age recognizes the existence and scope of this subconscious information gathering, and puts it to use. Perhaps the most important way to do this is to use your intuition.

Develop Your Intuition

Intuition is a subtle experience of inner knowing, a way of understanding that is not dependent on our usual rational, analytic processing. When we have a problem to solve and look within ourselves, we sometimes intuit the answer. We don't know why it's true: we can't prove it yet with external data. We just feel confident in our judgment—and in a remarkable number of instances, we are right. But how?

It is always with excitement that I wake up in the morning wondering what my intuition will toss up to me, like gifts from the sea. I work with it and rely on it. It's my partner.

Dr. Jonas Salk

Some researchers speculate that intuition may be the process of accessing our subconscious "files." Somewhere or other, this theory goes, we have picked up the relevant information subconsciously, without being aware of it. Intuition is therefore the brain's way of saying, "Hey, I know the answer to that!" Numerous studies have shown that in the business world, the higher up the corporate ladder a person is, the more likely that person is to trust and use intuition in problem solving and decision making.

Trusting your intuition means learning to respect the validity of those delicate impulses that speak from the quieter levels of your mind. A Master of the Information Age listens for those faint inner suggestions and puts them to use wherever possible. Here are ten ways you can improve your intuition.

1. Learn to reduce "mental noise" when you want to consult your intuition. Use meditation or relaxation techniques to settle your mind. Intuition favors a mind that is calm and alert.
2. Be flexible; don't straitjacket your mind with rigid habits and etched-in-stone procedures. You need to be open-minded to listen to what your intuition has to offer.
3. Don't reject your hunches prematurely. Learn to suspend judgment long enough for your intuitive ideas to gel.
4. Use techniques such as brainstorming and free-form writing to stimulate the flow of ideas.
5. Be willing to risk being wrong; don't stifle your intuition because you fear criticism.
6. Expand your horizons. Exposure to a wide range of information and experiences broadens the database for the unconscious mind.
7. Get familiar with your own intuition. Learn what it feels like when it turns out to be right.
8. Get away from it all. Stop dwelling compulsively on the problem you are trying to solve. Sometimes the best ideas and solutions pop into the mind when least expected.

9. Don't *try* to be intuitive; intuition comes spontaneously and effortlessly to a receptive mind.

10. Believe in your intuition. Not blindly, of course, but a little faith will keep you from suppressing your hunches.

A great deal has been written on developing our intuitive powers. The prior list is adapted from *The Intuitive Edge* by Philip Goldberg. Intuition is one of our most powerful information gateways, and we'll discuss it in more detail as we explore techniques to improve your reading skills in later chapters.

Tap into Your Subliminal Power

Related to subconscious information gathering is the field of subliminal learning. Although it is controversial, subliminal learning may be a technique from which you can benefit in your exploration of new methods to improve your learning and productivity.

Subliminal is defined as "below the threshold of conscious awareness." The difference between subliminal and subconscious processing lies in whether you can become consciously aware of the information if you choose to do so. Whereas *subconscious* processing refers to information (as in the earlier example of cars you pass while daydreaming) that you *could* bring to consciousness if you chose to shine your light beam of conscious awareness on it, the term *subliminal* is used to describe information that is *not available* to be consciously heard or seen no matter how hard you try.

Nevertheless, there does seem to be some support for the idea that subliminal learning can be effective. In the 98th Congress of the United States in 1984, the House Committee on Science and Technology held a hearing on subliminal communication technology. Numerous experts testified on the many applications of subliminal learning. One of the facts brought to light was that subliminal stimulation has been used successfully by doctors in a therapeutic context. For example, by reducing anxiety through the subliminal presentation of positive, reassuring messages, patients have been able to reduce neurotic overeating. Similarly, students with "math anxiety" have been able to improve their performance, and various more serious phobias have been successfully treated by presentation of appropriate messages below the conscious threshold.

In addition to these carefully monitored therapeutic uses of subliminal techniques by psychologists and physicians, many people today are using subliminal tapes at home and in their cars to help them overcome fears, develop dynamism, quit smoking, and improve their love and sex relationships, among many hundreds of available programs. Literally millions of these tapes are sold every year, and the anecdotal evidence of their effectiveness is mounting.

The underlying theory behind their use is that they function as an antidote to negative messages and beliefs deeply implanted in our subconscious mind. As we saw in chapter 2, we are all governed by self-evaluations and beliefs of which we are not aware, concerning such basic and crucial factors as our intelligence and abilities. Many, if not all, of our personal limitations and self-defeating habits are the result of early programming that has created negative expectations in our subconscious mind, which then influence much of our conscious behavior and attitudes.

In the words of Eldon Taylor, a leading subliminal tape producer and theorist, the effectiveness of subliminal programs lies in the fact

> that the conscious mind cannot argue with their positive content and thereby diminish them. Subliminals go directly into the subconscious and immediately begin to reprogram the old biocomputer scripts, replacing doubt, fear, and negative attitudes and expectations . . . with powerful new positive computations.

Taylor suggests that subliminal programs offer "an affordable alternative" to the individual seeking to improve aspects of his or her life. In your personal quest to become a Master of the Information Age, they may be a powerful ally.

EVERY EXPERIENCE IS A LEARNING OPPORTUNITY

One of the worst consequences of information overload is that many people simply tune out to new learning experiences.

It is now a generally accepted and scientifically well supported view that subliminal perception does occur—that people are capable of receiving and responding to information presented to them at levels below the threshold of conscious recognition.

Maureen Phillips
Olivia Goodkin

There is information everywhere, and a Master takes advantage of that fact to learn in every situation. There is always something to read, someone to talk to, something to observe, something to reflect about—all valuable opportunities for learning.

For example, you are no doubt occasionally presented with the opportunity to read magazines or other materials outside your usual fields of interest. As an information Master, it is important to use these sources to uncover new ideas and insights that might enrich and perfect your work or personal projects.

Admittedly, this may be difficult if you are already overwhelmed with information. However, the more you allow yourself to read selectively in a variety of areas, the less you will experience the feelings of information anxiety. The more free time you give yourself to play in the world of information that you apparently do not need at all, the more you will make new connections and serendipitous discoveries. The sports page, for instance, may offer you an unusual perspective on the competitive world of business. Even a work of fiction may provide you with insight into the solution to a problem.

Another arena for extending your knowledge is conversation. Whether it's talking to a friend or to a stranger, such as on an airplane or a commuter train ride, you should make an effort to learn from him or her. Here are some unusual questions you might ask others to stimulate conversation from which you can open new horizons of knowledge.

Any perception can connect us to reality properly and fully. What we see doesn't have to be pretty, particularly; we can appreciate anything that exists. There is some principle of magic in everything, some living quality. Something living, something real, is taking place in everything.

Chögyam Trungpa

1. *What book have you read recently that has most informed you or changed your views on an issue?* This might identify an interesting information source or lead to a discussion of an issue from which you can learn.

2. *What are your favorite magazines?* Asking this question might lead you to sources of information that you're not familiar with from among the hundreds of magazines available in this country.

3. *Whom do you most admire and why?* From this question you might find out about people you weren't aware of, from whose life or works you might gain insight or inspiration.

4. *How do you keep up with information on your job?* This might provide you with ideas and techniques that you might profitably learn and use.
5. *What's the one thing you might like to learn?*

Use Your Time More Productively

Another aspect of using every opportunity to learn begins with the recognition that most of us do not get full use out of much of our time. Ask yourself how you might use your time more productively to learn and to reduce your information anxiety. For example, most of us spend literally hundreds of hours a year in our cars.

How much time do you spend commuting?

daily one-way trip in minutes	round trip	hours each year	equivalent number of 40-hour weeks
5	10	40	1
10	20	80	2
15	30	120	3
20	40	160	4
25	50	200	5
30	60	240	6
35	70	280	7
40	80	320	8
45	90	360	9
50	100	400	10
55	110	440	11
60	120	480	12

Think how much you could become acquainted with or accomplish in those hours by using the time creatively.

One way would be to listen to audiotapes. Thousands of books, from current best-sellers to the literary classics, have been recorded onto tape. You can listen to biographies of famous people, novels, poetry, seminars, or business and management books. Most public libraries have a reasonable supply of audio cassettes available for borrowing, or you can purchase your choices at most bookstores.

There are also dozens of excellent self-development programs on tape, designed to help you expand your capabilities. Programs exist for just about any self-improvement issue you may wish to work on, such as overcoming procrastination, improving memory, generating positive attitudes, and so on.

Of course, you don't have to restrict your use of these rich audio information sources to your car. Listen to your tapes at home in place of television, or while simply relaxing in your favorite chair.

Consider how much you could learn or how much more effective your training or personal work on yourself could be if you spent only half an hour a day listening to a tape. At that rate you could listen to a one-hour tape every two days, 15 tapes a month, 180 tapes a year to expand your knowledge and improve your skills. Particularly if your career involves a lot of reading, taking advantage of taped material can add to your knowledge and keep you more up-to-date in an easy and enjoyable way. To find tapes that interest you, check your library for the publication *Books on Tape*, or visit your bookstore to see what they carry.

DEVELOP POWERFUL WORK HABITS AND STUDY SKILLS

Developing work habits that promote efficiency and bring you greater success in all your projects is one of the most critical aspects of being a Master. Whether you are a student or a professional, you need effective methods of information/time management: developing concentration, setting goals, prioritizing your projects, overcoming procrastination, and so on. Following are some habits a Master strives to maintain.

Concentration and Focus

Sharp focus and the ability to concentrate are extremely important to success in any kind of mental activity, whether learning, thinking, creating, or problem solving. Before you begin any study or work task that requires you to be fully focused, you may wish to use one of the following techniques to en-hance your concentration.

CENTERING. A surprisingly effective and quick way to gain or regain concentration is to fix your eyes on something for a short time. Tibetan Buddhists use intricate visual mandalas as a meditative aid to help them quiet their minds. You can use the second hand or digital readout on your watch. Simply focus on it for one minute. This technique reduces the input of your senses to a single source. As you center your focus, you direct your awareness away from extraneous thoughts and toward a fixed point. This gives your brain the message that it is time to stop wandering and regain concentration.

DOWNLOAD DISTRACTING THOUGHTS. Sometimes distracting thoughts are your way of worrying that you will forget some-thing important. If you feel this is the case, simply write the thought down. The act of writing it down will relieve the sub-conscious worry, and you will be able to get back in focus. Before you begin your work or study, give yourself a few min-utes to attend to these distractions, to clear your mind for undisturbed activity.

USE BREATHING TO SETTLE YOUR MIND. The alpha breathing technique presented in chapter 3 is also effective for narrowing your field of attention to a single focus. I suggest you use it before any learning session to establish concentration. If your concentration wanes in the midst of a task, stop what you are doing and use alpha breathing to reestablish focus.

Don't Be a Perfectionist

Psychologists have found that the tendency toward perfection-ism often springs from a fear of failure. For example, if you hold off turning in a report until it's perfect, clearly you will never turn it in, because you can always find a way to improve it. If you don't turn it in, you won't have to deal with the possibility of rejection or criticism. This is an extremely self-defeating tactic, but it is so common that perfectionism may rank as the Master's number-two enemy, after stress.

I've got to keep breathing. It'll be my worst business mistake if I don't.

Sir Nathan Rothschild

A Master knows it is impossible to read or investigate everything and that we must sometimes act on incomplete information and hunches. In some cases, if you simply cultivate your intuition you will do as well as when you spin your wheels worrying and trying to track down enough information to make the project "perfect." Do the best job you can in the time you have—and then go on.

Nothing is so fatiguing as the eternal hanging on of an uncomplicated task.

William James

Plan and Prioritize Your Day

Every morning, or before you go to bed the night before, make a list of priorities for the day. Here is an effective way to do this.

1. Start by listing everything you need to do.
2. Categorize each item "A," "B," or "C," depending on its importance to you.
3. Prioritize the As and Bs (A-1, A-2, A-3, etc.) in the order you intend to do them. Tackle the Cs only after you've finished the As and Bs.
4. A tricky but vital point to remember: "Urgent" does not equal "important"—try to focus on the things that are really the latter. Many people interrupt important tasks to do something that seems urgent. This is, however, a major obstacle to concentration and productivity. Whenever possible, save urgent tasks for a later time, and you will realize they were not so urgent after all.

Set Goals

In order to organize your priorities, you have to know what your goals are. Take some quiet time to think about what you want to accomplish in different aspects of your life, both in the long run and in the near future. Think about where you want to be 1, 5, and 10 years from now, in terms of your career, your social/family life, your spiritual and intellectual development, your health, and so on. When you know your goals, use your visualization skills to determine what concrete steps and actions you need to take in order to achieve them. This will also help make your most important daily priorities clearer,

Tips for Overcoming Procrastination

1. Break large projects down into parts. Divide large, intimidating projects into smaller, more do-able, clearly defined segments. Finishing the smaller parts will give you satisfaction and confidence.

2. Start with something you enjoy. The first step is the hardest, so begin with something you find pleasant and easy, just to get going. Try something you can polish off in fifteen minutes.

3. Set a series of small but realistic deadlines instead of one final date for the whole project.

4. Motivate yourself again and again. Use your visualization skills. Imagine the project completed. Using all your senses, experience the feeling of successful achievement.

as you will then take the steps that bring you closer to realizing your short-term and long-term goals. From the point of view of information, knowing your goals will also alleviate anxiety about keeping up with information that actually means little to you.

Use Your Prime Time for Priority Work

Some people function most effectively in the early morning, while others don't get into gear until nearly noon. Whatever your "prime time" for accomplishment is, work on your priority projects during those hours when your brain is most lively and your energy highest.

Remove Distractions from Your Workplace

Keep food, TV, magazines, and other temptations out of sight, and out of the room if possible.

Give Yourself a Break

Concentration can deteriorate as a result of mental fatigue. Studies indicate that forty to fifty minutes is about the maximum time most people can effectively concentrate. At the end of that time you begin to experience fatigue and drift out of the peak learning state. A short break will revitalize you.

When faced with deadlines, many of us have a tendency to "power through" even though our ability to think has declined. This is counterproductive, since our natural body rhythm is telling us that we cannot continue business as usual without a respite. A ten- to fifteen-minute break will reenergize you and increase the quality and quantity of what you produce when you return. You might even find that your best insights come during the break, when you "let go" of what you are working on and give your creative unconscious and intuition a chance to be heard.

When you take a break, get some exercise, stretch, relax your neck and back muscles, drink water, or participate in a nonmental activity to clear your mind.

Touch Paper Only Once

Handle letters, memos, articles, and so on only once. Make a decision if necessary and act. Write your reply, note it down, throw it away—but get it off your desk! It is amazing how many people spend vast portions of the day shuffling the same papers around. If you are in this category, you will find that adopting this habit can add many more productive hours to your day.

Clear Your Desk

At regular intervals, whether every day or once a week, clear your desk. Act on what seems necessary or required. More importantly, throw away things you haven't acted on and know you won't act on. This is like cleaning out your mental refrigerator—don't let things get stale.

Choose a Reading Time

Schedule into your week a period of time to read *uninterruptedly* professional magazines, journals, newsletters, or general-interest materials of potential value for your work or studies. Sticking to this schedule will eliminate haphazard reading or not reading at all.

Don't Read Extraneous Material

Many of us could gain several hours every week if we stopped reading obviously irrelevant material: newspaper accounts of Hollywood celebrities, unimportant local events, articles on recurrent themes we've already read about. Many people have a tendency to browse through useless articles in newspapers and magazines (even advertising material) as a way of relaxing. But there are much more effective ways to relax. A simple rule of thumb: *Don't read anything that doesn't provide you with information you might need.*

This is not to discourage you from pleasure reading or reading you might do to amuse or entertain yourself for a few minutes. The point is that there are not that many minutes in a day available for information gathering, and if you want to be a Master you need to use all of them wisely. Instead of reading magazines and newspapers as if you had all the time in the world, give yourself only ten to fifteen minutes to read each one, and you will quickly see that you can accomplish your significant reading in just that time.

5. Make a conscious effort to realize that no matter how well your project turns out, it *can't* be perfect: there is no such thing. Perfectionism—such as the compulsion to turn a five-page report into a literary or artistic masterpiece—is probably the leading cause of procrastination.

6. Don't wait until you have a big enough block of time for the whole project: get started NOW. If you can only work for 15 minutes, you're 15 minutes closer to completion.

7. Promise yourself a reward after each accomplishment—and keep your promise!

Make Appointments with Yourself

To make sure you will have enough time to work on your priority projects, schedule into your calendar appointments with yourself—times when you will schedule no other appointments or meetings and, if possible, take no telephone calls. Here are a few other suggestions for efficient time management.

- Write short letters.
- Keep phone calls and meetings short.
- Schedule a "quiet hour" every day for planning, relaxation, and stock-taking.
- Organize your workspace and files to minimize lost time.
- Make minor decisions quickly.
- Say no more often.

To close this chapter, the following Activator brings together much of what you have learned thus far.

■ ■ ■ ■

LEARNING ACTIVATOR #10
VISUALIZE YOURSELF AS A MASTER OF INFORMATION

Use your mind's silent power of visualization to *see yourself as a Master of the Information Age*. First take a moment to think about what that means to you. Look over the principles in chapter 1, where we defined what a Master is.

Now feel yourself as a successful Master of information. Picture yourself at your desk, on the phone, and in your various roles at work. You are confident of your abilities as you handle the flow of information. See your posture, hear your voice, watch the way you move as you talk to other people. Note that you wisely spend time only on important matters. See yourself reading and learning new material, quickly understanding the essence of information sources, effectively communicating to others. Feel your mind sparkling with intelligence.

I hope this sense of yourself and your possibilities has been developing throughout your reading of this book. You have learned that it is important to uproot self-sabotaging beliefs and promote positive beliefs about your abilities. You have gained the mental tools to transform negative beliefs, and to relax and put yourself in an ideal frame of mind for learning. Now combine these skills with your knowledge about visualization, and plant this image of yourself as a Master of information deep in your brain and in your awareness.

As you go through the remainder of the book, you will continue to gain the *practical* tools to make this image of yourself a reality. From time to time as you read and work on the Learning Activators, and whenever you have a quiet moment, bring this vision back to mind. See, hear, and feel yourself as a Master of the Information Age. This change in your self-image will help you mobilize your inner and outer resources and operate at peak performance levels in all phases of your life.

■ ■ ■ ■

Take a moment now to look back at the statement of purpose at the beginning of this chapter. Ask yourself whether you have assimilated all the material. If you don't feel you have, take the time now to go back over any sections you feel you neglected before proceeding to chapter 5.

RESOURCES

Intuition

Goldberg, Phillip, *The Intuitive Edge.* (Los Angeles: Jeremy P. Tarcher, 1985). Excellent as both a study describing intuition and as a workbook for developing it within yourself.

Vaughan, Frances. *Awakening Intuition.* (New York: Doubleday, 1979). An excellent description of intuitive experience varieties, with a special focus on dreams.

Listening

Burley-Allen, Madelyn. *Listening: The Forgotten Skill.* (New York: John Wiley & Son, 1982). A practical analysis of techniques that help you hone listening skills.

Right brain and left brain

Edwards, Betty. *Drawing on the Right Side of the Brain.* (Los Angeles: Jeremy P. Tarcher, 1989). An excellent book explaining the functions of the brain hemispheres and how to increase creativity.

Jaynes, Julian. *The Origin of Consciousness in the Breakdown of the Bicameral Mind.* (Boston: Houghton Mifflin, 1982). A provocative theory on the origins of the differences in the two sides of the human brain.

Peak intelligence

Gardner, Howard. *Frames of Mind: The Theory of Multiple Intelligences*. (New York: Basic Books, 1983). A standard reference on the multiple intelligences theory.

Houston, Jean. *The Possible Human*. (Los Angeles: Jeremy P. Tarcher, 1982). A rich collection of exercises to stretch the mind and enliven the senses.

Subliminal understanding

Harman, Willis and Howard Rheingold. *Higher Creativity*. (Los Angeles: Jeremy P. Tarcher, 1984). Based on a study of techniques used by the highly creative to spark the flow of inspiration, this work includes methods to trigger your own unconscious creative forces.

Taylor, Ph.D., Eldon. *Subliminal Learning*. (Salt Lake City, UT: Just Another Reality Publishing Company, 1988). Exploration of parallel information processing by a leader in the subliminal research field.

Time management

Fiore, Neil. *The Now Habit*. (Los Angeles: Jeremy P. Tarcher, 1989). Offers a comprehensive system for overcoming procrastination.

Lakein, Alan. *How to Get Control of Your Time & Your Life*. (New York: Signet, 1974). A classic by the founding father of time management.

Winston, Stephanie. *Getting Organized*. (New York: W.W. Norton, 1978).

Visualization

Epstein, M.D., Gerald. *Healing Visualizations*. (New York: Bantam Books, 1989). A guide that draws on recent scientific evidence supporting visualization as a healing tool.

Gawain, Sahtki. *Creative Visualization*. (San Rafael, CA: New World Library, 1978). This has become a classic on visualization skills, full of explanations, techniques, and exercises.

Simonton, M.D., Carl. *Getting Well Again*. (Los Angeles: Jeremy P. Tarcher, 1978). A well-documented work based on the author's use of visualization to successfully treat cancer.

Organizations

Audio Renaissance, 5858 Wilshire Blvd., Suite 210, Los Angeles, CA 90036.

Career-Track, 3085 Center Green Drive, Boulder, CO 80302.

McCarthy Learning Institute, Sunshine Mesa Ranch, Box 900, Hotchkiss, CO 81419.

Monroe Institute, Route 1, Box 175, Faber, VA 22983.

Nightingale-Conant, 7300 North Lehigh Avenue, Chicago, IL 60648.

Valley of the Sun Publishing, P.O. Box 3004, Agoura Hills, CA 91301.

Whole Brain Learning Institute, 1049 Camino Del Mar, Del Mar, CA 92014.

■ ■ ■ ■

C H A P T E R 5

DEVELOP THE MEMORY HABIT

The purpose of this chapter is twofold: first, to convince you that you have a better memory than you think you do, and second, to show you some simple ways to have an even better, more active memory than you are now using. This chapter won't give you a perfect memory, although appropriate work on your part can bring you as close to that as you'll ever need to come. It will, however, lead you to the techniques and tools for a truly excellent memory that will be far more satisfying than the one you now have.

Much of what you will find in this chapter is what I would call basic memory tools, but the fact that they are simple doesn't mean that any significant portion of the population actually uses these techniques. In my seminars and workshops I deal with hundreds of intelligent people in various positions of management and education. Many have heard of the techniques that follow in this chapter (and many that can be found throughout the book), but an astonishingly small number of them ever actually use these memory techniques.

It doesn't take great wisdom or mysterious teachings to make an enormous difference in the effectiveness of one's memory. What it does take is doing the simple things and doing them consistently.

Memory is the mother of all wisdom.

Aeschylus

■ ■ ■ ■

One of the obvious challenges of the Information Age is that there's so much information that we can't possibly remember everything. The quantity of data that bombards us every day —ideas, facts, names, faces, dates, numbers, trends—seems far beyond our capacity to remember. The cumulative amount of material we must take in and process over time in our jobs and personal life is staggering to contemplate.

A Master of the Information Age must therefore have a reliable but selective memory. A powerful memory significantly contributes to our ability to operate at peak performance levels in many ways. First, it saves us time, because we can easily call to mind the specific information or data we need. Second, our ability to remember, and our trust that we can and will remember what we need, reduces information anxiety. Working more quickly and with reduced stress results in increased efficiency and effectiveness in all our activities.

However, a Master also knows that it is not necessary to remember every shred of information read or heard. We only need to be able to bring to mind the important and relevant information required by a particular situation. Sometimes this will be a number of specific facts, but usually it is only the essence or gist of the material encountered. For instance, we may read an entire book or a five-page memo filled with facts and figures, but usually all we really need to remember are a few key points and a statistic or two.

FOUR KEYS TO AN EXCELLENT MEMORY

Given this dichotomy in our memory requirements, there are four major components of memory you need to develop in order to become a Master of information.

TRUST YOUR MEMORY. If you believe you "have a bad memory" or that memory ability is something that can't be changed, this chapter will help you eliminate once and for all those useless, self-defeating, and incorrect beliefs. Each of us has an amazing memory capable of prodigious feats. We just haven't been taught to use it at anywhere near its potential. Volumes of research indicate without any doubt that memory can be improved.

INTEND TO REMEMBER. A major component of good memory is simply the conscious intention to remember. This entails several skills most people do not practice, such as defining your information target zone (deciding beforehand what you want to remember), and being consciously attentive and focused when new information is presented.

EXERCISE YOUR MEMORY. Many psychologists believe that memory works on the "use it or lose it" principle. That is, exercising your memory strengthens it and enlivens your whole brain. "If you do not seek intellectual stimulation and use your memory abilities regularly, you will lose them," Dr. Robin West writes in *Memory Fitness over Forty*.

Over the centuries, hundreds of techniques and "tricks" have been developed to help you remember more effectively. In this chapter I will introduce you to some of the most powerful ones. "Given the use of good techniques, practice, and daily mental stimulation, there is no reason why you can't improve your memory by 50 percent," writes Dr. West. I believe that estimate is conservative.

DECIDE WHAT YOU DON'T NEED TO REMEMBER. One of the greatest skills of a Master of the Information Age is knowing what *not to remember*. You simply cannot afford to spend your time absorbing the enormous amount of irrelevant material that crosses your desk, comes in through the mail, and bombards your senses day after day. You need to know what is worth remembering and what is not. It is easier and more efficient simply to know where to find information than to try to store it all in your head. Because information in all fields

becomes obsolete or modified so quickly, it is often best to know where you can go for the newest fact or theory rather than retaining outmoded information.

I will also introduce you to the concept and practice of mind mapping, a visual whole-brain system to help you take concise, organized notes that you can use to consolidate your understanding and to review whenever you need to spark your memory. Lastly, I will tell you about a few low- and high-technology information retention devices to supplement your memory.

Before we explore these four points in greater detail, it will be helpful to gain a deeper understanding of how memory actually works.

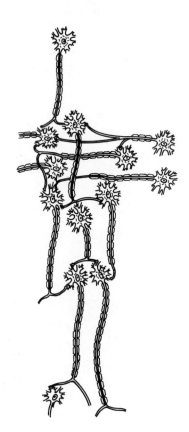

HOW MEMORY WORKS

There are many theories about how memory works and where in the brain our memories can be found. The most widely accepted theory today was originated by neuroscientist Donald Hebb in the 1950s. Hebb believed that information is stored in the interconnected networks of brain cells. Hebb's term for these interconnecting neuronal circuits was *cell assemblies*; others call them *neuronal networks*.

Each neuronal network is one of millions of similar networks that form pathways or highways of neurons stretching throughout the brain. According to Hebb, each piece of incoming information either becomes part of a preexisting network, or creates its own new one.

A cell assembly is like a woven net, consisting of millions or even hundreds of millions of neurons connecting together to hold a specific piece of information. Many of the nets are connected to others, depending on the relationship of the information in one to the information in another. These interrelationships are known as associations.

According to this theory, there are cell assemblies in your brain for everything you have ever learned and experienced in your life. Learning means the creation or modification of a neuronal network; memory results when specific existing neuronal channels become activated.

The neuronal network theory of memory gained support from the famous experiments by neurosurgeon Wilder Penfield. Attempting to locate the specific site responsible for epileptic seizures, Penfield probed the brains of epileptic patients with an electrode. Because the brain has no pain receptor cells, the patients were able to remain fully conscious and to communicate with the surgeon during the operation. To his surprise, Penfield discovered that direct electrical stimulation of particular regions of the brain caused the patient to recall specific experiences vividly, including some from early childhood that had been totally forgotten. Penfield first thought he had touched the specific spot in the brain where the memory was stored. He later realized that he had actually touched one portion of a neuronal net that stretched to other areas of the brain.

Penfield's research suggests that clear memory traces exist in the brain, perhaps for everything we have ever experienced. Many scientists now agree that the brain stores every bit of information it picks up. Because we never use most of it, it never gets reinforced, and we don't know it's there.

There are other indications that we ''remember'' everything. Under hypnosis, for example, many people are able to recall long-forgotten incidents in great detail. Individuals with ''photographic'' memories, and prodigies like the great conductor Arturo Toscanini, who memorized every note of 100 operas and 250 symphonies, also suggest that the brain can store everything it receives. Information theorist John Von Neumann estimates that if indeed nothing is forgotten, the total number of memories stored in an average lifetime would be 2.8×10^{20}, or 280,000,000,000,000,000,000, memories!

With this brief background, we will now examine the many ways you can improve your memory. Some require new habits and active practice of skills and techniques to facilitate your recall of information that your brain naturally stores, but the first involves your attitudes and beliefs.

TRUST YOUR MEMORY

In chapter 2 you learned what a powerful effect your beliefs have on your performance. You saw that if you have a negative

When one of these flashbacks was reported to me by a conscious patient, I was incredulous. . . . For example, when a mother told me she was suddenly aware, as my electrode touched the cortex, of being in the kitchen listening to the voice of her little boy who was playing outside in the yard.

Wilder Penfield

belief about your capabilities, your performance will be limited by that belief. You also saw that beliefs can be changed, that you can turn limiting beliefs into their positive opposites, which will enhance rather than restrict your progress.

This correlation between belief and performance is equally strong regarding your memory abilities. Since memory seems to be capable of retaining virtually everything, effective memory begins with trusting and believing in your ability to remember.

The first step you must take, therefore, is to inventory your memory beliefs. How do you feel about your memory powers? Do you trust that your mind has retained enormous amounts of information and is ready to deliver exactly what you need when you need it? Is your memory your ally in mastering the Information Age? Or do you think you have a terrible memory that fails you all the time and is a major cause of your information anxiety?

The advantage of a bad memory is that one enjoys several times the same good things for the first time.

Friedrich Nietzsche

■ ■ ■ ■

LEARNING ACTIVATOR #11
LEARNING TO TRUST YOUR MEMORY

This Activator will give you the opportunity to discover, diminish, and eventually eliminate any limiting beliefs you have about your ability to remember.

Begin by taking a few minutes to answer the first question below. Write down as many answers as you can. Don't think much about it, just jot down the answers that occur to you, which may come in the form of feelings, statements, or pictures. The answers I hear most frequently from my students include:

"I have a terrible memory."

"I never have been able to remember things accurately."

"It is right there but I can't quite get it."

"I can't remember details."

"I thought I understood it at the time, but now I don't remember."

If these sound like your responses, no chapter in any book could be more appropriate for you than this one.

What limiting beliefs do I have about my memory?

When you have made your list, take a few more minutes to choose what you think is the most significant, the one belief that holds you back and keeps you from trusting your memory. Now, identify the positive opposite of that belief by asking yourself, What is the opposite belief that would serve me and encourage the emergence of my peak intelligence? Then, one by one, look at the other beliefs and find their opposites too.

The positive opposites of my major limiting beliefs are:

Now create a personal affirmation, a positive statement derived from your positive opposite. If, for example, your limiting belief was "My memory is getting worse," and your positive opposite was "My memory is improving," then your affirmation might be, "My memory gets better every day." If you want to personalize it even more you can state it this way: "I, _____, have a memory that gets better every day."

Write the affirmation on a card and keep it on your desk, or write it a number of times in your notebook. Repeat it to yourself several times every day. Say it with conviction! Although repeating an affirmation will not in itself change you, it will begin an internal process by which change may come about. You begin with a change in attitude; you continue with a change in behavior.

It is important to honor your positive beliefs about yourself as well as to modify your limiting beliefs. Therefore I would like you now to spend a few minutes writing down your responses to the following statement and thinking about how well your memory sometimes serves you. By focusing on your memory successes, you will begin to develop the confidence you need to get better and better at this skill.

I honor the following qualities about my memory, which demonstrate that it can function very well.

■　■　■　■

Dwelling on the positive aspects of your memory and eliminating the self-sabotaging effects of your negative beliefs will help you develop a greater trust in the ability of your memory to retain information and to provide you with clear images and data when you need them. You will find that the more you trust your memory, the better it will become.

INTEND TO REMEMBER

"The art of memory is the art of attention," wrote Samuel Johnson. When you can't remember something, it may be because you never really paid attention to it. If you don't encode it in memory, it won't be there when you look for it.

Thus the first concrete step toward remembering is the effective inputting of new information. You cannot take out of memory what does not get properly put in. The quality of the information in your memory is dependent upon your mental state at the time of learning. Are you awake, alert, and focused, or are you inattentive, tired, distracted?

For example, how often has it happened that someone talks

to you but your mind is really somewhere else, and afterward you have no idea what the person said? Have you ever found yourself reading a page two, three, and four times because you aren't processing what you are reading?

If you want to be a Master of the Information Age, you need to wake up and pay full attention to what is happening in each moment. You need to actively intend to remember.

The first step is to practice the art of observation. Many of the suggestions and Learning Activators in chapter 4 were designed to help you with this. You can also simply observe everyday events more carefully, thus training your mind to be more alert.

To put more energy into your observations, practice every day making a mental image of something that is an ordinary part of your experience, such as a building you pass on the way to work, a person who works in your office, a garden on your street. Try to imagine it in detail. Ask yourself questions: "What flowers are growing in that garden?" "How many stories tall is that office building on the corner of Jefferson and Main?" Don't just look for visual details, but recall sounds, smells, and so on. If you regularly give yourself the challenge of asking questions like these, you will soon find yourself observing with more depth and remembering with more clarity.

By learning to observe even the smallest, insignificant details of life, you will find yourself being generally more alert whenever you are presented with new information, whether in reading or in listening to someone speak. The more wakeful and alert you are each moment, the more you will be rewarded with a treasury of clear impressions easily called to mind.

Think of your mind as a camera. When you are not attentive to your surroundings, the lens is out of focus, and when your memory "develops" the picture later on, it will be fuzzy. But as you build a habit of being observant and aware, your memories will become increasingly vivid.

Another way you can expand your intention to remember is to put yourself in the best state for learning whenever you have information to take in. We have already discussed the value of the alpha brain-wave state for learning and recall. Keep in mind that your brain absorbs information best when

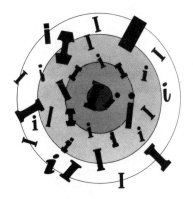

you are relaxed and stress free. Take responsibility for your learning state by doing a set of alpha breathing exercises or spending a few minutes with your favorite relaxation or meditation technique to calm your mind before you begin to read or study.

Be Purposeful—Define Your Information Target Zone

Once you have learned to be as observant as you can be, the next most important method you can use to enhance your intention to remember is focusing on what you wish to recall. For example, if you are invited to a business cocktail party at which fifty to sixty people will be present whom you don't know, you can't expect to remember everybody's name. Before you go, you might decide to "set" your brain to remember certain specific names, such as all potential clients, all people in managerial positions, any people from a specific city, or some other category meaningful to you. In this way, you plan ahead and preselect what is important to you. This is what I refer to as defining your information-target zone.

Defining your information target zone for each task will save you time. It will enable you to skip quickly over material that is not important to you and to focus your attention on understanding and reinforcing the important ideas and facts. You may decide, for example, that you don't need to recall any details at all but only need to grasp the essential theme of a report or of a few of its sections. Or you may decide by glancing briefly through the report that the details on pages 3 and 4 contain the information most relevant for you; you can then skip through the rest and focus only on the material that you intend to remember.

In chapter 7, I will offer you a detailed system for previewing printed material and defining your information target zone. When you learn and apply the basics of that system, you will take a giant step toward becoming an effective information manager and a Master of the Information Age.

Have a Memory Place

The physical surroundings in which you learn influence your ability to remember. Research has shown that when people are tested in the same environment where they learned something, their recall is significantly better than when they are tested in a different environment. A striking example of this comes from a British study in which two groups of divers were taught a list of forty words. One group learned under water, the other group on land. The lists learned on land were remembered almost twice as well on land; the lists learned under water were recalled best under water.

As unusual as this may sound, you can support your intention to remember by setting up a specific learning environment, where you sit in the same room in the same chair at the same desk. Doing so helps your brain get into a powerful learning state where all the cues help you lock in information.

If you are having trouble remembering something, try to visualize the place you learned it. If you can't remember someone's name, calling up the visual memory of where you met the person will often bring the name to mind. We will say more about visual memory shortly.

Exploit State-Specific Memory

A number of interesting studies have revealed that people tend to recall information best when they are in a psychological state similar to how they felt when they learned it. Information you learn when you are happy is recalled best when you are happy; information you take in when you are sad is recalled best when you are sad. You may have observed this in people who are depressed: typically they have great difficulty recalling pleasant or happy experiences, but they are able to recall sad events quite well.

You can put this phenomenon to work for you. Instead of being a prey to how you happen to feel, take control of your feelings. Remember that you are the "CEO" of your brain and your inner life. You can determine to a large extent how you feel.

Perhaps the easiest way to apply this principle is simply to relax, as suggested above, using meditation or alpha breathing before learning and again when you want to recall learned information. Although specific moods are difficult to turn on and off at will, a settled, alert mental state is relatively easy to create using these techniques and will stabilize your feelings and enhance your recall.

Take Advantage of Your Brain's Natural Memory Patterns

Our memory mechanism is divided into two different faculties, called short-term memory and long-term memory. Short-term memory is where all our conscious sensory inputs go. It holds information for a few seconds to a few hours. For example, we use our short-term memory when we look up a number in the phone book and retain it just long enough to dial it. If we have to redial, we often have to look up the number a second time. When we read, short-term memory enables us to remember the first part of the sentence while we are reading the end.

Long-term memory, on the other hand, is our main storage capacity. It holds billions of bits of memory material in its neuronal networks. Once information reaches long-term memory, it stays there indefinitely.

The transfer of information from short-term to long-term memory takes place by a process known as consolidation. Essentially, consolidation is accomplished by reinforcement. The first experiments in this area were conducted by the German psychologist Hermann Ebbinghaus in late 19th century. Since then, thousands of other studies have provided a great deal of information about the brain's natural cycles of remembering and forgetting. Ebbinghaus found that most forgetting occurs immediately after learning: Within one hour, more than half the original material is forgotten; nine hours later about 60 percent is lost; within a month, 80 percent.

However, we also know that if material is reviewed periodically, retention can be almost perfect. The review reinforces the neuronal networks created by learning the new material, and by the process of consolidation, establishes the new information in long-term memory.

If you intend to remember anything, it is therefore important to review it. I suggest reviewing in two ways. First, as you read material you want to remember, stop occasionally and think briefly about what you are reading. Summarize it to yourself in a word or a phrase; connect it to what has come before or to the context of your study. This simple act of thoughtful

review is one of the most powerful tools for learning and remembering. Second, review the material according to the following schedule.

After 10 minutes, review for 5 minutes.
After one day, review for 2–3 minutes.
One week later, review for 2–3 minutes.
One month later, review for 2–3 minutes.
Six months later, review for 2–3 minutes.

This schedule, which adds up to a mere 15 minutes of review
over six months, can improve your retention from about the
20 percent level predicted by the Ebbinghaus curve to 90 percent or better.

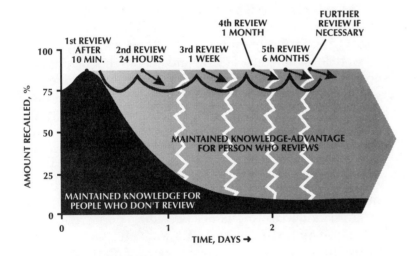

You can also improve your memory of new information by
taking breaks in your learning sessions. Doing so takes advantage of the following "special effects" that have been discovered
by psychologists.

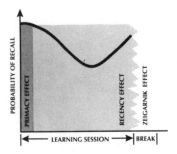

- You remember more from the first part of a study
  session. This is known as the *primacy effect*.
- Material learned during the tail end of a learning
  session is also recalled better later on. This is termed
  the *recency effect*.

- If you interrupt a period of learning, you automatically increase your recall. This is called the *Zeigarnik effect*.
- A few minutes after learning something new, the memory of it often increases for a short time. This is known as the *reminiscence effect*.

If you try to learn everything in a single long session, you get the benefit of the primacy and recency effects only once, and the other two not at all. If the session is divided into several smaller segments, with breaks in between, you enlist all four of these natural phenomena in your aid.

I have already suggested (in chapter 4) that you take a break about every 45 minutes. The recommended length of the break is 5 to 10 minutes.

EXERCISING YOUR MEMORY

Take a moment to recall the enriched environment studies by Rosenzweig and colleagues (see page 67), in which the brains of rats were found to grow in size, and the number of neuronal connections increased, when their environments included increased sensory stimulation. Those studies suggest that the more information we take in (the more the brain is stimulated), the more extensive our neuronal networks become.

The implications of this are important. Exercising the brain not only generates new neuronal networks and modifies existing ones, but also produces greater connectivity between networks. That means there is a greater chance of any specific bit of information triggering associations that connect it to other bits of information. The more you know, and the more you are accustomed to accessing your knowledge and keeping the connections lively, the better your memory will be.

Let's take a look at a number of effective ways you can exercise your memory to make it more powerful and accurate.

Use Multichannel Input

When you have something to learn, try to use more than one sense channel to take in the information. Using several input channels increases the number of neuronal networks processing and storing the information. It also links the new input to a larger number of previous pieces of information and sets up the possibility of finding it more easily.

I have a memory like an elephant. In fact, elephants often consult me.

Noel Coward

For example, if you have to remember points for a lecture you are going to give, write them down and then read your list to yourself out loud, thus using your senses of sight and hearing (as well as the kinesthetic sense while you write). If you want to remember how something looks, try describing it in words as well as making a visual picture. Then if you can't remember your picture later, you may remember the words (or vice versa).

One of the most complete and unfailing memories ever known belonged to a journalist referred to in psychological literature as "S." He was studied for 30 years by the famous Russian psychologist Alexander Luria, who sought to uncover the basis for S's accurate memory of intricate details of events and experiences. The main factor Luria found to account for S's phenomenal memory was his ability to merge his sensory input. He remembered how each thing looked, felt, sounded, tasted, and smelled; he consciously experienced everything with all of his senses simultaneously. He would also cross-reference his sensory experience. He would "hear" the sound of a feeling, experience the changing smells in a conversation, or "see" the sounds in music. For example, he described a musical tone as "something like fireworks with a pink-red hue," and a strip of color as "feeling rough and having an unpleasant taste—rather like that of briny pickle." This richness of sensory connections enabled him to remember everything vividly.

You have the same potential ability to combine your sensory input. It is just a matter of exercising each of your senses as they report to you throughout the day. As we have seen, the more vivid and complete the input, the clearer the memory.

The Importance of Understanding

Rote memorizing—reading or repeating something over and over—is the most common way people attempt to memorize. However, it is the least useful. Material that is repeated without involvement or motivation simply goes in one ear (or eye) and out the other. It seldom transfers from short-term to long-term memory.

The most important factor in memory is comprehension. Although it is possible to memorize a list of nonsense syllables or random numbers, essentially you have to understand in-

Nothing we use or hear or touch can be expressed in words that equal what we are given by the senses.

Hannah Arendt

A word to the wise is not sufficient if it doesn't make sense.

James Thurber

129

formation if you are going to recall it for any significant time and if it is to become useful to you. As I have been saying throughout this book, raw data is not truly information; it becomes useful when it is processed by a human mind into meaningful concepts.

As we have seen, the prevailing theory of memory holds that information is recorded in vast interconnected neuronal networks in the brain. Each idea, image, or item of information has hundreds or thousands of associations to other ideas or images and is thus connected to many other points in the brain's "circuitry."

Now let us expand this understanding. Scientists believe that what is recorded in the brain are not isolated letters, syllables, or words, but ideas and concepts. These ideas are connected to others in what may be called "semantic networks," networks of meaning. Committing something to memory thus means making new links in the networks by making meaningful associations.

That is why it is so important to understand what you are reading or hearing. When something is meaningful to you, your brain knows how to link it up with other related facts, ideas, memories, or images. When it is not meaningful, your brain doesn't know what to do with it or how to store it. It may store a record of it somewhere, but how will you access that record? On the other hand, you may have hundreds of associative approaches to a piece of information you do understand.

Studies have repeatedly proved that we remember better what we understand. Michael Epstein of Rider College found that subjects who were instructed to find meaningful relationships between pairs of words recalled more than twice as many words as others who were simply told to memorize the words. Epstein believes that the greater "depth of processing" of the words when they are approached meaningfully somehow activates more of the brain than rote memorization.

In another study, subjects were divided into groups to learn new words. The first group simply read the words aloud; the second group was instructed to sort the words by category; the third group was told to form a sentence using all the words. The second group learned better than the first, and the third remembered 250 percent better than the second!

To increase comprehension, therefore, you must use some ingenuity to create meaning for nonmeaningful material such as lists of facts or data. One effective way to do this is to make up a story utilizing the items on the list. Devising a story to help you remember information has many neurological implications. First, it supplies a meaningful context for the items to be recalled. Second, the plot provides an associative thread, a flow of ideas such that one triggers the next. Third, making up a story causes you to create scenes with verbal, visual, and other sensory associations, all of which strengthen the encoding. These rich images are easier to recall than a mere list.

Organize the Material and Get Involved

Organizing information helps to give it meaning. This was brought out in an experiment by the world-famous Canadian researcher Endel Tulving. Tulving gave two groups of students 100 cards with words printed on them. One group was told to learn the words by memorization. The other students were told that their task was to sort the cards into categories. When they were tested for recall later, the "organizers" remembered just as well as the "memorizers" even though they had not tried to remember! The active involvement in organizing the material provided meaningful patterns and associations that facilitated learning and memory without a conscious effort at memorization. There are numerous ways to organize material.

CLASSIFY. Find ways to divide the material into categories of some type. It might simply be alphabetizing, but the most powerful categories are ones that have some meaning for you.

"CHUNK" OR GROUP INFORMATION. Organize material into smaller, more manageable groups. For example, a list of ten numbers

2127629175

can be broken into three groups

212-762-9175

for easier recall even if they are not a phone number.

FIND PRINCIPLES. Look for underlying patterns or guiding principles. Once you know the principle, the specifics are easy to recall. You may not even need to recall the specifics precisely if you know the principles.

For example, if you have a set procedure to follow, knowing the principle behind each step will help you remember what needs to be done. If you have a memorized speech to deliver, knowing the logical sequence of your argument will remind you of the points and exact words you want to use.

FIND THE CONTEXT. Try to see the overview, the big picture into which the parts fit. This is another way of finding meaning in the information you are working with. It is difficult to remember something that has no meaningful context. We have all been to movies, for example, where the first several scenes made no sense until we figured out the context of the story; then they fell into place. Charles Schmid, a pioneer of accelerated learning, compares the importance of grasping the context to looking at the picture on the cover of a jigsaw puzzle box while you're trying to assemble the pieces.

Whenever you want to learn something, establish the context before working on the parts. In chapter 7 you will learn a method of previewing written material that will allow you to get the overview quickly, so that when you begin to read you will know how each part fits into the whole.

In these and other ways of your own devising, organize information that you want to remember. Whatever system you use, simply becoming actively involved in the organizing process will help your recall. This is because we remember what we care about. Whenever we are personally involved in information processing, when what we are trying to learn is personally meaningful or emotionally charged, it will stick in our memory. When we are interested in something, we naturally and spontaneously pay closer attention. Our senses and intellect are alert. Our brain works closer to its peak potential. When we give this kind of attention to our experience, our recall is bound to be better.

It is more difficult, of course, to build up your emotional involvement and motivation when you don't really care about the material but still need to remember it. Here are two ways to stimulate your motivation.

TEST YOURSELF. As you are reading or learning something new, repeatedly test your knowledge. Ask yourself questions to verify your understanding. This helps memory because we generally remember obstacles overcome and problems solved more readily than we recall situations that don't challenge our abilities.

SUMMARIZE. Try to summarize in your own words what you are learning. To make the process more enjoyable, explain the information to someone else. Conveying the information will force you to clarify it in your own mind, and the repetition and increased understanding will help to fix it in long-term memory. Explaining it will also show you the places you're not really sure of, which you may need to study more carefully.

Engage Your Visual Memory

Visual images are generally remembered much better than words. This is why memory improvement systems frequently utilize visual image-making techniques to encode information in the neuronal pathways.

The accuracy of our visual memory is astounding. In a study at the University of Rochester, subjects were shown 2,560 slides over several days. One hour after the last slide was seen, 280 pairs of slides were shown, in which one of the pair was from the original set. Subjects regularly recognized 90 percent correctly. The experimenter commented that the results "suggest that recognition of pictures is essentially perfect. The results would probably have been the same if we had used 25,000 slides instead of 2,500."

In a similar study, researchers presented 600 slides and tested their subjects immediately afterward. This time recognition was found to be 98 percent correct.

You can apply your naturally powerful visual memory ability in two ways. First, carefully observe people and things you want to remember: faces, places, objects, events. As I mentioned before, if you want to encode vividly, you have to be consciously attentive and really "see."

The other way to use your visual abilities to strengthen your memory is to create vivid mental imagery. Make use of the following methods in creating your images.

EXAGGERATE. We tend to remember things that are outstanding in some way—unusual, extreme, bizarre, colorful, frightening, vulgar—especially when they occur next to more ordinary things and events. Use this in your imagery by purposely exaggerating and making your images striking. Change proportions (visualize giant mice and tiny elephants, for example), change the colors of familiar items, and so on.

BE MULTISENSORY. Although vision is most people's dominant sense, the inclusion of other sensory images helps recall. (Remember the case of "S.") Imagine how things sound or smell, or imagine them in motion. Use images from sports or one of your hobbies to connect with material that is not inherently interesting to you.

BE INTERACTIVE. This is very important. Several studies have found that interactive imagery, where the things you want to remember are connected and related to each other, is remembered much better than more static imagery. For example, students in a test were asked to memorize a list of paired words such as *dog* and *bicycle* by creating visual images. When the images were static—such as a dog sitting next to a bicycle—recall was only 46 percent; when the images were interactive—a dog riding a bicycle or running after a bicycle, for example—recall was 71 percent. So put action and interaction into your visual images.

BE SEXUAL. If you seem to recall easily words or images connected to sex, you're not alone. Researchers say this happens to most of us. Since your visual imagery is private, feel free to make use of this tendency to create memorable images.

BE CREATIVE. Being inventive and original in the creation of your imagery involves you in the process. Involvement, as we have seen, increases focus and fixes the images in your mind. Give your imagination free rein.

Information is recorded in vast interconnecting networks. Each idea or image has hundreds, perhaps thousands, of associations and is connected to numerous other points in the mental network.

Peter Russell

Use Association

Along with visual imagery, association is your most powerful memory aid. Association simply means connecting a new piece of information to something—or many things—that you already know. As we have discussed, memory is an enormous system of interconnecting networks, in which each idea or image has hundreds or thousands of associations and is linked up with numerous other points.

Thus, memory is not like a container that gradually fills up, but more like an infinitely expandable telephone system. Each new memory is like a new telephone installation, which can access and be accessed by countless other telephones in the system. Each new link simply means more possible connections. As Colin Rose writes in *Accelerated Learning*:

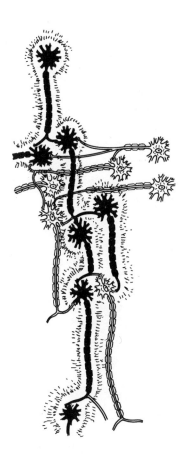

> Every new fact or concept you learn adds to and links up with the existing network. So when you encode something new, it not only forms a link to the existing network, it also provides yet another hook onto which still more associations can be hung or connected. So the more you learn and remember, the greater is your capacity for future learning and remembering.

When we want to remember something, our memory system does not go into a linear search, going through one item at a time. It reaches out simultaneously in many directions and pulls in information from many networks in the interconnecting circuitry of the brain. To use the process of association as a memory aid, we have to consciously and intentionally link new input to information that we already have.

■ ■ ■ ■

LEARNING ACTIVATOR #12
MEMORY AND ASSOCIATION

To experience how associations work, try this experiment: If you have moved your home or place of work, recall where you were five years ago. Remember the city, street, house or office. Think of the names of two or three people you knew at that time, or what a few of your friends or family members were doing then. Sit for a few minutes and think about this.

You will note that you do not only get memories of the things you asked for, you get much more. You recall not only the name of your street, but the exact address and a view of the neighborhood. You get pictures of the inside of your home or office, certain rooms, colors, arrangements. Not only do you remember the names of people, you also get images of their faces and bodily appearance, visual movies of events you shared, memories of things you knew about them, their interests, things they did that annoyed you, times they helped you out. Once you start the process, all sorts of additional information flows. This is association.

▪ ▪ ▪ ▪

MNEMONIC TECHNIQUES

Memory improvement systems are known as *mnemonics* from the Greek word *mneme*, "to remember." Actually, a mnemonic is any technique that helps you remember better, and we have already surveyed more than a dozen. Here are some more, beginning with two rather elaborate systems utilizing intentional association and visual imagery, followed by several simpler suggestions.

Loci Technique

Roman orators used to organize their speeches in the following way. First they would memorize a standard series of places, which they would then use to help them remember every speech. (The Latin word for place is *locus*, plural *loci*.) For example, they might pick out a fountain, a statue, a doorway, a chair, and so on. Then they would memorize the main points of their speech, associating each point to one of the places.

You can adapt this method to your own needs by memorizing your own set of easily recalled, familiar places. You can use the rooms of your house, or just the items in one room: doorway, sofa, TV, lamp, picture on the wall. Set that sequence in your memory by running through it several times a day for several days until you're sure you've got it. Then, whenever you have material to recall for a lecture, presentation, exam, or meeting, simply associate each point with one of the places.

Use active visual imagery rather than simply trying to remember words. If you are memorizing your shopping list, instead of thinking, "doorway . . . eggs," visualize hundreds of eggs rolling through the doorway. The more bizarre or dramatic the image, the better. See a cow being milked on your sofa. If you can hear the milk splashing into the pail and a "moo" or two (your sense of smell might come in handy here too), you can be sure you won't forget the information you associated with that image.

Pegword System

This is similar to the technique of loci but here the items to be recalled are linked to objects that rhyme with the numbers one to ten. As with the loci system, you prepare to use the pegword technique by choosing a series of objects. A typical list:

one—sun	six—sticks
two—shoe	seven—heaven
three—tree	eight—gate
four—door	nine—vine
five—hive	ten—hen

Memorize this or your own chosen list. When you have items to store in memory, associate them to your list of objects. Make a mental image linking the information, facts, names, or concepts to the objects you have selected to rhyme with the numbers. When you want to recall them, simply go through the numbers in your mind.

For example, suppose you want to recall several points to bring up in a staff meeting: expanding the telephone system, finishing projects in a more timely manner, and allocating tasks for a specific project. For the first point (one—sun—telephone), imagine a giant telephone floating in the sky with rays of the sun radiating out from it. For the second point (two—shoe—timely completion), see yourself at your desk stamping stacks of paper "Completed" with a giant shoe. For extra inputting strength, hear the "thud" of the shoe as it hits the pile of papers. For the third point (three—tree—allocation), visualize the people in the office sitting on branches of a tree, working away at various aspects of the project. If you take a moment to fix these images in your mind, you will be amazed at how easily you recall them later on.

Use Acronyms and Other Word Tricks

To recall a list of unrelated words, make up a word or sentence using their initials. For example, some people learned the names of the planets by memorizing an almost unforgettable sentence, "My very excellent mother just sells nuts until Passover" (Mercury, Venus, Earth, Mars . . .). Generations have learned the musical notes on the lines of the G-clef by memorizing "Every Good Boy Does Fine." Others memorized the Great Lakes by making one word of their first letters: HOMES (Huron, Ontario, Michigan, Erie, Superior).

Making up your own acronymic memory device is even more powerful since it calls for extra focus and usually carries a personal meaning for you. Personalizing information, as we saw earlier, helps you to recall it more readily.

There are many books on memory techniques, most of which could help you attain an active memory far beyond what you thought your capacity was. The Resources guide at the end of the chapter lists several of these books.

MIND MAPS

We remember best the information we have consciously processed and turned into knowledge. As we have seen, knowledge is the result of personalizing information, converting the incoming mass of data into meaningful concepts and images. This process takes place through thinking about the information input, understanding it, evaluating it, and translating it into terms we can use.

One of the best ways to consolidate your knowledge on a topic is to make mind maps. Mind mapping is a method of distilling the essence of what you know and organizing it in visual form. It is one of the most valuable whole-brain tools for mastering the Information Age. Mind maps can help you learn, stimulate your peak intelligence, and greatly improve your recall of information.

How to Make a Mind Map

To make a mind map, take a clean sheet of paper, place it horizontally, and begin by writing a central topic or main idea

WHEN WE WERE TAUGHT TO MAKE OUTLINES AND TAKE NOTES TO TURN INTO THE TEACHER, THE *RULES* SATISFIED ONLY THE LEFT HEMISPHERE. SOME OF THESE RULES WERE:

- BE LOGICAL
- USE BLACK INK
- BE NEAT
- SPELL CORRECTLY
- USE SCRIPT
- CONFORM TO TEACHER'S MENTAL PICTURE
- BE PERFECT

in large block letters in the center. The key ideas important to understanding and remembering the entire topic then radiate out from the center like limbs from the trunk of a tree or spokes around the hub of a wheel.

Write each corollary idea as a keyword or a short phrase. Then create sub-branches to carry subordinate ideas relating to the key idea represented by the branch. Each branch should contain only information relating to that specific key idea.

To enhance the visual power of your mind map, try these suggestions.

MIND MAP

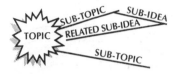

- Print each word rather than writing in script. Use lower case for easy reading, occasional capital letters for emphasis. Abbreviate words by deleting vowels.
- Place words above the lines (no more than three words per line). Join all lines to the central structure for organizational coherence.
- Use colored pens or pencils, and alternate them for each limb on the mind map. Reserve red for emphasis of major points.
- Include images other than words. Use stick figures, faces, trees, keys, mini-graphs, arrows to connect related ideas, question marks, anything that will fix an idea in your mind and stimulate recall later on.

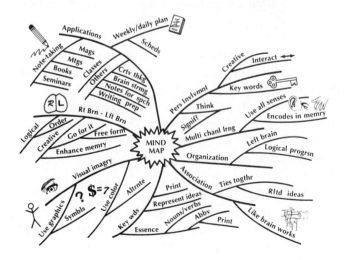

Why Mind Maps Are Effective

Mind maps are tremendously effective as memory aids because they utilize a large number of the factors critical to learning and memory:

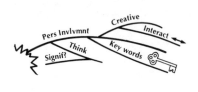

PERSONAL INVOLVEMENT. In constructing a mind map, you have to think about the information and decide what is significant. You simplify what you have heard or read, boiling it down into a few keywords or phrases that elegantly express the main points. You interact with the information. This is different from, for example, passive note taking in a class, where you often just try to copy down as many of the words as possible. You are also involved because you do something creative as you plan and draw the map.

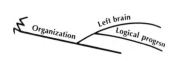

MULTI-CHANNEL LEARNING. The information in your mind map becomes encoded in your neuronal circuitry effectively because you use writing, hearing or reading, visual imagery, as well as thinking about the material.

ORGANIZATION. Creating a mind map forces you to organize the material in a clear visual pattern that shows the relationship of the various points to each other and to the central theme. This process both tests and reinforces your comprehension. Personally organizing information has been shown to be a powerful aid to memory.

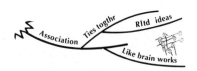

ASSOCIATION. As we have seen, the brain works largely through association, connecting ideas in a nonlinear fashion. Mind maps use this same structure of association and therefore mimic how the brain works. Ideas that are closely related are grouped together, reinforcing the association. This makes the mind map a powerful means of embedding knowledge in memory in a form that will make it easy to retrieve later.

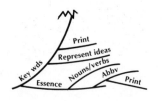

KEYWORDS. Mind maps contain only a few keywords. These are the words of most significance and power, the concrete words that carry the essence of the communication and generate vivid imagery. They are usually nouns and verbs. Again, we do not remember complete sentences but ideas, and it is ideas that are represented by keywords.

VISUAL IMAGERY. Since visual imagery is recalled much more perfectly than words, mind maps by nature are excellent memory stimulators.

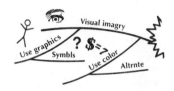

INTEGRATION OF RIGHT AND LEFT BRAIN. Mind maps combine the left brain's verbal, analytic, and orderly proclivities with the right brain's penchant for spatial design, visual sense, and artistic sensibility. The typical outline form of note taking and planning generally serves only the left brain's style.

    I. Topic
       A. Subtopic
          1. Related idea
             a. Subsidiary idea
       B. Subtopic

The more free-flowing form of the mind map, while still highly organized and intelligently condensed, also utilizes artistic and associational, intuitive abilities. This creative aspect and the use of graphics enhance your memory in themselves, and they also encourage your active involvement in the process of distilling the essence of the information and depicting it in a concise and memorable fashion. Therefore, let your creativity flow! The more attention you lavish on your mind map, the better you will recall the material.

When to Use Mind Maps

The most obvious use of mind maps is for taking original notes on books, articles, lectures, and meetings. In addition, you can use them to retrieve stored information from time to time. In studying for an exam, preparing to deliver a talk, and any time you need a review of information, a glance at a mind map gives you a quick capsule of all the essential points in just a few seconds—far less time than reading through paragraphs or pages of notes.

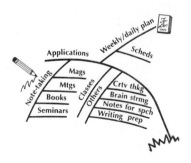

You can also use mind maps for planning and organizing your own work. Any writing task, lecture or presentation, meeting agenda, even your daily list of things to do, can be easily prioritized (main topic in the center, subtopics branching out in spiral fashion) in a mind map so that the entire project can be seen as a unified whole with all its parts in proper place.

Mind maps are also useful as a visual aid in making presentations. A large mind map in front of a group shows in an attractive and meaningful format the main points to be covered—and may help to keep the speaker on target as well! These simple devices will revolutionize your working habits, cut down on your preparation and reviewing time, exercise your brain, sharpen your thinking, enhance your creativity, and improve your recall.

DECIDE WHAT YOU DON'T NEED TO REMEMBER

With regard to memory, we can say that there are essentially three types of information.

- Information you need or want to remember.
- Information you want to be able to find when you need it.
- Information you don't need at all.

An essential part of being a Master of information is having a game plan for determining which is which. This is another aspect of defining your information target zone.

Whenever you have information to process, take a moment to decide which of these three categories it falls under. If you don't need it at all, don't waste time with it. If you want to remember it, relax, focus your attention, and fix it in your memory using an appropriate strategy from the methods contained in the first part of this chapter.

If you want to have it available but don't need to remember it, use one of the memory aids that we will discuss below. These various techniques and devices can help you alleviate information overload. They can help you take and organize your notes, and in general make your mental habits as well as your working habits clearer, cleaner, and more efficient.

Memory Ticklers

Self-adhering note papers have become one of the simplest but most effective memory ticklers and organizational devices. You can attach these easily removable notes to letters or memos ("Answer by 3/15," "Good info on p. 17," "Basic idea here is . . ."), make notes to yourself or someone else on your desk calendar or on the pages of a book, and use them for an infinite variety of information-highlighting purposes. You can use them to make marginal notes of important points as you read, and review them instead of rereading the entire memo or book.

Keep a Filing System

A good filing system serves as part of a Master's personal library. A well-organized file of materials you want to be able to review will save you search time and help you access important information. Instead of letting your newspapers and magazines pile up, clip out those articles you've read that you wish to keep for future reference. Photocopy passages from books or borrowed materials.

Periodically go through the files, review, and discard what you no longer need. Throwing away is as important as collecting. Glancing at the article for a second or third time will do a lot to help you recall its contents.

Notebooks

In this complex age, we are all information managers regardless of our jobs. We are all thinking individuals. Especially when we are operating at a peak performance level, we get good ideas and insights at unexpected moments. We remember things suddenly that we don't want to forget. How many times have you had an important idea while waiting for an appointment, taking a walk, or standing in line?

A small notebook that you can carry in your briefcase, pocket, or purse is indispensable for those moments. When a thought comes to you that you think might be important or that is part of your information target zone for a project at work or for something in your personal life, write it down. This will allow you to keep track of ideas easily and free your mind from trying to remember them.

It is not a good idea to have several notebooks, such as one

Paradoxically one of the greatest advantages of mind maps is that they are seldom needed again. The very act of constructing a map is itself so effective in fixing ideas in memory that very often a whole map can be recalled without going back to it at all. A mind map is so strongly visual and uses so many of the natural functions of memory that frequently it can be simply read off in the "mind's eye."

Peter Russell

143

for your personal life and ideas and another for your business and professional life. This can get too complicated. It is more efficient to have just one pocket-size notebook, with one section for personal entries and another for professional entries.

Keep your notebook handy at your desk so that when you come up with an idea at work that you don't have time to think about or put into action right away, you can jot it down and come back to it later. You can also record titles of books or articles you want to read, or points from things you have already read that you feel might be useful to think about in more depth at a later time. Reviewing the information later, when you're not stressed from the pressures of the day, can be useful for planting it in your memory. Use your mind-mapping skills whenever you can. Make it a habit to date all your entries.

I recommend reviewing your notebook at the end of every day. Doing this will enable you to think about the new ideas at greater length, to elaborate on them, and to decide if they are really useful and in what way they can be useful. This is the time to

- fix into your long-term memory things you want to remember,
- transfer ideas into files where you can refer to them later on,
- put ideas into immediate action, or
- decide to forget about them.

Pocket Dictating Machines

If you don't like to write, or if you're stuck in traffic or otherwise unable to use a notebook, you can catch your thoughts before they evaporate by recording them on a pocket microcassette dictating machine. Technology has made these available at low cost and with a high storage capacity: one minicassette can hold several hours of talking. You can review your spoken notes as you would your notebook, and transfer your ideas to their appropriate places for action or future reference. One advantage of a pocket dictating machine is that we can speak much faster than we can write, and therefore spoken notes tend to be much more complete.

Keep a Learning Journal

Many successful information Masters keep a personal learning journal in which they store special ideas, articles clipped from magazines and newspapers, lecture notes, and mind maps for topics they are interested in. This might be a three-ring binder or large spiral notebook. A learning journal is different from a personal diary, different from the small notebook you carry around to jot down ideas, and different from your general files in that it is a tool you use regularly as a focused learning device. Use it to write down reflections about yourself and your progress in life, to collect quotes that have lessons for you, and to gather materials relevant to your unique interests and concerns, whether personal or professional.

Keeping a learning journal can help you excel in your field and quickly master topics of personal interest. You can learn who the experts are in the area you are learning about, and gather their ideas to study and assimilate.

When you paste articles or quotes into your learning journal, I strongly recommend that you use a "double entry" method. Paste the article on the left-hand page and use the right-hand page to record your own ideas and reactions or a summary or mind map of the article.

Organizers

Even if you are not using an "executive organizer," you have no doubt seen ads for them. These pocket or desktop organizers are premade for busy people and contain a number of subdivisions and sections—to schedule appointments, note expenses, list goals, prioritize tasks, and so on. Some organizers have a small removable notebook for each month, others contain a whole year's worth of pages.

If you use one of these, you won't have to spend the time to develop your own style and technique of organizing. On the other hand, you will have to get accustomed to working with someone else's organizational principles.

Electronic Notebooks

These recent high-tech devices look like pocket calculators but have an alphabetic keypad and a word-processing system in addition to numeric keys. You can use them exactly as you would use a pen and notebook to record and store your personal thoughts and ideas and any information that you learn during the day. You can create a number of different personal or work files for your data storage. You can also use an electronic notebook as an address book, to store the equivalent of hundreds of business cards with names, addresses, and telephone numbers.

Using one of these devices is like having a miniature computer in your pocket. They are about the size of a small paperback book and can be carried in a briefcase or purse, or even in a breast pocket or back pocket like a wallet.

Computers

At the top of the line of memory aids, personal computers are becoming increasingly useful and affordable. It seems that each new model has greater storage capacity and can accommodate a wide diversity of software, allowing you to store volumes of information using database programs, to outline your thoughts using idea-generating programs, and to write and design your reports using word-processing and desktop publishing programs. The entire field of computers and software has expanded rapidly in the past few years. Rather than going into detail here on how these extraordinary devices can help your memory needs, it will be more useful for you to read one of the many excellent books devoted to explaining the variety of software currently available.

Of particular note, however, are lap-top computers, which have become quite affordable and may be well worth the investment if your work or schooling presents you with an unusual amount of information to remember. No bigger than an attaché case, a lap-top computer can be taken to meetings, lectures, classes, or anywhere else, allowing you to record important information and ideas that you can then review and "massage" at a leisurely pace. Many people prefer to type rather than take written notes (especially those who know touch typing, which is usually much faster than writing), but your personal preference is what matters most. Whatever method of note-taking you choose, the key is to use it consistently in order to improve your memory.

BE YOUR OWN INFORMATION MASTER

Throughout this chapter, I have attempted to show that with the right attitude and a few practiced skills, you can truly enhance your memory. You don't need to have any special genius to become a master of memory. If you implement even a few of these techniques, you will be amazed at how much improvement you will find. As I said at the start of the chapter, there is nothing mysterious about self-improvement: all it takes is doing the simple things, and doing them consistently.

Now take a moment to review the opening statement of purpose for this chapter, and consider whether you have achieved the goals. Because there are so many suggestions and techniques in the chapter, you don't need to learn them all at this point. If you have truly grasped the fact that your memory can serve you as well as you would like it to, and if you have mastered a few key methods that you can practice regularly to bring this about, go on to chapter 6. If you want to work on more of the memory-enhancing methods later, you know where to find them.

RESOURCES

Memory

Buzan, Tony. *Use Both Sides of Your Brain.* (New York: E. P. Dutton, 1984). The first author to cover mind mapping; includes study skills and reading.

Buzan, Tony. *Use Your Perfect Memory.* (New York: E. P. Dutton, 1984). Filled with useful memory techniques.

Lorayne, Harry and Jerry Lucas. *The Memory Book.* (New York: Ballantine Books, 1974). A best-selling compendium of memory-enhancement techniques and tricks.

Russell, Peter. *The Brain Book.* (New York: E. P. Dutton, 1984). Comprehensive treatment of memory and how to improve yours.

Mindmapping

Rico, Gabriele Lusser. *Writing the Natural Way.* (Los Angeles: Jeremy P. Tarcher, 1983). A superior book on the art of writing, which includes a chapter on *clustering*—Rico's version of mind mapping.

Yepsen, Roger B. *How to Boost Your Brainpower.* (Emmaus, PA: Rodale Press, 1987). Improve your memory and think creatively, with helpful information on nutrition for the brain.

C H A P T E R   6

THINK CRITICALLY
ABOUT INFORMATION

Mastering the Information Age means more than working efficiently, reading faster, and remembering more. The ability to think with clarity, precision, and depth is also vital to being a Master. In every phase of your life, you have countless decisions to make and precious little time to make them. You need to know how to evaluate the information related to your decisions, how to analyze facts and distinguish them from opinions, and how to organize, prioritize, set goals, and develop strategies to achieve those goals. Yet few of these thinking skills were ever taught to you.

This chapter will present a short course in thinking skills. We will begin by considering what thinking and critical thinking are. Then we will look more deeply into the reasons why we need to develop thinking skills. We will move on to the characteristics of good, powerful thinking. That section will present you with a 13-step program to strengthen your own thinking and decision-making skills.

Next we will consider the flip side: faulty thinking. Here you will learn how to avoid making the most common thinking mistakes, and how to detect and defend yourself against dishonest communications from the many forces in our society trying to "sell" you a point of view. We will look briefly at some of the "fallacies" taught in logic classes.

This is a vital and exciting chapter, from which you can benefit in every phase of your life.

■ ■ ■ ■

America has suddenly awakened to the importance of clear, powerful thinking. In 1980, all the articles published on critical thinking could have fit into a small file folder. By mid-decade, however, there were over 2,500, and the number of articles, books, and courses on thinking skills continues to rise rapidly in the 1990s.

Why is this? First, as we discussed in chapter 1, one-half of American jobs now involve the processing or communicating of information, and even more will do so within a short time. These jobs, and the jobs of the future, will require primarily mental skills, skills our education did not give us.

Second, we need better thinking skills simply to live effectively. In the image of British psychologist and educator Edward De Bono, we are all like "two-finger typists" when it comes to thinking. Obviously, we have all learned "to think" in order to cope with school and with life. But there are many methods of thinking that we can acquire that will vastly improve our ability to master the Information Age, to solve problems and make sound decisions. We will focus on some of those methods in this chapter.

We in America have everything we need except the most important thing of all—time to think and the habit of thought.

Norman Cousins

WHAT IS CRITICAL THINKING AND WHY DO WE NEED IT?

Critical thinking simply means a way of thinking intelligently, carefully, and with as much clarity as possible. It is the opposite of what we might call sloppy thinking. When we think critically, we weigh the truth and falsity of statements instead of accepting them on faith. We ask questions about the information presented to us to determine if it comes from a reliable

149

A man's life is what his thoughts make of it.

Marcus Aurelius

source, is backed by evidence, and is believable. We make sure we understand what is being conveyed to us. We make connections to knowledge we already possess, to see if the new information makes sense in terms of what we know.

When we think critically, we look for the truth. We don't want to be fooled by false arguments, advertising slogans, or emotional appeals. Instead, we rely on the principles of logic. We know how to define the terms we use, and we make distinctions between those terms and words that mean something else. We analyze data and facts and draw conclusions based on rational reasons and evidence, not opinions or feelings. In short, we use our mind actively and carefully in order to reach the best decisions.

Critical thinking can occur only if you keep your mind active. Consider the following list of some of the mental activities you can perform.

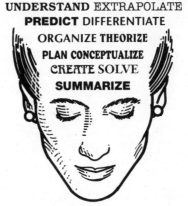

ANALYZE COMPARE DRAW CONCLUSIONS EVALUATE **RECOGNIZE**
IDENTIFY *FANTASIZE* INTERPRET **CONNECT** CATEGORIZE
CONCENTRATE DREAM SYNTHESIZE **REASON** CRITICIZE
IMAGINE CHOOSE **CLASSIFY** MAKE INFERENCES
MAKE DECISIONS DEFINE RECALL
UNDERSTAND EXTRAPOLATE
PREDICT DIFFERENTIATE
ORGANIZE THEORIZE
PLAN CONCEPTUALIZE
CREATE SOLVE
SUMMARIZE

If you examine this list thoughtfully, you will see that virtually all these activities of the mind are conscious and directed. Unfortunately, as the American educator and philosopher John

Dewey pointed out, the majority of people let their mental activity become "idle and chaotic," "automatic and unregulated."

> More of our waking life than most of us would care to admit is whiled away in this inconsequential trifling with mental pictures, random recollections, pleasant but unfounded hopes, flitting, half-developed impressions.

In short, most of us have a decidedly passive relationship with our mind. Thoughts float by. Only once in a while do we aggressively take hold and use the powers of our mind as an instrument. The majority of the time it does what it likes.

The range of thinking we are talking about in this book—the kind of thinking you need to develop if you are going to become a Master of the Information Age—is of an entirely different magnitude. Since critical thinking has come to have so many different meanings to different people, let's simply call it *active thinking*.

Active thinking requires a high level of control of the mind, an ability to hold a subject in your awareness and give it serious consideration, to reflect over time and come up with a final product, such as an analysis, comparison, evaluation, or plan. Active thinking means using your brain, not letting it be simply a screen for the mind to play out its movies. It means questioning, observing, evaluating, synthesizing, being able to perform all the functions in the list above. It is an active, directed, inquisitive, and conscious processing of information.

Why We Need to Learn Thinking Skills

Let's consider three main reasons why it is vital to develop thinking skills.

THINKING IS THE BASIS OF ACTION. As Dewey says in his book, *How We Think*, thinking "makes possible actions with a conscious aim." It enables us to "direct our activities with foresight, and to plan according to ends-in-view." That is, thinking allows us to establish goals, to plan how to achieve our goals, and to act to accomplish the plan.

The mind is powerful and primary. Whatever the depth, clarity, and accuracy of our thought, our actions depend on it

There is no expedient to which a man will not resort to avoid the real labor of thinking.

Sir Joshua Reynolds

and follow from it. As the British philosopher John Locke wrote 300 years ago,

> The ideas and images in men's minds are the invisible powers that constantly govern them. . . . It is therefore of the highest concernment that great care should be taken of the understanding, to conduct it aright in the search of knowledge and in judgments it makes.

The principal goal of education is to create men who are capable of doing new things, not simply of repeating what other generations have done— men who are creative, inventive, and discoverers. The second goal of education is to form minds which can be critical, can verify, and not accept everything they are offered.

Jean Piaget

CHOICES AND DECISIONS REQUIRE A SHARP MIND. Almost everywhere you turn, someone is trying to sell you something: a product, a service, an ideology, a point of view. The average American sees 30,000 television commercials a year and receives countless pieces of promotional advertising. Beyond this obvious selling, remember too that even writers of books and articles have an outlook or point of view that they would like us to accept. The media daily bombard us with conflicting points of view; today we see one position defended that may be valid, but tomorrow we are shown another perspective, equally worthy of consideration.

In today's Information Age, how do you know what to believe? How can you tell whether the supposed facts you are given are accurate? Is there any way to get past the hyperbole and the impassioned—or wily—advocacy of a point of view to the truth? One of the most important skills you need in order to master the tidal wave of information flowing in upon you is therefore the ability to think carefully about what you read, hear, and see.

PERSONAL AND SOCIAL PROBLEMS REQUIRE CLEAR AND POWERFUL THINKING. According to psychologist Robert Ornstein of the Institute for the Study of Human Knowledge, "Solutions to the significant problems facing modern society demand a widespread, qualitative improvement in thinking and understanding." We are realizing, slowly and painfully, that the difficult problems of our society, such as environmental pollution, crime, drug abuse, health care, and meaningful education, are not being met by the piling up of more and more data or the expenditure of larger sums of money on research.

"In view of the increasing pressures imposed on our society

by these problems," says Ornstein, many people are becoming aware that we "cannot sit back and hope for some technological innovation" to cure the illnesses of our culture. Rather, "we need a breakthrough in the *quality* of thinking employed both by decision-makers at all levels of society and by each of us in our daily affairs."

Look at it this way: our world is a product of our thinking. We have created our problems using a certain level of intelligence and thinking skills, and so if we want to create a better world, the only way is to use more intelligence, to think with more insight and foresight, to really use the great powers of the human brain.

Our nation's founders based their hopes for the future on an informed and intellectually capable citizenry. For a democratic society to succeed, its citizens must understand how its institutions work and be able to think critically and clearly about issues based on information, facts, and personal wisdom.

Effective thinking is particularly important today, as local as well as national and international issues are becoming increasingly complex. If people are not able to interpret information, to understand or think through the various sides of an issue and the ramifications and implications of the decisions that are to be made, they will leave the decisions to someone else, and that is the beginning of the end for freedom.

Sooner or later, false thinking brings wrong conduct.

Julian Huxley

The level of the development of a country is determined, in considerable part, by the level of development of its people's intelligence.

Luis Albert Machado

CHARACTERISTICS OF SKILLFUL THINKING

A Master of the Information Age embodies the following two fundamental habits of thought. If you remember to use these two principles when you deal with any information, whether written or spoken, you will find yourself thinking more clearly and effectively. You will feel on top of information and not intimidated by it. You will feel more in control of your life.

Thinking for Yourself

A Master never accepts anything as true without thinking about it and scrutinizing its validity. Don't accept anything without applying your own native intelligence. Just because you read it in a magazine or saw it on the seven o'clock news does not mean it is true.

People should think things out fresh and not just accept conventional terms and the conventional way of doing things.

R. Buckminster Fuller

As we discussed in chapter 1, our education often did not train us to think as individuals. Rather than think deeply or critically about information, we usually looked for only the "right" answer needed to pass an exam. In addition, teachers wore an aura of unquestioned authority that encouraged us to accept what we were told without evaluating it. As adults we often unconsciously pass this authority on to the people who write for broadcast and print media.

We all need to rely on experts or researchers for some information—performance ratings of items we purchase, for example, or data about social issues—but ultimately we need to make decisions for ourselves. Experts and researchers have their own points of view; they weigh various factors according to their own criteria. You may have different criteria. Trust yourself. Only you can decide which decision, direction, or information is right or useful for you.

Asking Questions

A major part of clear, critical thinking is asking questions—of yourself and your information source—whenever you are presented with new information. Questioning gives energy to your thinking. It encourages your mind to investigate, check sources, uncover hidden biases. Every time you read or discuss an issue, ask questions, such as:

- Is it believable?
- Is there any evidence or support for this statement (statistics, authorities, experiments) or is it just a point of view presented as a fact?
- Is this important? (Should I spend my time reading, watching, doing, thinking about this?) How does it affect my life?

Thirteen Steps to More Skillful Thinking

The principles of thinking for yourself and asking questions form the basis of the following 13-step program for more skillful thinking. Applying even half of these principles to your thinking and planning processes on a regular basis will dramatically change the quality of your thought and contribute to greater mastery of information.

1. GET ALL THE INFORMATION YOU NEED. When you have a problem to solve or a decision to make, begin by asking yourself: What do I know about this? What other facts, data, or opinions might I need in order to make my decision? Is there another way to see this issue that might be more useful? Be as sure as you can that all the information you have is correct.

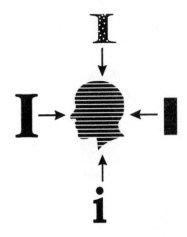

Getting sufficient facts and data is clearly a vital step in mastering information, yet it obviously presents certain problems. For instance, how do you know when you have enough? Information gathering can go on forever, but at some point it is time to stop gathering and make a decision. Some of the remaining steps can help determine this, but only you can decide when that point is reached. In any case, it is useful to periodically ask yourself: Do I have enough information now for what I need?

2. CHECK THE SOURCE OF INFORMATION. Get in the habit of asking whether the information comes from a reliable source. All sources are liable to be biased in one way or another. Is there some reason this source would like you to believe what is being said? (Is it an oil company claiming that solar-powered cars simply aren't feasible? Is the tobacco industry arguing that there is insufficient evidence to prove that smoking causes cancer? Is the research cited in the article funded by a particular company with a vested interest?) Is the person communicating the information a genuine authority? What is the person's position, credentials, or prior publications? Do you need to seek other sources to balance this or to fill out what is missing? If so, you know that you need to continue gathering information.

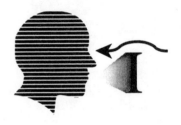

Find experts or publications whose opinions and judgments you can trust, but remember, even though certain magazines and professional journals (such as the *Harvard Business Review, New England Journal of Medicine, Scientific American*) have a reputation for accuracy and high standards, they are not infallible, and their editors have a point of view. Also, as new research comes out, yesterday's "truths" are often disproved. So don't abandon your quest for truth: Question the authors' conclusions and draw your own.

The man who never alters his opinion is like standing water, and breeds reptiles of the mind.

William Blake

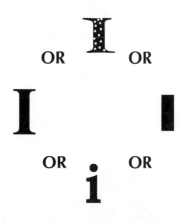

It is not best that we should all think alike; it is difference of opinion that makes horse races.

Mark Twain

3. BE FLEXIBLE AND OPEN-MINDED. Each of us has our own point of view, but hard as it is to admit, it is not the only way of seeing things, nor is it necessarily the "right" way.

Try to free yourself from rigid adherence to your belief system. Be open to new information. Don't get stuck in a pattern of thought so that you fail to recognize a good new idea or a valid viewpoint that may differ from your own, especially if it includes information you have not been aware of.

To combat this tendency, encourage yourself to listen to more sides than one, and pay attention to facts that may be inconsistent with your notions. Accept the potential validity of alternative solutions and views. Cultivate your curiosity and reach out for the new. Seek out people with contrary points of view. Learn to enjoy the opportunity to modify your position or to hold it even more surely because you have tested it against an opposing viewpoint and found it sound.

Try subscribing to a magazine or newspaper with a philosophy opposed to your own, and try to understand *what* its editors believe and *why* they believe it.

Also try this technique, often used by debaters: Write a sentence or two that expresses as clearly and fully as you can a view that you don't agree with. Putting yourself in the mindset of another person can help you understand the other viewpoint and solidify your own thinking.

Get feedback on your ideas. Share them with people you trust, and really *listen* to their reaction.

4. BE SURE YOU UNDERSTAND. If you don't understand what is being communicated, how can you possibly think properly about it? We all have a tendency to camouflage our ignorance behind nods and grunts of agreement, when inside we are wondering what's going on. Good thinkers are never afraid to admit their ignorance. Any honest person today knows that he or she is ignorant about many things. That's not a fault, nor does it detract from our expertise in what we *do* know about.

It is important to ask a speaker, "What does that mean?" "Can you explain that?" "Would you mind defining that?" "Could you go over that again?" If you are one of those people who feel reluctant to ever admit ignorance about anything, practice saying these phrases out loud a few times, and push yourself to use them. You will find that people often admire those who can admit ignorance, and people generally love to explain what they know. Tell others when you don't agree with them and why. Their clarification may be just the information you need to expand or change your point of view.

If something you are reading is difficult to understand, you may need to refer to the dictionary to define unfamiliar words. Read the passage or chapter again, then stop to think about it. Try summarizing the argument in a few words or phrases. If you can't, ask the author (in your mind), "What are you talking about here?" Don't assume the difficulty is your fault. Not every writer has thought his position out carefully or conveyed his meaning clearly.

In order for information to be of any value to you, you have to understand it. You have to convert the data into meaningful patterns. Do whatever you need to get it straight.

5. MAKE CONNECTIONS. Every time you come upon a new idea or piece of information, ask yourself: How does this relate to something I already know? Make connections from the new idea to other ideas. Your brain does this subconsciously with every bit of sensory input, but you can help the process along with your conscious thinking process.

Making conscious associations will help you in many ways. You will understand ideas better by relating them to past experiences and other concepts and facts. By tying the new material into existing neuronal networks, you will also improve your memory, for all the brain's "cell assemblies" seem to connect to other related ones.

Making connections also gives you a basis for the thinking process of *evaluating*. It allows you to compare and contrast what you already know about the topic, the speaker, the speaker's purpose and biases. This kind of active evaluation will enliven your brain and allow you to enjoy every encounter with new information.

6. CONSIDER ALTERNATIVES. As Alvin Toffler predicted many years ago in *Future Shock*, one of the central features of con-

The path of least resistance and least trouble is a mental rut already made. It requires troublesome work to undertake the alteration of old beliefs. Self-conceit often regards it as a sign of weakness to admit that a belief to which we have once committed ourselves is wrong. We get so identified with an idea that it is literally a "pet" notion and we rise to its defense and stop our eyes and ears to anything different.

John Dewey

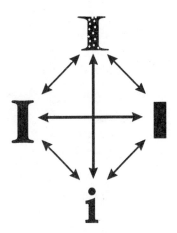

Genius, in truth, means little more than the faculty of perceiving in an unhabitual way.

William James

The typical human life seems to be quite unplanned, undirected, unlived, and unsavored. Only those who consciously think about the adventure of living as a matter of making choices among options, which they have found for themselves, ever establish real self-control and live their lives fully.

Karl Albrecht

Today is the tomorrow you didn't plan for yesterday.

Anonymous

temporary life is a multiplicity of choices. We rarely find clear-cut "right" and "wrong" decisions or courses of action. Usually many possible pathways lie open before us. Even when we think we see the direction we should take, it is helpful to look for other alternatives, other possible ways of seeing the problem or dealing with it.

Psychologists sometimes call this openness to alternatives *divergent thinking*. Divergent thinking involves creating a bigger picture by gathering facts and data, looking at a problem from several points of view, and generating as many possible options and solutions as you can think of. To help you generate new ideas, you can use techniques like brainstorming or "freewriting" where you simply allow your mind to flow freely, generating as many new ideas as possible, postponing evaluation until later. The chapter on sharing information explains these writing techniques in more detail.

The complementary mode of thinking is called *convergent thinking*. Convergent thinking is a selective process that consists of narrowing down options, evaluating, analyzing, and zeroing in on the factors that will lead to a decision. Doctors, for example, use convergent thinking as they narrow down possible diseases or conditions toward making their diagnosis.

Effective problem solving can be seen as a combination of divergent and convergent thinking. First, clarify the problem and generate alternative solutions. Then zero in on the most appropriate and desirable solution. Follow these steps:

▪ Clearly define your goals.
▪ Think of as many possible solutions as you can and analyze these various alternative courses of action in terms of factors such as feasibility, long- and short-term consequences, and how likely you are to hit your target.
▪ Consult your subconscious to see if any new solutions come bubbling up. (First spend a few minutes with alpha breathing or one of the meditation/relaxation techniques you have learned, in order to relax and quiet your mind.)

■ Formulate a decision that you can support. Define it clearly in your mind. "Turn it" in your mind as you examine it carefully. See whether it feels right intuitively.

■ Take action. Implement your plan.

7. THINK AHEAD. Our ability to think permits us to imagine the future and plan for it. We can mentally look ahead, visualize the progress of our life, and decide how we want to spend the time and what destination we desire to reach, planning a course of action.

This applies to major and minor aspects of life. When you take a weekend trip, you think about where you are going and what is likely to happen, and you pack what you expect to need. If you don't plan well, you may be caught without your boots when it starts to snow. Life offers many opportunities for planning and countless unpleasant consequences when we neglect to plan.

Use your mind, and all available information about current trends, to foresee and to plan. Think about possible changes in the economy, your profession, your company, or your family. Plan for contingencies and have alternate plans ready.

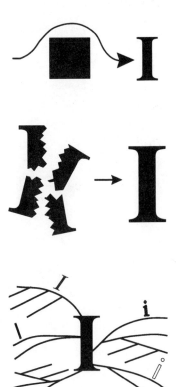

8. ORGANIZE YOUR THOUGHTS. Does your mind leap about haphazardly from one thought, memory, or image to another? Learn to think about things systematically, one step at a time. Organization is power. Control over your thoughts gives you control over your life.

One of the best ways I know to develop and organize your thoughts is to make a mind map (see chapter 5). Mind maps let you see the whole picture and how all the parts relate to each other and fit into the whole.

9. USE WRITING AND MIND MAPPING TO HELP CLARIFY YOUR THOUGHTS. Setting your thoughts down on paper can help you to think clearly. Is there something you need to do—a memo to write, a project to carry through? Write it at the top of a page, then write down alternative means of achieving it. "I

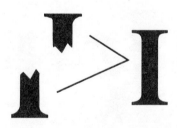

need to . . . I could do it by . . . or . . ." Underneath, to help you evaluate the alternatives, compile lists of pros and cons. If one alternative has the most "pros" but you still feel you don't want to do it that way, write about that feeling. Your intuition might be right.

Again, a mind map can help you see the whole picture at a glance. Put the goal in the center and use one "branch" for each alternative, with pros and cons as twigs.

10. READ TO STIMULATE YOUR THINKING. We usually use reading as an information source, but you can also read to stimulate your thinking. (When you begin to practice Active Reading in chapter 7, you will *feel* how it enlivens your brain.) Many people have learned that when their ideas seem blocked, picking up a favorite book or a stimulating article can get their creative juices flowing again. Try it next time you have a problem to solve and you're running out of new ideas.

Using the techniques you are learning in this book to sharpen your senses, activate your brain's peak intelligence, and read more quickly and intelligently, you will be able to process a great deal of information that you can use to generate new ideas.

11. ANALYZE AND LEARN FROM SETBACKS. Every active person is bound to experience many failures. Learn to be grateful for them. Don't call them "mistakes"—rename them "teachers." This minor shift in terminology can produce a major shift in attitude. When a "teacher" comes along, ask yourself, What can I learn from this experience? Use your mind to see more deeply than an immediate annoyance or setback.

Perhaps the most important characteristic of successful people is that they use defeats and difficulties as opportunities to learn and to grow in strength or perseverance. Analyze the situation, note what you did or said, what the reactions were, what you might have done differently, whether some other action might have been more appropriate, and so on. In this way you can learn to do better next time.

12. TUNE IN TO YOUR INTUITION AND INNER KNOWING. There are times for rational analysis and all the other conscious thinking skills we have been discussing; there are other times to trust your intuition and your innate intelligence, to "tune in" to another level of your being.

Use your intuition to tell you both what is wrong and what is right. If an answer to some question doesn't "feel" right to you, if a number is presented to you as being "what the computer readout says" but you feel it couldn't be right, if a fact doesn't make sense in the light of your previous experience—trust your intuition and examine the situation with care. It may turn out that your intuition is inaccurate, but more often than not you will discover why you are disturbed by what you are being told, and in that discovery you will find something that is important to you.

In chapter 3, I referred to the concept of "peak experiences" introduced by Abraham Maslow, the psychologist who was an early leader of the human potential movement. Peak experiences are those times when we function at our highest and best. We *feel* wonderful—blissful, energetic, certain to succeed, connected to the universe—and we perform at the height of our abilities or even beyond what we might have thought we could do. In these moments, it can perhaps be said that people tune in to the Creative Intelligence that operates in all of nature. Galaxies move in space, trees grow, kittens become cats, all without conscious thought but with tremendous intelligence and order behind every movement and stage of growth. When people enter "the Zone," they let go of conscious thought and turn in high-quality performances effortlessly and unreflectingly. Often they feel that they did nothing at all; the performance just "happened."

When we discussed intuition in chapter 4, I mentioned that studies have revealed that top executives rely on their intuition far more than lower-level managers do. Intuition is real. Be open to it, and you will take another giant step toward mastering the Information Age.

13. BE PATIENT. Thinking takes time, and we are in a hurry. Most of us are constantly under pressure to make decisions and put them into action. We already feel we don't have enough time, and we are not willing to make time to sit and think.

If a man sits down to think, he is immediately asked if he has a headache.

Ralph Waldo Emerson

161

But as you become a Master of information, you know that you must occasionally do just that. You know that thinking is the basis of action, so that if your course of action is to be powerful, you must take whatever time you need to make the best decision you can. As the Chinese political leader Sun Yat-sen said, "To understand is hard. Once one understands, action is easy." Therefore as a Master you have to be sure you have enough information, that your information is correct and that you understand it, that you have considered alternative points of view. All of this takes time.

A Master knows the importance of thinking and weighing information and therefore is comfortable taking time to think even when under pressure. Simply remembering to take time to think can be helpful when you feel overwhelmed by information anxiety.

If you don't find yourself leaping eagerly at every opportunity to think deeply and carefully, you are not alone. It is much easier not to. This is particularly true of what we might call "higher level" thinking. It does not require much time, concentration, or energy to perform simpler mental functions. But applying your knowledge to a new situation takes longer. Analyzing new information, synthesizing ideas into a new whole, and making evaluations and decisions are more demanding.

As Bertrand Russell noted, "Many people would sooner die than think. In fact they do." But there is too much at stake to be like that. It is vital for us as individuals and for the welfare of our human family that we learn to use our brains at their peak capacity to meet the challenges of life in the 21st century.

AVOIDING FAULTY THINKING

We do not always think clearly, nor is the thinking we encounter from others always a model of logic and accuracy. Many of the things we read or hear appear to have well-thought-out arguments, but this isn't necessarily so. Since the time of Aristotle, who formulated the basic rules of logic still followed today, Western philosophers have noted many "crooked" ways of thought and urged us to avoid them. At the beginning of the modern scientific era, Francis Bacon described four main classes of erroneous thinking.

1. *Idols of the Tribe.* Errors that have their roots in our common human nature, such as the limitations of our senses, or our tendency to see only what supports and accords with our beliefs. "Having first determined the question according to his will," says Bacon—that is, having made up his mind—"man *then* resorts to experience, and bending her into conformity . . . leads her about like a captive."

2. *Idols of the Cave.* Errors arising in specific individuals, due to their particular upbringing and state of consciousness, their character and tendencies, prejudices, likes and dislikes.

3. *Idols of the Marketplace.* Errors arising from the powerful effect that language has upon our thinking and understanding, such as the way we can be misled by language or "hard-sell" opinions of any kind.

4. *Idols of the Theater.* Mistakes "which have migrated into men's minds from the various dogmas of the philosophers." "In my opinion," Bacon wrote, "all the received systems of philosophy are but so many stage plays, representing worlds of their own creation." The ideas that have been handed down to us not necessarily reveal the truth of how things really are, which is to be discovered (according to Bacon) by the empirical observations and critical thinking of the scientific method.

Minds are like parachutes; they only function when open.

Lord Dewar

Tribe. Cave. Marketplace. Theater. If every time you started to really think about some idea or proposal you were to examine it in the light of those four words, you would be on your way to a level of critical thinking few people ever attain.

We all have the tendency to believe what suits our desires; we all jump to conclusions; we all distort, generalize, and make sweeping assertions. All our thinking is influenced by the prejudices and paradigms of our family and society. We all have to contend with these and many other kinds of faulty thinking every day, in addition to the intentionally dishonest tricks of argument deployed against us by those who want to convince us of something.

In the remainder of this section I will identify a few of the most common faulty ways of thinking that we are apt to encounter in reading printed material or in listening to other people. If you will remember these tactics and watch for them, you will find that much communication, including your own, is filled with such techniques, used to convince others of what well may not be true.

GENERALIZATION. Such phrases as "politicians are corrupt," "lawyers are in it for the money," "students are apathetic," imply the word *all* for the sake of making a point, where *some* is surely a more truthful evaluation.

This is a common trick, and in most cases it is easily exposed. Even *one* exception invalidates the generalization. Simply put the word *all* into the statement and you will immediately see whether it is really true.

USING EMOTIVE WORDS. Words can be used to elicit feeling as well as convey information. For example, consider the three words *adamant*, *stubborn*, and *pig-headed*. Each word escalates the speaker's negative judgment, although the trait being described is the same. Words with strong emotional connotations may be justified under certain circumstances, but at other times may be used to overwhelm your critical judgment. Whenever you hear an emotion-laden word in an argument, be suspicious that someone may be trying to convince you with an insufficiently rational argument.

Try substituting a neutral word with approximately the same meaning as an emotionally charged word, and see if the argument still appears so convincing.

PROOF BY SELECTED INSTANCES. Here the trick consists of selecting, out of a large sample, some specific cases that support one's argument and leaving out the rest. If I wanted to "prove" that women prefer to go to work rather than stay at home, I could interview working women, gathering up anecdotes supporting my point, perhaps interviewing a few disgruntled housewives for extra support. I would carefully avoid reporting on women who prefer to remain at home with their children.

The way to counteract this method is not to make your own selection to support *your* point of view; it is to ask for or supply numerical, statistical facts (if they can be found) or simply to point out that your opponent does not actually have a wide-based foundation, but only selected instances.

QUOTING CELEBRITIES AND EXPERTS. Just because So-and-So the "expert" espouses an idea doesn't make it true. Just because a basketball player or Hollywood star endorses an idea or a candidate is no reason for you to agree. Endorsements and opinions are not evidence of truth. Try taking the endorser's name out of the discussion and see if the argument is still convincing.

DIVERSIONS. This tactic lures people away from the argument by raising distracting points, such as, "It's all very well to talk about the dangers of drinking and driving, but what about people who speed on the highways?" No matter how many people speed, using alcohol before driving is still the problem under discussion. Arguments unrelated to the topic and intended to throw us off the track are commonly called "red herrings."

UNDEFINED SOURCES. Sometimes we're told information from inadequate sources that are made to sound authoritative, such as the all-too-familiar, "Informed sources revealed today . . ." Other times we are left totally in the dark as to the origins of information. How can you trust information if you don't know where it came from and consequently have no way to verify it?

Ask for the facts. In cases where you can't communicate directly with the speaker, realize that what you are hearing may not be the whole story.

DENIGRATION OF INDIVIDUALS TO AVOID DISCUSSING ISSUES. A standard technique of many persuasive speeches, this is called an *ad hominem* argument, meaning "against the man." For example, someone in your community is supporting a new proposal for a town project, and another person attacks the proposal by saying that the first person has no experience in this area. Even if the first person has no experience, his view might be reasonable and right and his proposal worthwhile. You need to consider the issue itself.

REPEATED AFFIRMATION. Much of what we read or hear capitalizes on the fact that mere repetition of a statement tends to make us believe it. Just the repeated command to "Vote for _____," "Drink _____," or "Buy _____" is apparently enough to induce people in the desired direction, even if no valid reason—or any reason at all—is provided.

This trick is often accompanied by emotion-eliciting words, music, or visual stimuli. It reminds me of the joke about the clergyman who wrote in the margin of his notes for his sermon, "Argument weak here—shout." There is no counterargument against the tactic of repeated affirmation; one can only be on guard against it.

PREPARING THE GROUND FOR AN UNACCEPTABLE CONCLUSION WITH ACCEPTABLE STATEMENTS. A speaker may begin a speech with a series of jokes and statements designed to win the audience's favor, and then safely proceed to make false or doubtful statements that go unquestioned. Writers can argue in a similar fashion. Just because statements A, B, C, and D are true or easy to accept, does not mean that E will be true. It is necessary to remain alert and evaluate the logic connecting each component of a conclusion.

AMBIGUOUS LANGUAGE AND UNDEFINED TERMS. Vague language and the use of ambiguous terms hinder clear thinking. While numbers and concrete words let us know exactly what is meant, abstract words and phrases (such as "justice," "the market," "equality," "freedom," "liberal," "a large percentage") are capable of multiple interpretations. If these words are not clearly defined, you may feel you understand what is being said, but you never really know for sure.

In conversation, you can offset ambiguity or vagueness by continually asking for explanations until the terms become clear, or by offering clarifications yourself and asking the other person if that is what he or she means. In reading, use the dictionary to define terms; see if the writer is going by those definitions, and if the terms are used consistently or have multiple meanings.

ARGUMENT BY ANALOGY. An argument by analogy is a comparison in which it is assumed that because one instance has characteristics A, B, C, and D (or more), then another instance that also has characteristics A, B, and C must also have characteristic D. Analogies are a useful device in explanations and illustrations, particularly to help explain an abstraction in terms of something concrete and familiar; for example, "The mind is like an ocean; when it is whipped up into waves, it is restless and full of thoughts; when it subsides into a calm flat sea, it is at peace." No one has ever seen the mind, so the analogy helps us understand how a meditation technique can produce inner quiet.

But analogy can be misused. An analogy is never a *proof*, and conclusions drawn from analogies are never certain. An analogy is only an illustration or a way of showing a relationship or suggesting a probability.

You can deal with faulty analogies by examining them carefully to see where they break down; that is, locating where the relationship between the illustration and the reality does not exist.

At this point, please go back to the statement of purpose at the beginning of this chapter and think about whether you have achieved the goals and mastered the information presented in these pages. Take a few minutes to flip through the chapter again, and if you feel there are some points you haven't fully grasped, take the time to look more deeply into those areas. The principles in this chapter can help you deal effectively with information at work and in all phases of your life. Take the time to master them, and put them to use!

RESOURCES

Creative thinking

Ray, Michael and Rochelle Meyers. *Creativity in Business.* (New York: Doubleday, 1989). Examples and techniques for enhancing creativity in business, drawn from the authors' Stanford University MBA course.

Von Oech, Roger. *A Kick in the Seat of the Pants.* (New York: Warner Books, 1988) and *A Whack on the Side of the Head* (New York: "Harper & Row, 1986). Two easily understandable books on how the creative process works, with methods to unlock mental blocks and achieve fresh thinking.

Critical thinking

Albrecht, Karl. *Brain Power: Learn to Improve Your Thinking Skills.* (Englewood Cliffs, NJ: Prentice Hall, 1980). A theoretical and practical guide to problem solving, decision making, creativity, and intelligent thinking.

De Bono, Edward. *De Bono's Thinking Course.* (New York: Facts on File, 1985). Instruction on creative thinking by one of the western world's leading teachers.

Flesch, Rudolf. *The Art of Clear Thinking.* (New York: Harper & Row, 1973). Compares fallacious to clear thinking.

Thouless, Robert. *Straight and Crooked Thinking.* Fifty years old and out-of-print, this book is still pertinent and very readable.

Historical

Gardner, Howard. *The Mind's New Science: A History of the Cognitive Revolution.* (New York: Basic Books, 1987). A readable and enlightening history of the working of the human mind.

Organizations

The Institute of Noetic Sciences was founded by astronaut Edgar Mitchell to explore and expand the potential of the mind and spirit. It provides a newsletter and offers special timely reports. Institute of Noetic Sciences, P.O. Box 909, Sausalito, CA 94966.

■ ■ ■ ■

CHAPTER 7

Active Reading: Learn to Be a More Intelligent Reader

Information experts estimate that 80 to 90 percent of the information we receive comes through reading. Therefore, to master the Information Age, becoming a superior reader is clearly a necessity. This means much more than perfecting a series of techniques to move your eyes rapidly over the page. To be a truly expert reader, you need to be not only a fast reader but an intelligent reader as well. You need to read voraciously but judiciously.

This chapter is packed with useful, practical techniques and insights to help you become a more effective reader. Here is a preview of what you will accomplish:

First you will learn how to set up an ideal reading environment to support maximum learning with minimum fatigue. Then you will learn how to define your information target zone, one of the most powerful time-management skills you will ever encounter. As a Master of the Information Age you will know how much time you can devote to reading, how to decide what to read, and how to determine in advance what you want to gain from the material. By previewing a book or article, you can effectively discover in a few minutes whether it contains enough useful information for you to spend your valuable time reading it.

Previewing can help you understand material better by "priming" your brain with the essential ideas of the book. You can also determine how carefully you want to read it—for what level of detail and comprehension—and you can vary your approach accordingly.

The information time-management skills you learn in this chapter will make your reading much more efficient and offer maximum returns on the investment of your most precious commodity: time.

The flood of print has turned reading into a process of gulping rather than savoring.

Warren Chappell

▪ ▪ ▪ ▪

DETERMINE YOUR BASE READING SPEED

In order to measure your progress in reading more quickly and effectively, you need to know where you are starting from. In a moment I will ask you to read for a two-minute timed reading. From that you will be able to ascertain your present reading rate. Read the following guidelines before you begin.

1. You will need a watch with a second hand or a digital readout, and a pencil or pen. It would be helpful to have someone else time you, but you can easily do this yourself.
2. Begin reading below where the text lines are numbered and continue reading at your *normal* rate for two minutes.
3. At the end of two minutes, stop reading and mark with your pencil or pen the spot where you ended.

That is all you need to know for now. Do it now and check back after you have completed steps 1–3.

4. Now you can figure out your base reading rate. Note the numbers in the margin at every fifth line. Determine how many lines you read in two minutes. Multiply this by ten. This gives you the approximate number of words you read in two minutes.

5. Divide the total number of words you read by two so that the final figure reflects the number of words you read in one minute. This is your beginning base reading rate. Complete the following here or in your journal for future reference:

DATE: _____

BEGINNING BASE READING RATE: _____ WORDS PER MINUTE.

BEGIN TIMED READING HERE. If you are like most people, you read approximately 250 words per minute. This means it will take you nearly 7 hours to read a 100,000-word book, the equivalent of about 300 pages. If you could triple your current speed, you would be done in less than 2¼ hours. Think about it: If you compare 7 hours of reading—either over several days, with much forgotten in between sessions, or in one marathon session with tired eyes and aching neck and back—to 2¼ hours (one-third the time), easily accomplished in an afternoon or evening, the value of increasing your reading speed is obvious.

Using the Active Reading system, you will be able to accomplish three times as much with your time. In addition, you will find that you understand much more of what you read, retain it better, and greatly increase your enjoyment of the reading process.

Active Reading transforms reading from a passive to an active experience. It challenges you to think about the content and tone of what you read. It is like having a dialogue with the author, asking questions, presenting your own ideas and seeing what the author has to say about them. By asking you to think about what you are reading before, during, and after you read, Active Reading increases your comprehension and retention of the material. When you merely take in words without thinking about what is being said, most of what you read just slips away.

Active Reading involves not only the left-brain, analytic thinking and language skills usually used in reading, but also incorporates the visual/spatial skills of the right brain. This use of more of your "whole brain" gives you a more complete grasp of the material and has an enlivening effect upon your brain.

Surviving and thriving as a professionial today demands two new approaches to the written word. First, it requires a new approach to orchestrating information, by skillfully choosing what to read and what to ignore. Second, it requires a new approach to integrating information, by reading faster and with greater comprehension.

Jimmy Calano
Jeff Salzman

15

20

25

30

By training you to move your eyes rapidly over the page, Active Reading permits your subconscious to pick up words and meanings within the range of your peripheral vision. Conscious and subconscious are integrated and work together to produce deeper understanding.

Active Reading trains you to look for the *essence* of what you read. For most of your reading, the essence—not every detail and every word—is all you really need. Learning to apprehend the essence quickly and not bother with the rest greatly increases the speed at which you move through the material.

Active Reading gives you the tools to vary your reading speed according to the nature of the material and your interest in it. When you want to read a beautiful descriptive passage in a novel, savoring all the details, or when you need to study the fine points of any subject, you will go more slowly. When you need only the essence, you will have the skills to extract it quickly and easily.

SET UP YOUR READING ENVIRONMENT

In creating your reading environment, whether at home or in the office, it is important to set up conditions that enliven and stimulate your brain. In chapter 3 you were given suggestions for maximizing efficiency and comfort in studying and learning: proper light, cool temperature, pleasant surroundings, and the use of specific aromas and appropriate music to stimulate and focus your brain. Spend a few moments reviewing those suggestions, and be sure to implement them before you continue with this chapter if you have not done so already.

Proper reading posture is also important. The best posture for reading is sitting upright with your back straight or bent slightly forward. Lying down, lounging, or slouching are not conducive to alertness or concentration.

I suggest that you sit at a table, resting the book at about a 45-degree angle from the table. This gives your eyes a clear, flat view of the whole page without putting undue stress on your neck and back. This method will decrease eyestrain considerably. You can accomplish this by placing a two- to three-inch-thick book or notebook under the book you are reading.

35

50

55

60

65

In addition, minimize distractions when you read so that 70
you will not be disturbed. Whenever possible, do your reading
in a place that allows you to concentrate as fully as possible.
Remember also to *take breaks* about every 45 to 50 minutes,
since this helps you take advantage of several of the memory
effects we mentioned in chapter 5.

Take a few minutes to set up your reading environment.
How you sit to read may seem insignificant, but it can influence
how alert you are and how quickly you become tired. You will
find that your speed and comprehension will be increased just
by sitting in an appropriate reading posture and placing the
book in the optimum relationship to your eyes.

DEFINE YOUR INFORMATION TARGET ZONE

This is one of the most important parts of this book. Determining your information target zone—selecting from within a
larger body of data the specific information that is relevant to 85
you—is a vital skill because the vast majority of facts and data
in almost everything you read has little significance for your
personal or professional life. What is important to you in any
particular material is different from what someone else may
want to learn. 90

By learning to work within your information target zone
you greatly increase your efficiency, and so you will be able to
accomplish more in less time. You will feel more in control,
less overwhelmed and intimidated by the sheer volume of information. As a result, you will feel less stressed and oppressed 95
by information anxiety.

Defining your information target zone also helps you to
maintain an active involvement in the process of drawing information from the written page for conversion into knowledge. Your active involvement makes all the difference between 100
a lazy brain passively taking in data and forgetting it almost
immediately, and a lively, interested brain that makes sense of
the data and stores it away efficiently for future reference.

Active Reading Preparation

The key to defining your information target zone is to use the 105
techniques of the Active Reading preparation. These are skills

If you are possessed by an idea, you find it expressed everywhere, you even smell it.

Thomas Mann

that you employ *before you read* a book, article, memo, or anything else. They consist of the following five steps.

1. Set your purpose.
2. Ask questions.
3. Anticipate answers.
4. Preview.
5. Use your mind like a magnet.

SET YOUR PURPOSE. Before you expend your valuable time on a particular written work, it is vital to ask yourself, What do I want to know? Is there something specific I want to learn, understand, or accomplish? There is no reason to read something unless you know what you want to gain from it.

To get what you want you must know what you want. If you have no destination, chances are good that you won't arrive! Too often, people read material without any sense of what they want to get out of it. They find their mind wandering a lot, because it doesn't know where it is supposed to go. However, if you determine what you want to know, you will immediately recognize every paragraph and every page as either helping you gain the information you want, or as useless. If it is useless to you, you can decide not to waste your time. You can skip ahead until you find something relevant, or put the book away entirely.

In other words, setting a goal puts your "mental hooks" out to catch what you want. When your brain has a purpose, it is on the alert to locate and extract the information you require for your information target zone. Having a purpose in reading wakes up your brain and takes it from a passive mode of operation where you are just taking in words, to the active mode where you are looking for something. If you have a purpose, your brain will be lively, evaluating the material in terms of that purpose. When you are actively thinking, you will understand what you read. The better you understand, the more you will remember. Here are a few examples of what reading goals or purposes might be.

135

140

Book	Goal	
A book on Japanese business practices	To find out if and how Japanese management policies and procedures can be useful to me in my work.	145
A book on English history	To learn more about the specific roles of women in 17th-century England.	150
A book on procrastination	To learn how prioritizing and goal setting can help overcome procrastination.	

Often your purpose in reading will be evident to you without much thought. If you don't know your goal immediately, take some time to think about it. I suggest you articulate it clearly in a sentence or two and write it down. If the project has a multiplicity of purposes, you will find it useful to begin a mind map.

You can either read something many times in order to be assured that you got it all, or else you can define your purpose and use techniques which will assure that you have met it and gotten what you need.

Peter Kump

ASK QUESTIONS. The second step in Active Reading is to ask specific questions that you want answered. This gets your brain further involved in the active pursuit of potentially useful information. For example, if your purpose in reading a book is to learn about procrastination, you might ask questions such as: What is the psychological explanation of why people procrastinate? Is there "hard" scientific evidence? Can it be explained in terms of how the brain functions? Have counter-techniques been tried in controlled experiments? What sort of anecdotal evidence exists, and how reliable is it? Are there techniques I can learn to help me eliminate the habit of procrastination? How long does it take to master these techniques?

ANTICIPATE. Your next step is to predict the answers to your questions based on what you already know. This is important because it begins to connect your own previous knowledge with the new material. Don't be afraid to be wrong. The benefits are in the activation of your brain, not in the accuracy of your prediction.

175

There are millions of neuronal networks or pathways in your brain, relating to countless subjects, from cooking to understanding the theory of relativity. When you establish your purpose, ask questions, and then begin to speculate on the answers, you are alerting the relevant neuronal networks to be prepared for new related input. This process gives your whole brain a mission to accomplish: to gain maximum input from what you are reading.

Knowledge rests not upon truth alone, but upon error also.

Carl G. Jung

185

When you begin to speculate about answers, you really begin to think. It is fairly easy to ask questions but more difficult to call upon your own experience to try to answer them. Once you make some predictions, you will have a reference point from which to evaluate everything the author tells you. You will begin to think reflectively, examining the book's message in terms of your own understanding and experience.

190

As you read, refer repeatedly to your purpose, questions, and speculations. Is your purpose being accomplished? Are your questions being answered? Are the answers what you expected? Is anything surprising you? In this way the purpose, questions, and anticipated answers form a thread that runs through the book, giving coherence to your reading experience.

195

PREVIEW THE BOOK. The steps in the Activator below will help you gain an excellent overview of a book in just a few minutes. By performing these, you will get a sense of the whole; you will know the general theme of the material and some of the subthemes, and you will quickly grasp the skeleton structure, the flow of the writer's thought. This gives you several major advantages.

First, you may learn enough in just a few minutes to put the book aside. You might find that the book is just a rehash of material you already know and offers nothing new in your information target zone. Or you may be able to grasp its main

210

message quickly. If you can pick up the essence of a 100,000-word book in ten minutes, your effective reading speed would be 10,000 words per minute—not bad!

Once you grasp the overall big picture, all the pieces as you meet them will have a lot more meaning. A jigsaw puzzle is much easier to complete if you know what the finished picture is supposed to look like. Without a preview in reading, you might find yourself thinking, "Where is the author going with this? How does this fit in?" and you may not know the answer until you are halfway through the book. The overview is like receiving a map to a new territory. Once you have the map, you can move about more comfortably.

A preview lets you become familiar with the material. Numerous studies of reading verify what our common sense tells us: We can read faster, and understand more, when we read something familiar. If you are not a nuclear physicist, reading about quantum mechanics will be slow going. The terminology and concepts will be foreign to you. Reading about a subject you already know something about is much easier. As we saw in our study of memory in chapter 5, understanding is one of the most important factors in our ability to remember something.

Previewing not only gives you familiarity with the material, it also gives you a chance to look up any unfamiliar keywords you might have noticed in the text as you glanced over it. This will further facilitate your rapid reading and quicker, deeper comprehension.

Previewing serves both the right brain and the left brain. Your left brain likes logic, order, sequence. It prefers to know specifics and always wants to know why it is doing what it is doing. It does not like to explore uncharted waters but prefers to move along in accordance with a well-reasoned and articulated plan. Establishing your purpose, asking questions, and mapping out the organizational structure and main themes of the book clearly serves these left-brain tendencies.

On the other hand, the right brain is fond of patterns and wants to grasp the whole rather than get lost in parts. It enjoys the process of zipping through several hundred pages of a book, picking up main headings and putting it all together into a coherent whole. Once you start reading, the left brain's security with structure and order sets the right brain free to continue its pursuit of the essence.

Lastly, previewing gives you a feel for the nature of the

215

There are books of which the backs and covers are by far the best parts.

Charles Dickens

225

230

235

240

245

250

177

255 material so that you can determine how quickly to read it. Is it complex material in an unfamiliar field, or is it in an area you understand well, written in a simple style? Do you need a lot of details, or just an overview? Your decision about speed is one of the most important decisions you make before you start to read.

260 These are some of the many advantages of previewing. The following Learning Activator will familarize you with the process and give you an experience of putting it to use.

▪ ▪ ▪ ▪

LEARNING ACTIVATOR #13
PREVIEWING A BOOK

265 Choose a nonfiction book to use for this Activator and the many reading exercises in the remainder of the book. I recommend that you choose a book that is interesting to you and relatively simple.

270 Choosing an easy book is important. You wouldn't want to learn driving in the middle of the Los Angeles freeway system; an empty parking lot or a quiet country road is best. You wouldn't want to teach your child to swim in ten-foot ocean waves, but in a shallow lake or pool. In the same way, when you are learning new skills you want to enjoy the process, and you want maximum success. Don't pick something overly complex and make the learning process a struggle. You will have ample opportunity to read difficult material once you have

275 mastered the Active Reading techniques.

Here are the steps of previewing. Go through them now with the book you have chosen.

1. *Tune in to your intuition as you first pick up the book.* You are going to decide if you really want to spend your time with the book

280 and, if so, what your purpose will be for reading it. Look at the book and listen to your internal voices as you explore it through the following steps. Often people force themselves to read material even though their inner voice tells them they have little interest in it. When this happens, consider putting the book aside, or at least perform the next

285 steps to see if your interest increases as you get to know more about the book.

2. *Read the title and subtitle.* A lot of time and thought went into these, and they can tell you a lot about the book. Think about why the author gave it that title. What clues are buried in it? What other

290 titles does it remind you of?

3. *Examine the front and back cover and the inside flaps.* These are "billboards" upon which the marketing experts of the publishing houses have the opportunity to sell their books. More useful information may be packed into the blurbs and recommendations. Are the recommendations written by knowledgeable experts? Can you learn anything from the artwork on the cover? 295

4. *Read the jacket summary.* This is an excellent way to get a sense of the essence of the book and perhaps learn a bit about the author. Keep in mind that it is intended to sell you the book and may be written in inflated language. 300

5. *Evaluate the author.* What are the author's qualifications for writing this book? Has he written other books? Does he teach the subject? If you have read other books by this author, you will have a good idea of the quality and level of the writing.

6. *Read the table of contents.* This is the outline of the book. You 305 will learn not only the main themes and the logic of their unfoldment, but also about the book's structure, how many chapters there are and how long they run. This can help you begin to get a feeling for the book. In fact, you may be immediately attracted to one or more chapters as possible sources of information. If so, browse quickly through 310 those sections. You may be able to read only those sections and reach your information target.

7. *Check the date of publication.* In some cases where recency of material is relevant, this could be important to you. If you are familiar with the subject matter, it will give you a sense of where to place this 315 book in the context of other works in the field.

8. *Read the preface or introduction.* Here the author generally explains why she has written the book, why she cares about the subject, and what her perspective is on it. She often gives away the essence of her argument. You can learn a lot about both the material and the 320 author. You may find that you disagree with the thesis and want to read more to learn something new. Or you may find that you agree and do not need to read the book, since it is not offering you a new perspective.

9. *Look over the index and bibliography.* From the index you can 325 get a more complete idea of the subjects the book covers and how much space is spent on them. The bibliography tells you about the author's source materials. From both the index and bibliography you can learn whether you are in familiar territory or are likely to encounter a lot of new information. If the material is too familiar, you may not 330 need to read the book. If it is very *un*familiar, you may need to allocate plenty of quiet, concentrated time to read it.

335

*Our minds become
magnetized with the
dominating thoughts we
hold in our minds and
these magnets attract to us
the forces, the people, the
circumstances of life which
harmonize with the nature
of our dominating
thoughts.*

Napoleon Hill

360

10. *Flip through the book and briefly take in the layout and ty-pography.* Notice bold section headings and italicized words and phrases. These will continue to build your sense of the main concepts. Stop briefly at graphs, pictures, charts, illustrations. Since ''a picture is worth a thousand words,'' you may be able to greatly increase your grasp of the book's themes.

11. *Read the first and last couple of paragraphs in the book.* This will give you a taste of the writing style, and often announces the main theme and the conclusion. To go a little deeper, read the first and last paragraphs of several of the chapters that intrigue you.

12. *Establish your purpose.* If you had difficulty defining your purpose before previewing the book, you should find it much easier to do so now. If you identified your purpose earlier, you might wish to revise it now that you know more about the book.

Setting your purpose, asking questions, and predicting answers can be done either before or after you preview the book. In fact, Active Reading involves a continuous interaction with the material. You not only ask questions and anticipate answers in the beginning, but you continue to do so throughout your reading. As you master the technique, this interaction becomes a smooth flow that is primarily unconscious but that keeps your mind actively engaged. As your questions are answered, new ones often arise. As your anticipated answers are proved or disproved, you will have new speculations about the answers to new questions.

Since you did not define your purpose before we started this Activator, and you have just previewed your new book, take a few minutes now to write down your purpose for reading it.

My purpose for reading this book is:

What questions would I like to answer by reading this book?

I anticipate the answers to my questions will be:

■ ■ ■ ■

USE YOUR BRAIN LIKE A MAGNET. The last step in Active Reading preparation is automatic: your brain works like a magnet to locate the information you want quickly and effortlessly. I'm sure you have experienced this many times; you utilize your brain's natural ability to bring in just what you want in countless daily experiences. For example, if you are looking for a blue shirt you don't have to examine each shirt in your closet. If you are thinking about buying a car of a certain make, model, and color, you suddenly start seeing it everywhere.

When you know what you want, your brain locates it. This is a great principle of life, applicable in all spheres of living. For our purposes, we will talk about it primarily in the context of information, but as we go along, pause to consider the relevance of this principle to other aspects of your personal and professional life.

This is not just metaphor: there is scientific evidence that explains why the brain works this way. Edward Evarts, a physiologist at the National Institutes of Health (NIH), trained monkeys to pull a lever in response to a light. Measuring the monkeys' cortical activity, he discovered that there was a definite response in the brain following the turning on of the light but well in advance of the movement to pull the lever. In Evarts's words, there were "preparatory states for a particular direction of centrally programmed movement." This "preparatory state" sets the brain in motion to accomplish its mission.

Defining your information target zone is a way to con-

365

370

375

380

385

390 sciously direct your attention toward what you want. When your brain knows what you want, it will steer your senses toward achieving your purpose. You will find your eyes attracted spontaneously to relevant information. The following Activator will help you verify this principle.

■ ■ ■ ■

395 **LEARNING ACTIVATOR #14**
EXPERIENCING YOUR MIND AS A MAGNET

Here are several simple exercises to improve your brain's ability to get what it wants.

1. Where is the number "6" in the following number
400 sequence?

9753148157923983**2**653278

2. With a pencil, mark the letter "e" each time it appears on this page (or a page of a magazine). Note that you don't have to pause at each letter to consider whether to mark it
405 or skip it. Your brain is on the alert for the "e's" and you hardly notice what the other letters are.

Try this with magazines in waiting rooms, or modify it by using your eyes to pull in a specific letter or color on billboards and highway signs.

410 3. Look around wherever you are now and locate all the objects that are curved.

Did you notice that straight lines and rectangular objects had no relevance and your eyes went directly to the curved objects?

415 4. On the next page is a drawing containing numerous geometric patterns. Within you will find another square that looks like this:

☐

It is visible although it is surrounded by similar geometric patterns. Take a good look at this shape, then turn to the
420 next page and find it.

What was your experience? Did you find your eyes being drawn quickly to the small square?

Employ your time in improving yourself by other men's writings so that you shall come easily by what others have labored hard for.

Socrates

From this moment on, do not read any book or article without having a prior purpose or previewing to see whether a purpose and questions arise. If a purpose doesn't develop from the preview, the material probably has little value for you. Use your time for something better.

Although Active Reading preparation may seem to *add* time, and one of your primary motivations is to *decrease* the number of hours you spend reading, you will soon see that it saves you enormous quantities of time. It can be accomplished quickly. Depending on the nature of the book, anywhere from five to fifteen minutes is generally sufficient.

Here is a suggestion that can allow you to use your previewing skills to become an extremely well-read and well-informed person. Every week, stop off at the library and pick up half a dozen books that interest you. They could be current

425

430

435

440 best-sellers, classics, books in your field, or books on topics that you know nothing about. Each day, spend at least fifteen minutes—more if you have it—previewing one of the books using the twelve-step plan outlined above. In this way you can effectively increase your information input by well over 300 books a year!

445 You will be amazed to see how much you will learn by following this routine. It becomes even more effective if, after reading, you write a few brief notes summarizing what you've learned, add the information to a mind map you have on this topic, or tell someone about it. This will crystallize the knowledge and add it to your information storehouse.

450 You should also consider reading the book review section of your local newspaper, or subscribe to an excellent national publication such as the *New York Times Book Review* or the *New York Review of Books*. Few people make sufficient use of these valuable resources. Each week, several dozen books are re-

455 viewed, some at length and some in brief. Reading the reviews not only gives you a good notion of the content of many new books, but also points you toward books you may not have heard about. Indeed, reading book reviews is a vital step toward becoming a Master of the Information Age.

460 ## DECIPHERING ORGANIZATION: A KEY TO PICKING UP INFORMATION FAST

A valuable aid in your previewing process is an understanding of basic organizational structures used by writers. Most written works follow certain universal patterns. A nonfiction book or

465 article is almost always structured like this:

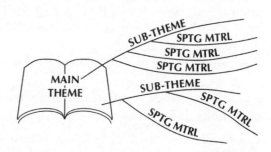

There can be any number of subthemes and any amount or kind of supporting material, such as explanations, graphs, charts, examples, statistics, anecdotes, and diagrams. There can be a kind of "infinite regression" of subthemes, sub-subthemes, sub-sub-subthemes, and so on, depending on how much detail the author goes into.

In a book, each chapter is likely to represent or explore one of the subthemes and in turn to have its own subthemes. Each paragraph also has a theme and its elaboration. Phrased differently, we could say that every level of a book has a main point and any number of subordinate points elaborating, exploring, or examining the main point.

The typography of a book is designed to help you recognize these levels of organization. In addition to the chapter titles, most books have major headings usually printed in boldface and capital letters, secondary headings in less dramatic typeface, and a succession of increasingly less significant headings with their own correspondingly less bold type styles. Italic or boldface type in the body of the text signals that an important point is being expressed, to which the author wants to draw special attention.

Before you read any further, take a moment to flip through the pages of this book or another nonfiction book of your choice and note the different type styles and how they are used. Ask yourself why these were used, how effective they are, and how they can help you.

As an active reader, the smallest unit of writing that you will generally be concerned with is the paragraph. Each paragraph usually contains one main idea or image. The first sentence of the paragraph usually states the main point. The final sentence is a wrap-up, conclusion, or nexus to the following paragraph. Sandwiched in between is the supporting information. The paragraph is usually a single mental image, fleshed out.

Since your goal is to read mainly for ideas, one way to save time is to read only the first and perhaps the last sentence of each paragraph. This is a common technique in "skimming" in which a reader looks only for the essence of what the paragraph conveys. In addition to what is explicitly stated in those sentences, your brain will take in much of the intermediate

He has only half learned the art of reading who has not added to it the more refined art of skipping and skimming.

Arthur, Lord Balfour

480

485

490

495

500

505

supporting information on a subconscious level through your peripheral vision. If anything important is contained there, you will intuitively slow down to pick it up.

510 Recognizing how books are written, designed, and published can help you in several ways. First, simply skimming through a book and reading all the chapter and section headings gives you a good idea of what the book contains. (This is step 10 of the previewing process.) In just a few minutes you can grasp the main points and their sequence of development.

515 Second, once you set your purpose and know how deeply you want to study the book—whether you just want a general idea of its contents and main ideas, or you need to look into the details—your knowledge of the organizational structure can help you accomplish your goals.

520 Articles, reports, and long memos, if they are properly written, are organized in a similar way, with main themes, sub-themes, and supporting material, usually indicated by sections and headings. If you apply this knowledge to all your reading, you will be able to read much more intelligently and efficiently.

▪ ▪ ▪ ▪

525 **LEARNING ACTIVATOR # 15**
HOW FAST DO YOU WANT TO READ?

Before you start the exercises in the next chapter that will help you increase your reading speed, you should set a goal for yourself. Now you know what your current reading speed is. How much do you

530 want to increase it? Don't take this question lightly; the answer is your commitment to yourself.

COMPLETE THE FOLLOWING. I will master the Active Reading skills necessary to increase my reading speed _____ times by the time I complete this book.

535 When I achieve this goal, it will benefit my life in the following ways.

Take a moment to imagine that you have achieved your goal and that you are enjoying the benefits you listed above. Visualize yourself as a faster reader than you are now. Keep this image of yourself in mind as you work on the next two chapters. 540

■ ■ ■ ■

At this point, take a look at the statement of purpose at the start of this chapter, and glance through the chapter itself. Do you feel you have understood the importance of defining your information target zone? Are you now so conversant with the five steps of Active Reading preparation that you could go 545 through them almost automatically every time you have something to read? If not, fixing them in your memory and practicing them a number of times will solidify your mastery of a useful Information Age skill. Please take time to really complete this chapter before proceeding to chapter 8. 550

CHAPTER 8

DOUBLE YOUR READING SPEED

The sad truth is that for the overwhelming majority of people, the last time they had any formal training in reading was in elementary school. The result is that even professionals who complete high school, college, or graduate school may still be reading at nearly the same slow pace as when they were children.

In this chapter you will learn how the way you were taught to read has limited your reading speed, and how you can take in information much faster. The exercises will then help you to at least double your reading speed. Tripling your speed is probable if you practice the exercises thoroughly and put them to use as often as you can. Your new skills will allow you to greatly increase the speed at which you extract useful information from your reading.

■ ■ ■ ■ ■

WHY MOST PEOPLE READ SLOWLY

There are three principal reasons most people read slowly.

1. word-for-word reading
2. subvocalization
3. regression.

An explanation of each of these reasons will help you understand why you can read faster than you do now.

Word-for-Word Reading

As children, most people were first taught to recognize the letters of the alphabet and recite them out loud, first one by one and then in sequence. The next step was to combine the letters into words, to associate a familiar object with combinations of letters. Sometimes this was done using flashcards where a picture would correspond with a word. More often, we were asked to sound out words by reading and pronouncing each letter or phonetic group.

To recapture your early reading experience (and the feeling of being back in first or second grade struggling through a phonetic rendition of a sentence in front of the class and the teacher), read this sentence aloud, taking about twenty seconds to sound it out *letter by letter*.

Learning to read has been reduced to a process of mastering a series of narrow, specific, hierarchical skills. Where armed-forces recruits learn the components of a rifle or the intricacies of close order drill ''by the numbers,'' recruits to reading learn its mechanics sound by sound and word by word.

Jacquelyn Gross

An old man stood far away from his fishing boat.

As you were reading, your eyes were stopping at each letter. The progression looked something like this:

An old man stood far away from his fishing boat.

As our skills progressed we were able to drop the letter-by-letter reading and began to recognize and pronounce whole words. This was a great leap in our reading evolution and greatly accelerated our reading speed.

The next step was combining the words into meaningful sentences and reciting the sentences aloud under the attentive ear of the teacher, who was careful to correct any mispronunciation. At this point the original objects referred to by the concrete words—cat, dog, sky, tree—became far removed from the visual image, and *sound* was established as the major processor of written language. In other words, we were judged on how well we could *say* "see Spot run" with no emphasis on whether we could really *see* Spot run.

Subvocalization

In later grades we began reading silently to ourselves. However, most of us continued reading at about the same slow pace we used for reading out loud. This is because, instead of audibly vocalizing the words, we simply repeated them internally, a process known as subvocalization. Many children actually move their lips to form the words as they sound them out mentally.

This procedure of learning to read is fine, up to this point. It is a natural and logical progression. Unfortunately, this stage of reading—word-for-word subvocalization—is as far as most of us have ever gotten. Once we learned how to read silently we received little or no further instruction, and most of us still continue to pronounce each word in our mind.

It is important to recognize, however, that our brain is able to grasp larger chunks of material, and that we can substantially increase our reading speed by picking up whole phrases or sentences instead of just single words. In the same way that we graduated to words from single letters, we can grasp ideas, concepts, and images, rather than just plod along with our old word-by-word method.

On the average, English-speaking people talk at about 150 words per minute. When we read we can move a little more quickly, but if we are subvocalizing or pronouncing the words mentally—which virtually everyone does—the top limit on our reading speed is 200 to 300 words per minute. This is too slow for the Information Age. A Master must learn to read in a different way.

Regression

In addition to word-for-word reading and subvocalizing, the third reason most people read slowly is *regression*, the process of backtracking to reread words, phrases, or sentences. Most regression takes place unconsciously; only a small percentage is due to deliberate rereading. It is usually caused by a lack of

Very young children eat their books, literally devouring their contents. This is one reason for the scarcity of first editions of Alice in Wonderland *and other favorites of the nursery.*

A. S. W. Rosenbach

confidence in our ability to understand the material. If we miss a word or a phrase, if our attention wanders for a moment, we instinctively feel that our comprehension will improve if we go back and read it again. With regression, our eye movements may look something like this:

An old man stood far away from his fishing boat.

In reality, regression does not increase comprehension, it actually diminishes it. This is because repeatedly stopping the forward flow of attention in order to go backward is disruptive to the brain's grasp of the incoming information. This causes poor concentration, characterized by daydreaming, mental wandering, and losing one's place in the reading material. These repeated distractions severely limit reading speed.

Because the brain is capable of receiving and processing information literally hundreds of times faster than we ordinarily read, slow reading fails to keep the brain challenged. Consequently the mind is free to fill in the gaps with extraneous thoughts. As you increase your reading speed to a pace that more faithfully mirrors your potential, your brain will exchange boredom for lively interest and heightened concentration. Your comprehension will also improve, and as a result your retention will increase.

Although you may now be convinced that word-for-word reading is not the most efficient method, you have been reading that way for many years. Such securely ensconced habits are the stuff of which our comfort zone is made; they do not die easily. Woody Allen once joked, "I took a speed reading class. We read *War and Peace* in twenty minutes. It's about Russia." His anecdote summarizes our fears about not "getting" the material if we don't employ our usual ponderous word-for-word reading style. The following Activator will help to smooth the transition from the old way of reading to the new way.

▪ ▪ ▪ ▪

LEARNING ACTIVATOR #16
MAKING THE TRANSITION TO FASTER READING

Part I
To help you eliminate any anxiety you might have about not fully understanding or missing something important when you read faster, complete the following sentence, listing as many concerns as you can. Express what you fear will happen if you do not read each word.

If I don't read each word, I may

Part II
Now think about the advantages of gaining more understanding by reading fewer words, and complete the following sentence, again putting down as many advantages as you can:

By not reading each word, I will

▪ ▪ ▪ ▪

WHY YOU CAN READ FASTER

We read with our eyes. This statement of an obvious fact holds the key to faster reading. The eyes are not limited to the same

200 or 300 words per minute that we can verbalize. In fact, the eyes can easily grasp thousands of words per minute and still maintain adequate understanding.

When light enters the eye, it is focused by the lens onto the retina, which lines the inner surface of the eye. Networks of nerve cells relay the information falling upon the retina through the optic nerve to the brain, which processes and interprets it. The eyes, then, should really be considered as information-gathering extensions of the brain.

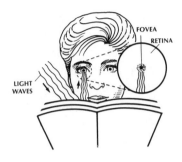

At the center of the retina is a tiny area called the fovea, where the light-sensitive receptor cells are tightly packed, and where the perception of images is consequently much sharper and clearer. Around that point what you see is blurry or hazy, not in sharp focus.

The central point of clear vision seen by the fovea at any time is only about one forty-thousandth of the entire visual field. As you look at this page, that central focus takes in only about three to five letters in perfect clarity. You can easily prove this to yourself by holding your eyes still for a moment on a short word or a few letters; you will see that everything around that central focus is seen, but is not sharp.

The physiology of the eye has two important consequences. First, almost all of our field of vision is *peripheral vision*: we aren't focusing on it, but we do see it. We will come back to this point shortly.

Pauses

The second consequence of your eyes' physiology is that in order for them to transmit useful information to your brain, they must temporarily pause at the information source in order to get a clear picture. The pause is normally so quick that you don't consciously notice it. When we read, the eye moves rapidly along the page, stopping again and again in order to bring words into focus. These minute pauses are called *fixations*. In between pauses the eye is actually in motion and we are not seeing anything clearly. Thus the eye takes in information in small visual gulps.

For nearly 100 years it has been known that the eye moves from one point of fixation to the next in about ¼ second. If we read word by word, this limits our reading speed to 4 words per second, or a maximum of 240 words per minute. Word-by-word reading thus locks us into a slow speed because of two factors.

1. subvocalization, which ties us into the speed of speech
2. the large number of fixations we make

Each group of words is processed by the brain as a single thought. And because the words are viewed in context, you retain them more accurately than if you processed the words individually.

Rose Saperstein
James Joseph

Add to this the phenomenon of regression, which slows the process down still further, and you will understand why we read so slowly even though our brains are capable of much more.

Miles A. Tinker of the University of Minnesota is a researcher specializing in eye movements as they relate to reading. Tinker is one of several researchers who have found that over 90 percent of reading time is spent on pauses. The critical questions for Active Reading thus become:

1. How many pauses do we *have* to make?
2. How much information can be taken in at each pause? Are we limited to pausing at each word and taking in that word only, or can we take in bigger gulps of information?
3. How long must the pauses be? How quickly can we move from fixation to fixation?

Clearly, the key to faster reading would be to make fewer pauses, each of shorter duration, and yet pick up larger amounts of information with every pause.

If every pause you make requires ¼ second, and you pause at every word on a 240-word page, reading that page will take one minute. If instead of reading every word you could take in larger gulps, perhaps of three words each, you would pause only 80 times and thus could read the same page in only 20 seconds. Because you would expend less energy—you would do two-thirds less work—you and your eyes would be less tired.

Numerous studies have shown that "better" readers—those who read more quickly and with greater understanding of what they read—do not read word by word, but rather take in several words or phrases, even several *sentences*, with each fixation.

Keep Your Eyes Healthy

Aside from momentary pauses when you blink, your eyes are on duty all the time. No wonder so many of us suffer from eyestrain or impaired vision! Here are some things you can do to keep your eyes healthy.

Be sure to get plenty of vitamin A. It is essential for the visual process, particularly for vision in dim light or at night. Good sources of vitamin A include yellow fruits and vegetables such as carrots, squash, sweet potatoes, and corn; green leafy vegetables; and dairy products and eggs.

Don't rely on a supplement for your vitamin A. Isolating "active ingredients" from their natural sources, where they exist in organic integration with other substances, may decrease their effectiveness. Research at Johns Hopkins University, for example, suggests that for vitamin A to be effective it needs to be ingested in conjuntion with zinc. Both are found together in vegetables and fruit, but not necessarily in a vitamin pill.

Prepare proper light when you read. Reading in dim light, or having a bright glare on your page, can cause eyestrain and fatigue.

Take breaks. Don't try to read or work at a computer terminal for hours on end. Get up at least once every hour, move around, get your blood flowing, give your eyes something different to do, or close them for a minute or two.

Learn eye exercises. Many doctors and researchers have helped people learn to improve their vision through eye exercises. Here are three to relieve eyestrain and sharpen your vision.

1. Sunning. To do this exercise, you have to be outside. If you wear glasses, take them off. *With your eyes closed*, look at the sun. Slowly move your head from side to side, letting the sun's warmth soothe your eyes. Move your eyes in small circles, as if painting a circle around the sun with your nose. *Do not do this sunning exercise with your eyes open.* At first, do this only for 15 to 30 seconds, but after you get used to it, you can do it for as much as 5 minutes if you have the time. You will find it relaxing to your eyes, and if you ordinarily wear glasses, you may be surprised when you open your eyes to find your vision sharper.

2. Palming. If you wear glasses, take them off. Briskly rub the palms of your hands together, creating an energetic friction heat. Then with your eyes closed, cup the palms of your hands lightly over your eyes. Don't apply any pressure to the eyes. Hold for at least 30 seconds. You will feel the warmth and soothing energy from your palms penetrating into your eyes. I recommend that you "love your eyes" with this palming exercise several times during the day, especially if you are reading or looking at a computer terminal.

3. Near and Far Focus. This is an active exercise to help keep the lens of your eyes pliable. Hold a book, a photograph, or a picture postcard about six to eight inches from your eyes. Look at it carefully; don't stare, but actively look at the words or details of the picture. After a few seconds, look across the room or out the window, and again actively focus your eyes. Look at a tree or run your eyes around the edges of a building; or look at a picture or a calendar on your wall. Do this for only a few seconds, then return to your close focus. Continue to shift back and forth several times. After you finish this exercise, spend a minute "palming."

RESEARCH SUPPORTS A BETTER WAY TO READ

In chapter 5 you were introduced to research indicating that although we can only process about seven items at a time, we can group together a number of elements, such as numbers or letters, and then treat the assemblage as one unit. For example, we usually memorize our Social Security number as three units, even though it contains nine digits, and telephone numbers as two units of three and four digits each.

The theory of Active Reading holds that we are not limited to seven *words* at a time either; we can process much larger chunks of information. Indeed it was George Miller, author of the quintessential essay on this apparent limitation of the brain to about seven items at a time, who also wrote, "It is as if we had to carry all our money around in a purse that could contain only seven coins. It doesn't matter to the purse, however, whether these coins are pennies or silver dollars."

Word-for-word reading is a purse full of pennies. In the series of Activators in the second part of this chapter, you will learn to decrease the number of pauses in your reading and increase the information taken in at each pause: to gather up silver dollars.

VISUAL READING. Some of the latest research on the functioning of the brain and the senses indicates that faster reading is possible if we receive training in it. The old way, word-for-word subvocalizing, was supported by the belief, generally held by neurophysiologists, that it was necessary for our brain to transfer incoming visual language into an auditory form before the semantic (meaning) centers could be triggered and we made sense of the input. In other words, this theory held that visual input to the brain necessarily followed a path from the visual cortex to the auditory cortex, before going to the frontal lobe for processing. Under this model, it made sense to think we were helping the process by subvocalizing each word.

However, in 1988, the prestigious journal *Nature* reported a study that gave credible support to what teachers of accelerated reading have long held: Purely visual reading is possible, and more effective than reading based on subvocalization. Using a positron emission tomographic (PET) scanner that gave a graphic color picture of what was happening in the brain, scientists at the Washington School of Medicine compared the reaction in the brain when stimulated with auditory input and visual input. In the experiments, subjects would either hear words repeated or see words flashed on a screen. The neural pathways were recorded by the PET scanner.

The results clearly showed that while auditory input followed a path from the auditory cortex (primarily in the left hemisphere) to the frontal lobe for cognitive processing, *visual* input followed a purely visual pathway, from the visual cortex directly to the frontal lobe. There was no intermediate stopover in the auditory cortex. Neural activity for the visual input was more evenly distributed in the left and right hemispheres than was found with the auditory input. Their results, the researchers said,

> favored the idea of separate brain areas involved in separate visual and auditory coding of words, each with independent access to supramodal articulatory and semantic systems. These findings fit

Thinking in words slows you down and actually decreases comprehension in much the same way as walking a tightrope too slowly makes one lose one's balance.

Lenore Fleischer

Once we have learned to read, meaning of words can somehow register without consciousness.

Anthony Marcel

well with the parallel models, but argue against the obligatory visual-to-auditory recording and serial nature of the clinical neurological model.

In short, your brain is structured to allow you to read *visually* instead of in the word-for-word way based on sound.

The lens of a camera opens and shuts at speeds up to several thousandths of a second. Even in this short amount of time the film receives enough information in the form of light waves to produce a picture.

Your brain has the same capacity. Even receiving input for a fraction of a second, your brain is able to register many bits of information.

The following Activator will give you an experience of the phenomenal ability of your brain to take in information quickly. You will be using your eyes like the lens on a camera, taking a picture at a very fast shutter speed.

■ ■ ■ ■

LEARNING ACTIVATOR #17
YOUR EYE AS A CAMERA

Read all the instructions before you begin.

Close your eyes and move your head to a fixed position. Blink almost as fast as you can, opening your eyes for about half a second to "take a picture." Do this several times, moving your head around and taking a different picture each time. Pay special attention to the vibrancy of the colors, clarity of the details, and the length of time the image remains visible after you have closed your eyes.

Clearly your brain only needs a split second to take in a lot of information. This has an obvious application to increasing the speed at which you read.

■ ■ ■ ■

Peripheral Vision
As mentioned above, our peripheral vision capabilities are another important part of why we can read faster. While only a tiny portion of our visible field is in sharp focus, things away

from that center still register in our brain, "out of the corner of the eye." Because we are not consciously aware of this information we might call it "subconscious"; that is, while we consciously read one or two words, subconsciously we are picking up much more than that.

This secondary processing is valuable when we read. As we are looking at a word or phrase, our eyes are picking up material ahead of the current point of focus and transmitting that information to the brain. Subconsciously, the brain is grasping the material and directing the eye toward its next fixation. That next focus may not necessarily be the next word. The brain may be content to skip "connecting" words like *and*, *the*, *a*, and instead move on to a word with more information. Indeed, research has shown that the eyes do not move along a line of print in a stepwise, orderly fashion; they move in a series of jumps, often skipping unimportant words, although you may subvocalize them.

The faster we go, the more information we can absorb. This is because individual words have much more meaning in context than they do alone. Like musical notes, which have "meaning" as part of a chord or a melody, words have meaning as part of an *idea*. I'm sure you have experienced this yourself many times: you begin to read or listen to someone speak a sentence, and well before the end you know the idea. When you read quickly enough to grasp whole groups of words and phrases, you are grasping ideas and images within a larger context. This gives much greater comprehension and better retention than if you processed individual words one by one.

In fact, if you read slowly and word for word, by the time you reach the end of a sentence you often forget where it started. You lose the *meaning*, so you resort to regression, you backtrack to pick up what you lost. This makes reading a slow, tedious process. Reading quickly as an active reader, however, your brain is grasping the essential content, the big picture, and the parts are simply adding to your understanding of the whole.

The following Activator will allow you to experience how your peripheral sensory system expands the base of information input to the whole brain.

▪ ▪ ▪ ▪

LEARNING ACTIVATOR #18
DISCOVERING YOUR PERIPHERAL VISION

Part I

Stare at a point on the wall or anywhere in the room, and notice all you can see around that point, both close to it and far away. As you do this, allow your stare to relax and soften, and notice how much detail you can actually see in the whole picture.

Practice expanding your peripheral vision capabilities often. Anytime you are looking at something, allow your focus to widen like going from a telephoto lens to a wide-angle lens in a camera. Go back and forth between a condensed, concentrated focus and a wider, more encompassing focus. You will actually be able to experience a shift in your brain as you do this.

Part II

Extend your arms out in front of you with the palms together. Start wiggling your fingers, while at the same time moving your hands away from each other and out to the sides. Stop moving your hands when you can no longer see your wiggling fingers at all with your peripheral vision.

How far apart were your arms when you reached the limit of your peripheral vision? Have you ever seen a page larger than that?

▪ ▪ ▪ ▪

As you are reading right now you are probably concentrating on each word just as you focused on one point in Part I of the above Activator. However, you have the ability to take in information on two levels, consciously and subconsciously. While you are fixating on the word, your eyes are actually taking in much more information than that word. *Your peripheral system is processing all the surrounding words.* This is a continuous process as you work your way from word to word along each sentence.

Think of how a motion picture works. When you sit in a theater you watch the action of the movie projected upon the screen. Actors walk, talk, run, shoot, and perform any number of scenarios, which you interpret as continuous action. What you see is actually a linked series of single frames that are being passed in front of the light of the projector at a rapid rate. The single frames become a continuous coherent whole when they appear on the screen, because your brain is taking in the *sequence* of pictures as it unfolds, not just the details of single frames.

In the same way, as you begin to move your eyes more quickly across the page utilizing the techniques of Active Reading, you will experience the printed material as a continuous whole. The images conveyed by the words will become more vibrant and visual as you glean the substance and don't get lost in the form. Using your parallel conscious and subconscious learning systems, you will be able to take in bigger gulps of information.

DOUBLE YOUR READING SPEED

You are about to begin the first in a series of Learning Activators that will enable you to make fewer pauses in reading and take in more information at each pause. It is important that you fully participate in each of these exercises. They are a carefully designed sequence, and they have a cumulative effect. Master them one at a time, repeating each one several times until you feel you have perfected it. Mastering the whole sequence will enable you to create a new neuronal network. Only then can your old patterns, regulating how often your eyes pause while you read, be replaced by this new reading skill.

Remember: Old habits cling with what seems almost like a survival instinct. It doesn't matter how much education you've had. Even people with graduate degrees and CEOs of large corporations arrive at my seminars reading word for word. Your reading habits were established many years ago and have been reinforced daily. You will be hearing from those deeply entrenched patterns often as you try to learn a new way of reading.

So don't be fooled by that inner voice telling you, *"You don't have to do these exercises. They're too simple for someone as bright as you. Skip them and get to the real stuff." This is the real stuff. These simple exercises will give you all the information and experience you need to double your reading speed.*

Don't try to go through all the Activators in one or two

marathon sessions. You will find it much more effective—and far less fatiguing—to have many shorter practice periods.

Your long-established reading habits *can* be broken using these exercises, but it will take consistent daily practice over a period of several weeks to establish new patterns.

Habits are formed by the repetition of particular acts. They are strengthened by an increase in the number of repeated acts. Habits are also weakened or broken, and contrary habits are formed by the repetition of contrary acts.

Mortimer J. Adler

An old man stood far aw

▪ ▪ ▪ ▪

LEARNING ACTIVATOR #19
EXPANDING YOUR PERIPHERAL VISION, PART I

You will find this series of exercises easier to do successfully if you focus just above the top of the letters rather than at the middle. When reading, your eyes normally progress through the middle of the line. This sets up a communication to your brain that the space between words is relevant, and consequently your eyes tend to pause on them. In effect, this creates a visual roadblock in the white space at the end of each word, which fortifies your word-by-word tendencies. When you change your focus to just above the word, you can glide along in smooth white space.

This small change in your reading habits takes practice to perfect, but will make an enormous difference in your ability to read more rapidly. Be sure to make this change as you do the following exercises, and in all your reading from now on.

In this Activator and those that follow, allow your eyes to pause just above the center letter of each line. *Without moving your eyes* from the center letter, take in the picture of the letters on either side of the center letter. Then move down to the next line and do the same thing. Simply fix your eyes just above the center letter and see, *without vocalizing*, the other letters.

Spend no longer than one second on each line. Let the letters form a picture in your mind without taking the needless step of mentally saying what they are. At first you may notice your eyes beginning to shift from letter to letter. Just keep your focus softly at the top of the center letter and it will soon become easy for you to grasp the whole line visually at one time.

You may want to use a straight edge, such as a 3 × 5 index card, or a larger card or sheet of blank paper, to move down the page, showing the line you are looking at but hiding the upcoming lines.

A	D	R
G	N	M
K	C	A
W	G	P
L	V	Q
K	A	J
S	M	P
K	V	H
P	T	R
L	H	C
G	O	B
G	D	U
F	S	T
U	F	R

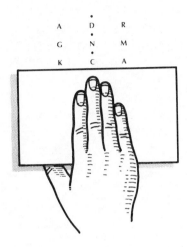

If you found yourself silently saying each letter, try this: Pause, with your eyes focused just above the center letter of each line. Then breathe through your mouth and relax until the subvocalization stops. Then move on to the next line.

■ ■ ■ ■

As you proceed through these Activators, do not be critical of your progress. You are learning an entirely new way to read and it takes time, patience, and practice.

It is not unusual to experience your eyes wanting to shift back and forth and to look at each letter. This is especially true if you are subvocalizing. However, you probably noticed an improvement in your ability to concentrate your vision on the center letter as you got to the end of the exercise. If not, repeat this exercise until you begin to maintain your focus just above the center letter and still clearly see the ones on either side without subvocalizing them.

■ ■ ■ ■

LEARNING ACTIVATOR #20
EXPANDING YOUR PERIPHERAL VISION, PART II

This exercise is performed the same as the previous one. Softly focus your eyes just above the center group of letters and then take in the picture of the letter to the left and the letter to the right. Relax and remember to keep breathing while you do this. Make it fun to discover the ability of your eyes to take in bigger gulps of information. Stay with each line until you can see all of the letters without saying them. Use a straight edge to isolate the line you are working with.

A	EFB	Z
D	KLY	P
H	YGF	C
J	IFS	F
G	UEB	D
L	SYM	Y
Y	PGS	G
J	YDM	T
P	HLF	D
H	DLJ	Q
G	YCW	R
R	ENP	H
Y	PHR	O
H	UKB	D

▪ ▪ ▪ ▪

You may notice your eyes getting a little tired. Part of what you are doing in these Activators is retraining your eyes to stay focused and not regress or jump ahead to one of the side columns. Each time the eyes start to move you are pulling them back. This can cause fatigue. To help ease the strain on your eyes, remember to practice the palming exercise. Be your own guide as you go through these Activators and take a break when you need one.

Remember: Master each exercise before you go on, but be easy on yourself. Allow this new learning to be woven into a neuronal network without strain or discomfort.

■ ■ ■ ■

LEARNING ACTIVATOR #21
EXPANDING YOUR PERIPHERAL VISION, PART III

Follow the instructions from the previous exercise. Focus just above the center letter and take in the letters from either side. Just to add a little variety, you will notice a number thrown in every once in a while.

A	D	G	J	K
Y	K	P	F	S
N	5	U	P	D
X	T	N	B	E
L	O	R	8	P
J	L	F	V	S
H	K	C	E	9
E	E	B	H	U
J	T	D	4	S
A	F	C	L	I
R	B	O	P	Z
K	X	S	O	Y
W	H	C	P	F
K	B	A	T	2

■ ■ ■ ■

Notice how much more your peripheral vision is beginning to register, and how much less you are subvocalizing the letters.

■ ■ ■ ■

LEARNING ACTIVATOR #22
EXPANDING YOUR PERIPHERAL VISION, PART IV

In this Activator, again focus on the central letter group, and take in the letters/numbers to the left and then to the right. Soften your focus and you can actually experience your peripheral vision expanding. This activator will extend your peripheral vision almost as wide as a line of type. That is about as far as you will be able to go at this stage. Think how much more information your eyes are taking in with each pause than when you read word for word!

If you have difficulty with this exercise at first, don't worry. Repeat it several times. With practice you will be able to master all the exercises. Be patient with yourself and you will achieve your goal.

S	G	GHK	T	I
I	K	LBD	P	W
J	B	SIH	O	D
H	9	FRD	R	T
S	D	HBG	S	O
J	S	TBJ	R	Z
S	T	XID	9	L
H	A	RCO	P	S
A	I	JSN	F	E
Y	5	YRT	P	J
C	S	JDF	D	I
H	U	EZD	J	F

Repeat this exercise several times, until you find it comfortable to keep your attention on the center group, yet fairly easy to take in the outermost characters.

▪ ▪ ▪ ▪

You are undoubtedly beginning to stretch your horizontal field of vision far beyond where it was when you started reading this book. The visual "bytes" you are now taking in are about the size an experienced active reader takes in while reading around 1,000 words per minute.

Now try this: Take the straight edge you have been using to cover the lines below the one you are reading (if you haven't been using one, get one now) and at a comfortable speed, pull the straight edge down through the lines in the last Activator as you focus above the central letter group. Repeat this several times, *increasing your speed each time* until you are going quite fast. Doing this will give you the feeling of how increased speed can maximize your peripheral vision and minimize your tendency to subvocalize and to make unnecessary eye movements.

Reminder: Are you taking frequent breaks to relax your eyes with the palming exercise as you do these Activators? This will reduce eyestrain and allow you to enjoy this process of expanding your capabilities much more.

The four preceding exercises were designed to increase your *horizontal* peripheral vision. In reality, as you experienced in the Activator in which I asked you to focus on a spot on a wall, your peripheral vision extends in all directions from the focal point. The next few exercises will give you the experience of those other dimensions.

■ ■ ■ ■

LEARNING ACTIVATOR #23
EXPANDING PERIPHERAL VISION MULTIDIRECTIONALLY

Keep your eyes focused just above the letter in the center and see the letters/numbers that radiate out from that center. Work with each figure until you have captured the experience of the multidirectional nature of your peripheral vision. Once you feel you have mastered it, move on to the next one. Cover up the figures you are not working on with a piece of paper.

Figure 1

F

T   W   Q

M

Figure 2

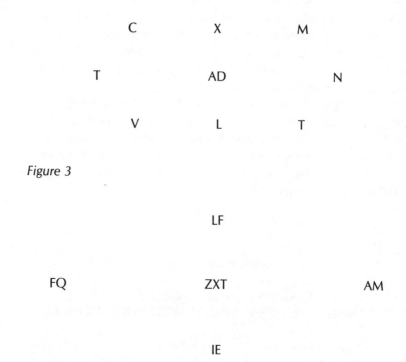

Figure 3

Now let's see how well your peripheral vision can bring you the information contained in a paragraph.

■ ■ ■ ■

LEARNING ACTIVATOR #24
APPLYING PERIPHERAL VISION TO TEXT, PART I

In this exercise, allow your eyes to follow the dots down the center of the text. Use a straight edge as a guide if this helps you. Pause briefly at each dot. Do *not* try to read the text for comprehension. Comprehension is not important now; it will come later. Right now just do the exercise and take what you get.

•
You are now

•
learning to take

•
in information with

•
only a few visual

•
pauses. You will find

•
that this exciting new

•
technique is now

•
changing the way

•
you relate to reading.

•
As you gain more

•
confidence you will

•
find yourself making

•
far fewer visual

•
pauses and learning

•
more and more from

•
the written word than

•
ever before.

Now stop for a moment and reflect upon what you have learned. What was your experience in this exercise? In the space below, write down any new discoveries you made about your ability to read more quickly.

Now write down any difficulties you experienced.

How would you advise someone to overcome those difficulties?

▪ ▪ ▪ ▪

Remember that you are in the process of rebuilding old habit patterns that held you back in the past. You are on the path to an entirely new way of using your intelligence. These exercises are simple but effective. If you do them carefully and practice each one several times, you will soon find that with little effort your reading speed has become twice as fast.

▪ ▪ ▪ ▪

LEARNING ACTIVATOR #25
APPLYING PERIPHERAL VISION TO TEXT, PART II

This Activator contains some text printed in paired lines. As before, allow your eyes to pause briefly at each dot. As best you can, continue to move down the page from dot to dot without saying any of the words. Remember, a faster reading speed with increased comprehension depends on switching from auditory to visual processing.

Once again, this exercise is *not* for comprehension. Its purposes are to develop confidence in the effectiveness of your peripheral vision to take in information and to reduce the number of eye pauses you make.

So don't expect to comprehend the content, but if you have some understanding or some visual imagery, enjoy them.

•
Many of the neuronal nets
that relate to the way the

•

way you learned to read
have their origin in the left

•

brain. The left brain likes
to stick with the familiar

•

and is resistant to change.
Also the left brain is con-

•

tent to read each word and
become immersed in the

•

details of what is being
read. Much of what you

•

will be experiencing dur-
ing the next two chapters

•

is the left brain wanting
you to forget all of this new

•

way of reading and stick
with the way you have al-

•

ways read. Your left brain
is very smart and will

•

come up with many per-
suasive reasons why you

•

should put this book down
and go back to reading

•

each word. It is true that
your left brain is a very

•

important part of your
"whole brain," but while

•

you are learning these new
skills it is a good idea to

•

let it take a vacation. Each
time your left brain criti-

•

cizes this new way of
reading, just thank it for

•

sharing and then send it
to the beach. Your left

•

brain has done a lot of
work over the years and cer-

•

tainly deserves a little rest.

■ ■ ■ ■

If you had any difficulty keeping your eyes focused during this Activator, you simply need a little more practice. If you found yourself silently pronouncing the words, don't be frustrated. With time and practice this old habit will loosen its grip and gradually slip away. You have been reading the old way for a long time. Be patient with yourself.

Slowly increase your speed as you practice the above exercises a few more times. You will find that your eyes will not wander as much as they did when you began.

Practice on Newspapers

There is a perfect place to practice taking in these larger gulps of information: newspaper columns. Practice this in three stages. In all three, always read right down the middle of the column. Do not read word for word or allow your eyes to jump to the left or right of the column.

1. If you want to start conservatively, use the one-line-at-a-time method you used to "follow the dots" in Activator #24.

2. If you feel more adventurous, or after you have

mastered the one-line-at-a-time method, take in two lines at once, as you did in Activator #25.

3. Finally, try taking in several lines in a big gulp, and notice how you can take in a vast amount of information with each pause.

Now that you have learned this technique, you should never need to read a newspaper word for word again.

When you feel comfortable with the scope and effectiveness of your peripheral vision in columnar reading, move on to the next section.

THE ACTIVE READING TWO-STEP

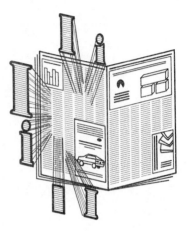

In the next exercise you will use text the normal width of a page. You will go back to reading one line at a time, but with an important difference: you will pause only twice per line. This is called the *Active Reading two-step*.

The two pauses are not made in order to allow you to read in your old way of subvocalizing each word. Rather, each pause is to allow your eyes to transfer information to your brain. Because your peripheral vision has been enlivened by the pre-ceding exercises, a lot of information will be transferred. From the start, you will begin to pick up bits of content as you go down the page, but don't stop to analyze them. As before, this exercise is only to train your eyes to reduce the number of pauses they make in reading and to pick up more information with each pause. *Comprehension at this stage is not important.* It will come later.

■ ■ ■ ■

LEARNING ACTIVATOR #26
THE ACTIVE READING TWO-STEP

Read the following text with only two eye pauses per line. Allow your eyes to *briefly* pause where the vertical line intersects with the top of the line of text. Keep your eyes relaxed and let them take in these big gulps of information.

To succeed at this exercise, you will have to discipline your eyes to resist the old pattern urging them to stop and read each word. Remind yourself that the purpose of reading is to gather information, to grasp ideas and form mental pictures, and that doing this does *not* require that you read every word. Writers paint word pictures for you; you don't need to scrutinize every brushstroke or daub of color to get the impact of the picture. You will do best if you relax and enjoy the exercise, without being critical and self-conscious. Take a moment to "palm" and relax your eyes before you begin.

As you read this portion of text you will begin to get the feeling of increased amounts of data coming to your brain. Although you are making two pauses per line you are finding that you are able to see all of the words even though the lines are getting longer. When you used to stop at each word you were wasting time and boring your brain. Imagine that you are driving cross-country and you stop at every mile marker to look around. Before long you would be tired and bored. Your brain works the same way. It wants to keep going with the minimum number of stops. As you continue reading, concentrate on making only two pauses per line. Your brain is making some new discoveries and it is up to you to practice the techniques you will learn in this book until they become a habit. In this chapter you have introduced your brain to some new reading tools that can replace the outmoded ways you originally learned to read. Your brain is pleased with the new information and is eager to read the next chapter and learn still more about Active Reading. Doubling your reading speed is not enough for your brain. It can go much, much faster. As you perfect the new techniques and begin to cut down on the number of stops your eyes make, you will notice several new things begin to happen. You will gain increased comprehension of what you read in a shorter amount of time. Your eyes will eventually be directed to pause at the places in the written piece where there is information valuable to you. Your whole brain will work like a magnet to get just what it is you need from what you are reading. Congratulations on how well you are doing. You are beginning to implement some important changes in the way you relate to the written word. You are experiencing the awakening of your peak intelligence.

▪ ▪ ▪ ▪

Go through the preceding Activator several times until you feel comfortable pausing only twice per line. Each time go a little faster, pushing for higher speeds. At first you will understand little, but the faster you go, the easier it will become to get beyond word-for-word reading and into the essence of the text. You will begin to notice additional information coming in with each reading.

In the next few days, practice the Active Reading two-step with other material as often as you can, at least for a half hour every day. If you like, you can pencil in two light lines with a ruler in the material you practice on, until you are familiar with the eye movements in the Active Reading two-step.

Another reminder: Don't worry about comprehension; just concentrate on perfecting the technique. You will begin to pick up more and more comprehension as you practice. The main purpose at first is to limit your eye pauses and minimize subvocalization and regression. As you practice, remember to pause only briefly and keep moving ahead, regardless of the temptation to slow down or go back to check out what was just said. Soon the fixations will become smoother, any jerkiness you experience as your eyes move from point to point will disappear, and it will seem that you are moving along the lines of text in one continuous flow.

After a few days of conscientious practice of the Active Reading two-step, you should be able to combine this technique with your Active Reading preparation skills to help you with all your professional and personal reading. By previewing, you will grasp the overall context and main theme of your material, so that word-for-word reading will become unnecessary. Then, using the Active Reading two-step, you will see that your speed can double (or more) while you maintain your comprehension.

TEST YOUR PROGRESS

If you have gone through this chapter systematically, participating in the exercises faithfully and practicing the Active Reading two-step for several hours, now is the time to monitor your progress. If you have skipped any of the exercises, it is worthwhile to go back and practice them in sequence.

His biographers report that while he was in the White House, Theodore Roosevelt used to read a book every day before breakfast; when he had the chance he would read as many as three books a day. Another president, John F. Kennedy, was well known for being able to read 1,200 words per minute. In his book Breakthrough Rapid Reading, *Peter Kump recalls a student whose speed went up to 5,000 words per minute. This woman was in the habit of reading a book every day, in less than an hour, while waiting for her husband to come home from work. (Can't you imagine her saying, if he got home a little early, ''I'll just be 5 minutes, dear; I only have 100 pages to go!'')*

Ascertain your current reading speed now in a two-minute timed reading just as you did in chapter 7 when you determined your base reading rate. Here is how to proceed.

1. You will need a watch with a second hand or a digital readout, and a pencil or pen. It would be helpful to have someone else time you, but you can easily do this yourself.
2. Begin reading on page 171 *using the Active Reading two-step*, and continue reading for two minutes. Read at a comfortable rate, at which you feel you are "getting" the material. Don't rush, but don't slow down and start reading every word. Continue to move ahead with the two-step method.
3. At the end of two minutes, stop reading and mark with your pencil or pen the end of the last line you read.

Do your reading now. Come back when you complete steps 1–3.

4. In the margin of the book, you will find the lines numbered in increments of five. Determine how many lines you read in two minutes. Multiply this by ten to determine the approximate number of words.
5. Divide that number by two so the final figure reflects the number of words you read in one minute. This is your rate using the Active Reading two-step. Complete the following here or in your journal.

DATE: _____

ACTIVE READING TWO-STEP RATE: _____ words per minute.

How does this number compare with the base reading rate you wrote down on page 171 or in your journal? More than likely, the new rate is at least twice as fast.

Congratulations! If you have come this far, you have made a major step forward in your reading and learned a significant new skill that can advance your quest to become a Master of the Information Age.

You now have most of the concepts and a good percentage of the skills needed to master the next stage of Active Reading, called "grokking." With just a few more hours of practice, you can tune up your brain to grasp large amounts of material quickly with comprehension that will astonish you.

If you are content with simply doubling or tripling your speed, that is a major achievement. Keep practicing and you can do even better. If you are adventurous and would like to increase your speed by 10 or even 20 times, then read on!

RESOURCES

Speedreading

Kump, Peter. *Breakthrough Rapid Reading.* (West Nyack, NY: Parker Publishing, 1979). Comprehensive book on skills and techniques for faster reading based on the Evelyn Wood Reading Dynamics courses.

Learn, Inc. *Super Reading.* (New York: Warner Books, 1988). A complete speedreading program.

Serling, Robert. *Accelereading.* (Studio City, CA: Hartford Press, 1988). A short reading course based on a speedreading technique developed by the author.

Vision

Goodrich, Janet. *Natural Vision Improvement.* (Berkeley, CA: Celestial Arts Publishing, 1986). Complete, well-illustrated guide to better vision through exercises, particularly visualization. Interesting psychological insights into the origins of vision deficiencies.

Huxley, Aldous. *The Art of Seeing.* (Berkeley, CA: Creative Arts Book Company, 1982). An explanation of the Bates method for vision improvement. Written by Huxley after the techniques saved him from blindness.

Saperstein, Rose and James Joseph. *Read Your Way to the Top with the Guide.* (Seattle, WA: Bluechip Publishers, 1987). A concise book with tips for reading faster.

CHAPTER 9

GROKKING:
GO FOR THE GOLD

This chapter is for extra credit. The giant step forward you have already taken in your reading abilities will greatly help you master your information-processing responsibilities, but if you truly want to stretch yourself, if you are interested in "super-reading," this chapter is for you.

In chapter 8 I referred to word-for-word reading as a purse filled with pennies, and contrasted it with the Active Reading two-step, a silver-dollar method of picking up larger amounts of information quickly. This chapter introduces you to "grok-king," a twenty-dollar gold piece way of reading.

Grokking is on the cutting edge of what is possible for your brain. Using this method you can actually learn to read up to ten times faster, still fully grasping the essence of the material you read. In my seminars, most students have experienced a definite shift in their reading speed, especially if they trained themselves to work at peak performance levels.

Like doubling your reading speed, grokking requires perseverance. You need to complete the exercises and practice the techniques over several weeks in order to get lasting results. Be patient and give it your best.

■   ■   ■   ■

GROKKING AND PEAK INTELLIGENCE

The term *grokking* derives from the popular science-fiction novel *Stranger in a Strange Land*, written in the 1960s by Robert Heinlein. The hero of the book, a human being born and raised on Mars, returns to Earth with some remarkable powers, including the ability to *grok*. As the hero explains, "Grok means to drink . . . to understand so thoroughly that you merge with it and it merges with you." The term is a metaphor for a profound concept and experience: the ability to understand something completely, to *get it* in an intuitive, "aha!" way.

To grok doesn't mean to have mastery over details; that is typically not the goal of a Master anyway. It means to understand the whole, the essence. It is the ability to gain a deep understanding of a concept or message in a short period of time. The process of grokking both arises from and activates the peak intelligence inherent in your whole brain.

There are several potential benefits you can gain by mastering the grokking techniques:

RETRAINING THE WAY YOU LOOK AT THE WRITTEN PAGE. Grokking helps you build a new neuronal network to keep your eyes moving forward quickly through written material. It eliminates regressions and minimizes subvocalization, far more than you were able to accomplish with the Active Reading two-step.

SHIFTING YOUR READING STYLE FROM THE VERBAL LEFT HEMISPHERE TO THE IMAGE-PRODUCING RIGHT HEMISPHERE. Proficiency in grokking helps you read much faster than your spoken language capabilities. You will depend less on your left brain and will develop a more integrated whole-brain approach to reading.

The guru, if he is gifted, reads the story as any bilingual person might. He does not translate—he understands.

Sheldon Kopp

I am not a speed reader. I am a speed understander.

Isaac Asimov

Reading is to the mind what exercise is to the body. It is wholesome and bracing for the mind to have its faculties kept on the stretch.

Augustus Hare

The words of my book nothing, the drift of it everything.

Walt Whitman

DEVELOPING MULTI-TASKING CAPABILITIES. Grokking is mental aerobics for your brain. It enlivens your intelligence and efficiency. Your brain has the capability to perform several tasks at the same time, although most of us do not do so. If you master the exercises in this chapter and begin grokking, in your reading you can be simultaneously picking up the content, forming mental images, and thinking about what you are reading—even as you move over the page at speeds up to several thousand words per minute.

DEVELOPING MORE COMPLETE COMPREHENSION. "Comprehension" doesn't mean remembering every bit of information in a piece you read, it means grasping and recalling what you need to know. When you grok, you move through written text at a speed that stimulates you. Your innate learning abilities can then truly focus on the information you have identified as your target zone.

INCREASING TRUST IN THE CAPABILITIES OF YOUR BRAIN. Grokking helps you further develop a trust in your own peak intelligence. Since this is one of the main objectives of this book, you will experience more of what your brain can accomplish, and your trust in its enormous abilities will increase, if you can successfully master the techniques.

FREEDOM TO READ AT THE SPEED OF YOUR CHOICE. By learning grokking (and all of the Active Reading skills) you can vary your speed when reading different kinds of material. The grokking techniques themselves enable you to use "freestyle" reading: that is, you can move down a page at whatever speed you determine is proper. This can change many times during your reading, depending upon such factors as the complexity of the material, your level of prior understanding of the subject, your purpose in reading the material, the level of detail required by your purpose, the writing style of the author, and so on.

When reading any book, magazine, or memo, your reading speed will usually not remain constant but will accelerate or slow down as your brain locates and absorbs the information of significance to you. This ability is one of the most useful in mastering the Information Age.

GROKKING: GRASPING THE ESSENCE

A writer begins his work with something to say (at least we must assume so, despite occasional evidence to the contrary!). Whether it is a strong feeling or conviction, or a clear idea or set of ideas, it is this essence that the writer attempts to communicate to you with words, sentences, paragraphs, chapters, examples, stories, diagrams, statistics, and so on. It is also this essence that you remember after you are finished reading.

If the writer's words are well chosen and artfully ordered, they will lead you to grasp the original idea. This is the heart of communication, one brain speaking to another.

The author begins with a mental image or concept he or she wishes to communicate. The writer's job is to embody the idea in words that have sufficient power to trigger your brain into forming a coherent retranslation of the idea in your mind. Your job as a reader is to apprehend the original conception, to "get" the essence of the writer's idea or image.

In creative writing, the original conception comes largely from the right brain, and the words tend to be imaginative, symbolic, metaphorical, and evocative rather than literal or factual. Such writing carries a sense of integrity and wholeness and is often rich in feeling or emotional intensity. Expository writing generally is more "left-brained"; its original spur may be an idea or series of ideas rather than an image or feeling.

However, even the most intellectual writing utilizes analogy, metaphor, and right-brain imaginative faculties. Similarly, in even the most creative writing the left brain is deeply in-

The thought pattern characteristic of the right brain lends itself to the formation of original ideas, insights, discoveries. We might describe it as the kind of thought prevalent in early childhood, when everything is new and everything has meaning. If you have ever walked along a beach and suddenly stopped to pick up a piece of driftwood because it looked to you like a leaping impala or a troll, you know the feeling of pleasure that comes from the sudden recognition of a form. Your Design mind [right brain] has perceived connections and has made a pattern of meaning. It takes logical, rational acts and facts of the world you know, the snippets of your experience, the bits and pieces of your language capabilities, and perceives connections, patterns, and relationships in them.

Gabriele Lusser Rico

volved, contributing order and analyzing the written text for logic, clarity, and felicity of expression. Because both hemispheres are involved in the creation of the written work, both must be involved in the reading to fully grasp the meaning.

Active Reading therefore employs methods to engage both hemispheres. The right brain, which tends to experience and perceive in terms of wholes rather than parts, gets activated in the previewing process where you look over the material quickly to get an overview of its main theme and organization. More importantly, when you learn to read faster and without your old word-for-word habit, the right brain's intuitive, image-making faculties come into play and enable you to quickly pick up the essence of the author's message.

The left brain also gets involved in the process when you set your reading goal, ask questions about the material, and analyze its organizational patterns. Then, as you read, you continue to employ left-brain strategies in the form of critical thinking skills: checking for logic and accuracy; asking more questions; committing information to memory, and so on.

To adapt an analogy from Gabriele Lusser Rico's book *Writing the Natural Way*, the author's original conception is like a melody and the words are like musical notes used to capture the melody and convey it to someone else. The melody is the essence, the real music; the notes put the essence into a communicable form. As a reader you read the notes, but only for the sake of hearing the melody. What you want is not the notes but the music.

When you read, your brain does not store every word or impression in verbatim fashion but distills the impressions into their essence. An entire chapter of a novel, for example, may leave you with a single feeling. You may end up with just a few mental images, or a series of words that verbally represent your brain's interpretation of the material.

Words, as is well known, are great foes of reality.

Joseph Conrad

Your Design mind [right brain] attends to the melody of life, whereas your Sign mind [left brain] attends to the notes that compose the melodies. And here is the key to natural writing: the melodies must come first.

Gabriele Lusser Rico

■ ■ ■ ■

LEARNING ACTIVATOR #27
REMEMBERING THE ESSENCE

Think of a nonfiction book you have read in the past five years that has made a significant impact on your life. If there is one special book that has meant the most to you, choose that one. Take out your journal or a blank piece of paper, and spend the next 10 minutes writing everything you can remember about that book. Begin writing now, and come back after about 10 minutes.

What you just wrote is the *essence* of the book, as you grasped it. If you are like most of the students who attend my seminars, you were able to write only half a page or a page. All you can remember of a book several hundred pages long, which was extremely important to you, can be expressed in a few sentences or paragraphs. In coming up with your response, your brain distilled many concepts with all their subthemes, elaborations, and examples into a few simple images or statements. You will not remember all the individual words or all the details even from the most important books you read, but the essence may remain with you for life.

■   ■   ■   ■

Researchers believe that what happens in the brain to transform the written material into the stored information of memory is this: First, the words you read are briefly stored in your short-term memory. As you saw in chapter 5, this is an ephemeral storage system that can hold new information for only a few seconds. After that the individual words are forgotten but the meaning, the essence of the phrase or sentence, is transferred to long-term memory, where it is stored in the form of semantic networks (networks of meaning). As little as a minute or so after you have read something, the actual words are forgotten, but you may be able to recall the essential meaning for 50 or 75 years.

A fascinating research project carried out at Vanderbilt University by John Bransford corroborates this essence-extracting faculty of the brain. Test subjects were read a group of sentences, and then later read a new set of sentences, often similar in meaning to the first but different in exact wording. When asked if they had heard the sentences before, the subjects generally answered that they had.

Discussing this research in *The Mind's New Science: A History of the Cognitive Revolution*, Howard Gardner notes that the subjects "seemed to listen, right through the surface wording of a sentence, to its meaning; were likely to accept a sentence that made the same point as one of the initial ones; and even com-

If you were designing the sort of information-processing system a brain is, it would be extremely unpractical to store memories permanently in their original form. You need mechanisms for transforming and recording them; for "chunking" information into categories. . . . Is your memory a phonograph record on which the information is stored in localized grooves to be replayed on demand? If so, it's a very bizarre record, for the songs are different every time they're played. Human memory . . . is more like the village storyteller; it doesn't passively store facts but weaves them into a good (coherent, plausible) story, which is recreated with each telling.

Judith Hooper
Dick Teresi

The successful Accelerated Reader is able to read larger than normal ''blocks'' or ''bites'' of the printed page with each eyestop. He has accepted, without reservation, the philosophy that the most important benefit of reading is the gaining of information, ideas, mental ''pictures'' and entertainment—not the fretting over words. He has come to the realization that words in and of themselves are for the most part insignificant.

Wade E. Cutler

bined the contents of disparate sentences if they fitted comfortably together.'' For example, if the subject heard the separate sentences, ''The ants ate the jelly'' and ''The ants were in the kitchen,'' they would respond that they had actually heard, ''The ants in the kitchen ate the jelly.''

What this suggests, Gardner says, is that we are ''actively and constructively processing information and are inferring meaning rather than recalling sheer strings of words.'' Most of this integrative and inferential processing is subconscious.

When you read as a grokker, this essence-generating faculty of your brain will serve you well. You will quickly scoop up pagefuls of words and instantly convert them into statements or images of essence.

PRINCIPLES BEHIND GROKKING

Grokking is possible because of many ways the brain operates. To begin with, you can create a more meaningful and comprehensive understanding of incoming information when the speed of input from the senses is increased.

As I have been pointing out, the mind is concerned with *meanings*, not the individual words or sequences of words that we read. We remember a picture or a concept, the meaning that the words convey to us. When we read slowly and word-for-word, we tend to lose the forest for the trees; the over-arching context that gives meaning to the words gets lost from our awareness. The faster we can go, the better we will grasp the whole, the essence that the brain is seeking to discover or create out of all the isolated pieces of information input.

A related principle is that the brain can take in, process, and store large amounts of information in meaningful patterns quickly and thoroughly. You have already experienced this when you did Learning Activator #17, Using Your Eyes as a Camera. In just the half-second your eyes were open, you were able to take in a great deal of information about color, shape, relationship of size and distance, and so on. Your brain also gave meaning to that information; it converted the raw sensory input into images that were meaningful in the context of your experience.

This same natural ability can serve you well in reading.

Even when your eyes move quickly over a page, a great deal of information is picked up and instantaneously given meaning.

You have also experienced another important faculty of the brain, the large amount of information brought in by your peripheral sensory systems. We tend to think we only "get" what we focus on, but from your practice of columnar reading and the Active Reading two-step, you know that your eyes perceive a large amount of information surrounding your central focus. If you have pushed yourself to higher speeds with these techniques, you have discovered that your brain is able to pick up more, not less, as you increase your speed.

Grokking is also possible because *your brain inherently seeks closure*, or a sense of completion. It has the wonderful ability to create the whole picture from a few of the parts. It can complete the puzzle even with pieces missing. It creates completeness even from what might seem like incomplete input. For example, complete the following aphorisms.

You reap what you _____.
Out of _____ out of mi___.
A _____ saved is a _____ ea___.
If at _____ you don't suc___, ___ ___ again.

■ ■ ■ ■

LEARNING ACTIVATOR #28
PERCEIVING A WHOLE PICTURE
FROM INCOMPLETE PARTS

On the next page are three incomplete pictures. Turn to the next page, look at each picture for a second or less. If you don't identify them all the first time, try again until your brain has sufficient information to put the picture together.

What was your experience? Did your brain have sufficient information to translate a few lines into Abraham Lincoln, a cat, and the Statue of Liberty? Did it get one more easily than another?

■ ■ ■ ■

Differences in speed of recognition may be due to discrepancies in previously stored information. As you know, the brain

analyzes all incoming data, comparing and relating it to previous impressions, searching for similarities, patterns, and ways to recognize and interpret the fresh input. How it interprets the incoming data is determined by what is already there.

This relationship of recognition to previous impressions plays a part in grokking. You will find yourself able to fly through familiar material quickly, but material with unfamiliar subject matter or terminology—such as an article in a medical journal for those of us not in the medical profession—will require a slower pace.

Here is another example of your brain's ability to create the whole from parts. Read the following paragraph. Don't study each word, but let your eyes move effortlessly through it. Trust your brain to fill in the missing letters. If you experiment reading the paragraph at different speeds you will notice that the faster you go, the easier it is for the brain to translate.

At the same tm yr brn is rcvng the infrmtn frm yr eys it i als recvg infrmtn frm yr othr sns. Ths r the sns of hrng, flng, sml and tst. We r cncntrtng on th vsl sns bcs it is mst applcbl to rdng. We cd also stdy our othr snss in ordr to mre fly undrstnd hw thy apply to lrng. All of th snss wrk clctvly to gthr the infrmtn whch yr brn uses to trnslt the otsid wrld into its own lnge.

Without much effort your brain filled in the missing vowels. The meaning received by your brain was as complete as if you had read the complete text.

Another principle behind grokking is that your brain seeks and recognizes patterns. When any new information comes in through the senses it is immediately compared to what the brain "thinks" is similar information previously recorded. The brain seems to ask, "Is anything familiar here? Is there a pattern to this?" If you see the information ABABABABA and you are asked what the next letter probably is, you would say B.

In translating the following number sequences, your brain will look for the pattern to make sense of the sequence.

    123456789 . . .
    8642097531 . . .
    1,4,9,16,25,36,49,64 . . .

The brain also searches for spatial patterns. Circle the triangle shapes that are alike in the following illustration.

The pattern-seeking faculty of the brain helps you to grok the material you are reading. As your brain gets tuned into the patterns of the author—writing style, organizational structure, belief system, metaphors, and so on—you become increasingly able to anticipate and understand the text. As this happens, you naturally begin to move more quickly through the pages with greater comprehension.

These principles, then, make grokking possible:

- Your brain can take in a large amount of information in a short period of time.
- Your brain works like a magnet, quickly locating information it needs.
- Your brain can generate a whole picture from only a few parts.

Grokking thus is a natural, effective, and powerful means of gaining knowledge quickly.

GROKKING WARM-UP

Before we engage in any physical activity, most of us do some kind of warm-up. Reading is also a physical activity, involving the eyes, the page-turning hands, and the neural pathways of the brain, and so it is equally important to warm up.

Many of the reading drills you learn in these chapters will be discarded as you move up to higher levels of competence. *The grokking warm-up is something I encourage you to do once every day.* It will enliven your brain, get your eyes accustomed to moving at a fast pace, and prepare you to take in large amounts of information quickly.

For the grokking warm-up and the remainder of the drills in this chapter, you will be using the book you chose in chapter 7 to practice previewing skills.

Breaking in the Book

Before you begin, grokking requires that you "break in" your book so that you can turn the pages extremely quickly. Here's how to do it: Hold the book in both hands and open it up to the middle. Then *gently* bend the two sides of the book back until they touch each other.

Now work your way toward the front, repeating the procedure 10 or so pages at a time. Then work your way from the middle toward the back, again bending the book back every 10 pages. The purpose of this is to make the pages lie flat so they will not curl up and interfere with your page turning and your view of the page.

Next, put the book flat on a table, opened to the middle.

Work your way backward and forward 10 pages at a time, pressing on each section close to the binding. Now open the book to the middle page and see if it stays open and fairly flat. If it does, the book is ready. If the pages close up, then you have been too cautious and you need to repeat the procedure a little more aggressively.

If the book is a paperback, you can get even more aggressive: knead it as if you are preparing dough. Twisting it back and forth may seem brutal, but it is the best way to prepare the book for reading.

The U-Stroke

Place your book in a slightly tilted position and turn on some appropriate music. You will use your full hand to make the warm-up stroke, which forms the letter U on the two open pages. Pull your hand down the left-hand page with your palm facing the book, flip your wrist at the bottom, and then run your hand back up the right-hand page with the palm facing you, fingers pointing downward.

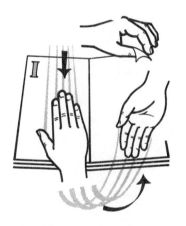

If you are right-handed, make the U-stroke with your right hand. If you are left-handed you will probably feel more comfortable using your left hand, but you should experiment with both; many left-handed people prefer using their right hand to make the strokes.

Page Turning

Probably you never thought you would need a lesson in page turning! But now that you are beginning to increase the speed with which you move from page to page, you will need a new way to turn pages to keep up with your speed.

If you are using your right hand for the U-stroke, you will turn pages with your left hand; if you are using your left hand you will turn with your right hand. Your turning hand is always ahead of your stroking hand, ready to turn the page when the stroke is completed. You will need to get your turning hand to the upper corner of the right-hand page quickly.

Use your chosen book and try it: down, up, turn the page! Down, up, turn! This may seem awkward at first, but after a little practice it will come more easily.

Important: At all times during this drill, keep the focus of your eyes just beyond your fingertips. This will be above your fingers as you move down the left-hand page and below your fingers as you move up the right-hand page. Perform the complete movement on each page, even if it is blank. This exercise is for warm-up and *has nothing to do with comprehension.* Do not worry that your hand is going up the right-hand page.

∎ ∎ ∎ ∎

LEARNING ACTIVATOR #29
GROKKING WARM-UP

Practice the warm-up stroke for five minutes, spending about *one second* on each page. Remember to keep your eyes moving with your hand. Your goal is to develop a smooth rhythmic stroke and easy page turning. Do not be concerned with your speed.

So that comprehension will not be an issue, *turn your book upside-down.* You will still be moving from left to right as you would ordinarily read, but you will be warming up both upside-down and backwards.

Warm up with your book upside-down for a full five minutes. When you finish, do the palming exercise, and for extra release and relaxation, laugh. Don't be shy: make it a good, hearty laugh that you can actually feel.

Do the grokking warm-up now.

You are beginning to establish a new pattern that can only become firmly established by repetition. Do the warm-up drill in five-minute intervals until you have mastered:

- a smooth stroke down and up the pages
- a smooth page-turning technique, and
- your eyes easily keeping up with the forward progress of your fingers.

Remember to take breaks to relax your eyes. As you begin to feel more comfortable with the warm-up drill you can increase the speed to one-half second per page. Continue to hold the book upside-down. You will keep the book in that inverted position until the end of this chapter. Continue to work with the warm-up drill until you feel comfortable with it.

∎ ∎ ∎ ∎

LEVELS OF GROKKING

The following exercises in different levels of grokking will give you practice in progressively faster rates of reading. The purpose of these exercises is to train your eyes and brain to work together at a speed that eliminates regressive reading and minimizes subvocalization. The next Learning Activator will give you a quick preview and insight into where you are headed.

■ ■ ■ ■

LEARNING ACTIVATOR #30
A PREVIEW OF COMING ATTRACTIONS

In a moment you are going to look at an object or a large picture in your immediate surroundings. Your purpose is to get as complete a mental image as you can in a short period of time. As you do this, pay special attention to the movement of your eyes. Notice how your eyes flow over the object, pausing only briefly at certain fixation points. Observe that these pauses are automatic, apparently outside your conscious control.

Look at the picture or object for no longer than five seconds. Again, notice particularly the path that your eyes are taking when processing the object. Do this now.

Did you notice that your eyes mapped their own route? They did not move in a linear left-to-right manner, or systematically cover every inch; rather, they bounced around and, like a magnet, brought you just the right information to form a coherent image of the whole. Try this a few more times until you have a deep understanding of how your eyes move to achieve the purpose of generating a complete mental picture. This is where you begin to move beyond the Active Reading two-step and into the world of grokking.

■ ■ ■ ■

With practice, you will eventually read in much the same way you just experienced your eyes working in their natural search for the whole picture. Your eyes will bounce down the page at varying rates and with a varying number of pauses per line, and you will comprehend completely.

Now let's move on to the four levels of grokking. You will be practicing levels 1–4 and gaining proficiency in them before you move on to freestyle reading, the highest stage of Active Reading.

In the grokking warm-up you used your full hand, but in practicing the levels of grokking you will use *only your index finger*. This gives your eyes a more concentrated focal point from which your peripheral vision can pick up information.

There are other reasons for using the finger as a guide in the beginning stages of learning this new skill. First, it produces an energizing effect on the brain. The area of the cerebral cortex responsible for the fingers is comparatively large. Research indicates that utilizing finger movement activates that part of your brain and also has an overall enlivening effect on other parts of the brain.

Dr. Per Roland of the Department of Clinical Neurophysiology at the Karolinska Hospital in Stockholm carried out a series of experiments in which subjects were told that they would receive a stimulus in their fingertips. The anticipation of that stimulus caused increased cerebral blood flow in the part of the brain related to the hands and fingers, and also in the nearby association areas and the anterior and mid part of the frontal cortex where our highest intellectual functions take place.

Second, and more importantly, using your finger as a guide for your eyes serves as a forward-moving target that trains the eyes to keep moving ahead, never regressing. As you begin these exercises you will still be working to some extent from your old habits that prompt you to pause at each word and reread words and whole passages. Using your finger will have the effect of creating a new neural pattern to support your mastery of Active Reading.

Once you have firmly established this new skill, you may continue to use your finger as a guide, or you can let your eyes move freely on their own, whichever is more comfortable and effective for you. This is a major difference between the system of Active Reading and most "speed reading" courses. Many other systems advocate use of a reading guide at all times, but I have found it preferable to use finger movements only in the skill-learning phase of my technique. After that you are on your own to pursue continually higher speeds of reading in the way you find most effective.

Work your way slowly through the four levels, making sure you have gained proficiency at each stage before moving on. You will no doubt want to move ahead as quickly as possible, and I encourage that. However, these exercises have a cumulative effect; one level builds on another. Give yourself time to completely master each level before moving on to the next. Don't try to complete all the levels in one session. Let your progress evolve at its natural speed.

GROKKING DRILLS

Now you will begin a series of drills to master the four levels of grokking. You will find specific instructions for each level as you get to it. Here are some general instructions for *all* the levels.

1. Repeat the exercises in each level at least five times. Increase the speed each time you practice until you are able to achieve your fastest possible speed in that level.
2. Use your finger as a guide to do the exercises. As you increase the speed, make certain you maintain your eye concentration just above where your finger is, and that you keep a steady, smooth rhythm.
3. "Love your eyes" (using the palming technique) and laugh after each practice session. Shake your hands and arms to loosen them if they are getting tired.
4. Take a break whenever you feel tired. One of the benefits of learning Active Reading from a book instead of a class is that you can progress at your own speed. On your break, take a walk or do some light exercise.
5. Any time you have been away from the drills for more than one hour, start your next session with the grokking warm-up for two to three minutes.
6. When you feel you have reached your highest potential in the mastery of each level, do it one more time for two minutes. This time mark where you begin and end and figure out your speed. Go as fast as you can while still maintaining proper rhythm and eye contact.

7. When you have completed the two-minute timed exercise, count the number of words on one average line of text and multiply it by the number of lines on the page. This will give you the average number of words per page. Multiply that number by the number of pages you completed and *divide by two* (since you read for two minutes). That is the number of words per minute you covered. Enter that number in the spaces provided below or in your journal.

8. All the exercises are to be done with your book upside-down.

Grokking Level One

Using your finger as a guide, run your finger under each line from margin to margin, turning the pages in the same manner as you did in the warm-up drill. Your eyes should be focused *at the top* of the lines you are underlining with your finger. Maintain a steady rhythm and start with a slow pace that feels comfortable. Make certain you run your finger under *each line*.

Remember to turn your book upside-down. Begin your first three-minute practice of level one now, and then proceed following the general instructions above.

My practice speed on level one timed reading was _____ words per minute (wpm).

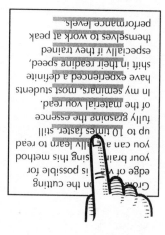

Grokking Level Two

This level is similar to level one. You still run your finger under every line, but now you underline *only the middle half of each line.* Your peripheral vision will pick up the rest of the line. Keep your eyes following just above your finger at the top of the line you are underlining. Maintain a steady rhythm. With your book upside-down, begin your first practice of level two at a rate comfortable to you, and practice for three minutes.

When you have practiced at level two at least five times, ascertain your speed using the same formula you used in the level one timed practice.

My practice speed on level two timed reading was _____ wpm.

Grokking Level Three

The finger/eye movement in level three is called the "tight snake." In this level you sweep your finger back and forth down the page, underlining only the middle half of the line as in level two. This time, however, you underline *only every third line*. Each time you come to the end of your finger stroke you drop down three lines and underline in the opposite direction to the beginning of the next stroke. Continue that pattern to the end of the page.

As always, keep your eyes following just above your finger at the top of the line you are underlining. Begin your first practice of level three at a comfortable rate, and practice for three minutes. Be sure to repeat this exercise at least five times before testing your speed.

My practice speed on level three timed reading was _____ wpm.

■   ■   ■   ■

LEARNING ACTIVATOR #31
BE YOUR OWN TEACHER

You have now achieved proficiency in grokking levels 1–3. Take a moment to be your own teacher. Write down any difficulties you may be experiencing.

If someone told you they were having these difficulties, what would you advise they do to overcome them? Write down your responses.

Write down the positive experiences you have had in learning the skills of levels 1–3.

Grokking is on the cutting edge of what is possible for your brain. Using this method you can actually learn to read up to 10 times faster, still fully grasping the essence of the material you read. In my seminars, most students have experienced a definite shift in their reading speed, especially if they trained themselves to work at peak performance levels.

▪ ▪ ▪ ▪

Grokking Level Four

In this level you make one smooth sweep down the page in the shape of a curved Z. Remember to keep your eyes following just above your finger, and to maintain a steady rhythm.

My practice speed on level four timed reading was _____ wpm.

At this point, congratulate yourself for taking the time to practice the foregoing drills.

USING GROKKING IN YOUR READING

Now that you have mastered the four levels of grokking, it is time to put your skills to use and actually *read* using the levels of grokking. The transition from practice to reading is an exciting moment.

The remaining exercises and Learning Activators in this chapter will continue training your eyes to move forward at a steady and increasingly rapid rate. As you continue to refine your eye movements, your old self-limiting reading habits—subvocalization, word-for-word reading, and regression—will eventually fall away, to be replaced by new habits that will open the door to your peak intelligence. By the end of the chapter, you can become an expert grokker, ready to tackle all your reading with confidence.

■ ■ ■ ■

LEARNING ACTIVATOR #32
VISUAL PROCESSING

This Activator is designed to give you the experience of how a word or phrase is translated into the "language of the brain" using primarily the visual pathways. It will help to facilitate your transition from auditory to visual processing of reading material. As you recall, the great value of visual processing is that visually we can easily pick up 2,000 words per minute or more, compared with a maximum of about 250 words per minute aurally.

Below you will find a set of single words and then a set of phrases. For both, *look* at the words and *without saying them* either out loud or subvocally, allow the translation of that word into the language of the brain to take place. Look at each word until the subvocalization ends and your whole brain experiences the translation. Allow your whole brain to get the picture the word represents.

book	table
frog	candle
football	carrot
neuron	flower
brain	love

Now do the same with each of the following phrases. Let the picture develop without saying the words. If you start to subvocalize, continue to look at the phrase as a whole until your internal voices quiet down.

glass of lemonade

sunset on the ocean

colonial southern home

bowl of ice cream

presidential debate

ink spilled on a carpet

snow covering a tree

communication between neurons

children on a swing

Many people can actually experience a brain shift between saying the word and picturing it. Saying the word is a cumbersome and

Levels of Grokking

Here is a quick review of the levels of grokking. You will be using all these levels in the next exercise, and progressing from one to the next without stopping, so it is important that you know them without having to break your stride to look them up.

Grokking is on the cutting edge of what is possible for your brain. Using this method you can actually learn to read up to 10 times faster, still fully grasping the essence of the material you read. In my seminars, most students have experienced a definite shift in their reading speed, especially if they trained themselves to work at peak performance levels.

Grokking is on the cutting edge of what is possible for your brain. Using this method you can actually learn to read up to 10 times faster, still fully grasping the essence of the material you read. In my seminars, most students have experienced a definite shift in their reading speed, especially if they trained themselves to work at peak performance levels.

unnecessary intermediate step between seeing it and incorporating its essence in a neuronal network. The exercises are designed to help eliminate that intermediate step whenever possible.

■ ■ ■ ■

As you practice the exercises and Activators in the balance of this chapter, you may find yourself successfully grokking right from the start, or it may take a little longer. In my seminars, I usually teach this progression of exercises over a five-day period, and many students require that much time to really "get" it. It is well worth the wait. Once you experience grokking and understand from that experience that you can achieve complete comprehension at a much faster rate, you will have passed a threshold into an entirely new way to read.

Before you begin the exercises, take a few minutes to reflect that your success with grokking will depend on your *beliefs*. Confidence in yourself and your capabilities will help you succeed; resistance to breaking old boundaries and learning something new will hold you back. Review chapter 2 and refresh your understanding of the power of beliefs. I also suggest that you review the affirmation you made in Activator #4, and the goal you set in Activator #15. Renew your determination to master Active Reading. If you want to revise your goal to a higher level, now is the time to do that.

Finally, take a moment to once again visualize yourself as a Master of the Information Age, having mastered grokking and all aspects of Active Reading. Sit quietly and relax with some music or deep breathing, close your eyes, and imagine yourself in a future situation, taking in information at the rate of your goal and utilizing it in your life.

For the next series of exercises you will need your chosen book. Before beginning, review your purpose for reading the book, and look at the questions you want answered and your anticipated answers.

A word of caution: I have noticed that beginning grokkers sometimes sacrifice the smooth flow of grokking to an analysis of how well they are doing and what they are getting out of it. This self-conscious watchfulness is a normal occurrence during the initial stages of learning any new skill, when the process is a deliberate, laborious series of steps. If you find yourself watching and self-commenting, don't encourage it; don't analyze yourself right out of the experience!

There is no way to master these skills other than to practice them repeatedly until they become second nature. To fully implement this new way of reading, you will have to restructure your old habits on the level of the neuronal networks of the brain. The only way to do this is to repeat the new skills again and again.

Now you are ready to begin. Start your reading session—now and always—by "loving your eyes" and turning on some suitable music. Then warm up with the grokking warm-up (the U-stroke) for three to five minutes. This will sharpen up your eye-hand coordination and get you ready for grokking.

Remember to *keep your book upside-down for the warm-up.* Go as fast as you want, but maintain a smooth rhythm and focus your eyes at the tip of your fingertips. Breathe deeply, and enjoy the warm-up.

Grokking Exercise #1

Keep your book upside-down during this entire exercise. You will begin with grokking level one at a very slow speed, making sure that your eyes are following along the top of the line above your finger and that you are maintaining a smooth, steady rhythm. You will then gradually increase the speed in level one until you have reached the maximum speed at which you can still maintain proper eye focus and a smooth rhythm. Spend at least one minute on level one.

Once you have reached your maximum speed in level one, you will switch to level two *at a very slow pace.* You will then gradually increase the speed in level two for at least one minute, and once you have reached maximum speed you will begin level three at a very slow pace. Continue with the sequence. Build up to top speed in level three, drop down to a slow pace to begin level four, build up to maximum speed in level four. Then, *drop back down to level one at a slow speed.* The flow from level to level is continuous with no stopping at any time.

Knowledge is a treasure, but practice is the key to it.

Thomas Fuller

They can do all because they think they can.

Virgil

Grokking is on the cutting edge of what is possible for your brain. Using this method you can actually learn to read up to 10 times faster, still fully grasping the essence of the material you read. In my seminars, most students have experienced a definite shift in their reading speed, especially if they trained themselves to work at peak performance levels.

Grokking is on the cutting edge of what is possible for your brain. Using this method you can actually learn to read up to 10 times faster, still fully grasping the essence of the material you read. In my seminars, most students have experienced a definite shift in their reading speed, especially if they trained themselves to work at peak performance levels.

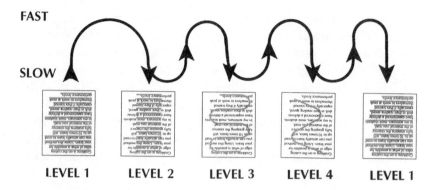

FAST

SLOW

LEVEL 1   LEVEL 2   LEVEL 3   LEVEL 4   LEVEL 1

Don't be afraid to speed ahead at the top of the level, but make certain you slow down and move at a snail's pace at the beginning of each level. With your book *upside-down*, begin this exercise now.

Before you move on, repeat this exercise at least two or three times to get the feeling of moving from level to level and making the transitions smoothly.

Grokking Exercise #2

This exercise is the same as the previous one except for one exciting difference. Like before, you will repeat the linked progression from levels one through four and then back to level one, increasing and decreasing the speed at each level change. But this time, when you have gone through levels one through four and are back at level one going slowly, *turn your book right side up* and continue for a minute or so on level one at a slow speed. This is where you will suddenly discover the quantum leaps you have been making in your reading evolution.

It is important to go through the entire exercise *before* you turn the book right side up. When you turn the book right side up at level one, keep going at a *slow but steady* pace, allowing your speed to increase only if you feel comfortable with the comprehension you are getting. Choose a pace that propels you past the speed where you are subvocalizing each word. Don't fall into your old word-for-word reading pattern in an effort to comprehend. Just keep going; you will be amazed at what happens.

Begin this exercise now, spending about one minute going through each level. The complete exercise should take you about four to five minutes.

You probably had the experience of the words beginning to jump off the page, even though you were moving at a much faster rate than when you started reading this book. Many of the words that jumped out at you were keywords, which gave you a clear idea of the essence of what you were reading even though you were not picking up all the words. Whatever your experience was (even if it was very good!), the results will only get better from now on.

Remember that you are still in the early stages of your journey to a higher level of performance. Think of it as similar to the first time you tried to drive, stand up on skis, or hit a tennis ball. You can't expect to be as competent now as you will be after years of practice and skill development. You will need to practice in order to achieve your maximum potential.

Some Common Problems

Here are some hints for dealing with difficulties you might be experiencing at this point.

EXCESSIVE SUBVOCALIZATION. No doubt you are still finding that you have a tendency to pronounce some of the words silently, but at this point it is normal. In order to minimize the distracting effect of this habit, try humming or whistling a tune while you are reading. You will find that it is impossible to do this and subvocalize at the same time.

TENDENCY TO REGRESS. If your eyes are still jumping backward to pick up parts of the sentence you have already underlined, you need to concentrate more on following your fingers. The purpose of using your fingers as a guide at this point is to retrain your eyes to continually move ahead.

As we have discussed, people often regress in their reading because of a lack of confidence that they have taken in sufficient information from what they just read. As you continue to use the Active Reading techniques, you will gain more confidence in the ability of your whole brain to get what it needs at a fast rate. The upcoming mind-mapping exercises will help you see that you *did* get the essence of what you read.

When you fully realize that you actually have a higher rate of comprehension when utilizing these new skills, you will find that the tendency to regress fades away along with your other limiting reading habits.

TIRED EYES. You are putting your eyes to a more demanding task when you read in this new way. They have the ability to rise to the occasion, but it will take a while for them to adjust to the demands of the new speeds. Take frequent breaks while you are in the learning stage, and continue to "love your eyes."

MUSCLE FATIGUE. If your arms and shoulders get tired, simply shake them by your side to loosen the muscles.

FRUSTRATION. In any new skill you develop, frustration can be attached to the learning process. At this point, you know enough about the enormous capabilities of your brain to understand that you are quite capable of mastering most every challenge. But you can't be perfect right from the start! You are still in the beginning stage; don't judge yourself in terms of the final results you wish to achieve. Whether your frustrations are large or small, continue to practice the Activators and you will surely progress. The investment of time you make now will pay off with hundreds or thousands of hours saved later on.

Grokking Exercise #3
Part I: Pick a chapter in your book that interests you. Let your eyes flow down the table of contents and choose whichever chapter jumps out at you for the next exercise.

When you have chosen your chapter, utilize your Active Reading preparation skills. Take a moment to determine your purpose for reading it. What might be in it of interest or benefit to you? What questions do you have? What do you think the essence might be? How does this chapter relate to your overall reason for reading the book?

What can you tell about the chapter from its title? Read

the first and last paragraphs to see what clues you might gain there and to gain some familiarity with the author's style. Close your eyes for a moment and imagine that these simple procedures are alerting specific neuronal pathways in your brain that there is some action coming their way.

Part II: The purpose of this exercise is to refine your proficiency in level one with the book right side up. You are not yet going primarily for comprehension, although you will probably achieve some anyway.

You will be reading for approximately two minutes. Chances are that you will not finish the chapter in that time. Maintain a pace that allows you to move comfortably through the lines. Begin now with your chosen chapter in level one and read for about two minutes. Repeat this exercise several times, increasing your speed a little each time.

During this exercise, there were undoubtedly some moments when you were moving quickly along the page taking in whole gulps of information. Were there also times when you felt that you could take in even more but you were being held back by the slowness of your fingers? Whatever happened, continue to trust in yourself and to let go of the need to read every word as your experience gives you increasing confidence in your ability to take in information at a faster rate.

GROKKING AND SUPERCONDUCTIVITY

A recent advance in technology parallels grokking in a fascinating way. It is the development of superconductors that are revolutionizing the way electrical energy is transported. In the old way, we used copper wire to conduct electricity. Copper is a good conductor but is limited because the copper atoms produce a slight resistance to the flow of electricity, which decreases the electrical power delivered at the end of the line.

The new way is called superconductivity. New specially developed substances derived from silicon allow the electrical current to run smoothly without encountering resistance. Thus there is virtually no loss of energy along the way and what is delivered at the end of the line is nearly the same as what went in.

Grokking is a method of eliminating *reading* resistances, such as regression and word-for-word reading, which slow down our absorption of new information. The result is a smooth, uninterrupted flow of information from the page to your whole brain.

As you move through the remainder of this chapter, monitor your energy and attentiveness and remember to take breaks when you need them. It is important to move along at a pace that is comfortable for you. Don't rush from exercise to exercise. Repeat each Activator or exercise until you feel you have gained all possible benefit from it and are truly ready to move on.

■　■　■　■

LEARNING ACTIVATOR #33
PUTTING IT ALL TOGETHER

This exercise will ask you to combine mind mapping with your new Active Reading and grokking skills. You will need a four-color pen or a set of colored pens or pencils. Have them ready so you can complete the mind map when you finish reading.

Use a chapter in your chosen book. Make certain to establish your purpose and questions before you begin. Using level one, read for about two minutes at a pace comfortable for you. Stay relaxed, and let the information flow out to you as you read. Remember to move your eyes along on top of the line above your fingers, and keep a steady forward rhythm.

When you have completed this short reading exercise, you will create a mind map to reflect how much information you took in. Take a moment to "love your eyes" after you have finished reading, and while your palms are still over your eyes, allow the mental image of what you read to fully develop in your whole brain.

Start with the central theme of the chapter, which may be a short version of the chapter title. Place that in the center of your mind map. Fill in the branches radiating out from the center with the main subsidiary ideas. As related concepts begin to emerge, fill in the appropriate limbs and twigs. (If a diagram or a drawing would express your understanding better than words, don't hesitate to use it.)

You don't have to fill in all the empty lines if you don't have anything more you need to say. On the other hand, you may need to add more lines to complete the mind map in order to do justice to what you got out of the reading.

Begin the reading now. Read in level one for about two minutes at a speed that is comfortable and easy, and then fill in the mind map.

Some books are to be tasted, others to be swallowed, and a few to be chewed and digested.

Sir Francis Bacon

■ ■ ■ ■

FREESTYLE READING: HOW FAST CAN YOU REALLY READ?

As an accomplished active reader and master of the Active Reading two-step and the four levels of grokking, you have the choice of how fast to read. This ability puts you in a select group comprising less than 10 percent of all readers.

Numerous studies by reading researchers have shown that people tend to read everything at the same rate, regardless of the nature of the material or their reason for reading it. Our reading speed is a deep-rooted habit, both behavioral and bioelectrical, deeply patterned in the cells of our brain. That is why it requires some effort to establish a new flexibility.

At first, learning to vary your reading speed requires conscious awareness and effort on your part. But once you have confidence and mastery of your new Active Reading skills, you will adjust your reading speed to the specifics of your situation just as you adjust your driving speed to road conditions.

Factors in Deciding Reading Speed
You will decide how fast to read based on three main factors.

YOUR PURPOSE IN READING. Your information target zone will determine what level of information you are seeking. Are you studying for an examination? Preparing to write a report or give a talk? Do you need to know many fine points and details, or do you just want to get the general idea? Perhaps you are simply skimming through the material, looking for a name or a date. Each of these purposes will result in a different reading speed.

Naturally, you can use a faster pace when your purpose is to preview a book, chapter, article, or memo to glean the main points. Speed is appropriate when you are not required to do much analytical thinking or interpreting. You can move your eyes swiftly and lightly over the page when you are merely trying to locate facts or data, to find a small piece of information—a name, a date, a number—in a large mass of words. This is common sense, and some good readers do it automatically. Even if your purpose is more complicated, such as sorting through a large amount of material in order to discover the parts that are important to you, you will be able to go quickly until you come to the places you want to study more thoroughly.

You will want to use a slower pace for in-depth study. To fully understand a concept or a procedure, to follow the logic of a complex argument or master the deeper aspects of any subject, you will read more slowly and carefully, pausing more often to think about what you are reading. You will want to apply the principles of critical thinking you learned in chapter 6. You will be weighing the material against what you already know, modifying your storehouse of knowledge with this new incoming information. This type of reading simply takes more time and care.

YOUR PRIOR KNOWLEDGE OF THE SUBJECT MATTER. Studies have proved that when you are familiar with the subject matter, you can read it more quickly. Your brain has a background of terminology and concepts ready to apply to the incoming data. The new material falls into an existent "department" in your brain. This sets you free to move quickly until you encounter material that your brain distinguishes as new; you can then slow down to pick it up.

If the subject matter is unfamiliar, you will have to pause repeatedly to think about new ideas or look up new words.

Previewing will help you go through the material much more quickly, but even previewing can't guarantee that you will always be able to read at super speed. However, my experience in teaching Active Reading to thousands of people is that even when you have to read more slowly, you will still go twice as fast as you did when you began this book.

THE DIFFICULTY OF THE SUBJECT MATTER. As we have discussed before, you should be able to go through easy material more quickly than material with new terminology and complex ideas. However, the fact is that *most people read even very simple material at the same speed as difficult material*. They read the sports page, or the pages of popular magazines written with a junior high school vocabulary, at the same speed at which they would approach writing that expresses truly abstract and complex ideas. They read word for word. They backtrack to pick up words they think they may have missed, even though the subject matter surely doesn't warrant getting every detail.

To eliminate this habit of reading all material at the same speed, use your previewing session to examine the complexity of language and density of content and *consciously* determine which level of grokking you will use to read it. Aim high: you can always cut back a level if you're not getting the material.

A STUDY PLAN TO MASTER GROKKING

You are now ready to progress through the levels of grokking, mastering them one by one at your own speed. You know everything you need to know: what the four levels of grokking are, how to relax your eyes, how to use your finger to guide you smoothly and steadily forward, and so on. You just need to practice.

Use the book you have been using so far, or choose a new one. Here is a suggested study plan for mastering the levels of grokking.

1. Begin by previewing each chapter (or significant section) before you read it.
2. Read several chapters at grokking level one, one chapter at a time, until you feel you have mastered that level.

3. After each reading session, mind-map the section you have just read to test and solidify your comprehension.

4. Proceed to level two and follow steps 1–3. Continue in the same way until you have mastered all four levels. If you run out of chapters in your chosen book, pick a new one and continue with that.

Whenever and whatever you read from now on, apply the following principles.

- Be actively involved.
- Don't read it if it doesn't serve you.
- Define your purpose.
- Formulate your questions.
- Anticipate the answers.
- Stay relaxed.
- Push your reading speed to the maximum appropriate for the material.
- Make mind maps for consolidation and review.
- Reduce eye stops.
- Eliminate distractions.
- Trust your brain to get what you need.

GRADUATION

You have now learned the skills necessary to master the highest levels of Active Reading and grokking. You have begun to loosen the grip of your long-standing reading habits. The way to completely accomplish the transition to a new style of reading is to practice and use these techniques in your daily reading. The more you practice and apply these skills, the more you will increase your mastery of the flow of information.

■ ■ ■ ■

CHAPTER 10

OVERCOME RESEARCH ANXIETY

As if the amount of information that comes to you every day isn't enough, there are times when you find it necessary to seek out more. You may need to write a memorandum, paper, or report on a particular subject for which you lack specific information, or you may be faced with a business problem and need to make a decision based on the most current and comprehensive data. Perhaps you just enjoy learning and want to expand your knowledge base about a particular topic.

This chapter is intended to provide you with an overview of the vast information landscape. You will learn how to use indexes, directories, databases, and libraries, as well as each of the major subdivisions of the information landscape: books, periodicals, newspapers, specialized reference sources, government documents, organizations, and other sources. In the final section of the chapter is a practical Learning Activator designed to give you experience applying the techniques you will learn to the act of finding information.

■ ■ ■ ■

What is research but a blind date with knowledge.

William Henry

Knowledge is of two kinds. We know a subject ourselves or we know where to find information upon it.

Samuel Johnson

You ask what is the use of classification, arrangement, systemization? I answer you: order and simplification are the first steps toward the mastery of a subject—the actual enemy is the unknown.

Thomas Mann

It is easy to feel overwhelmed by the quantity of information around us. Failing to find the right information when you need it can cause serious problems: low grades or job performance ratings, lost opportunities, and poor decisions based on inadequate information.

Our information abilities are limited in many cases by a malady related to information anxiety: research anxiety. The major cause of this ailment is unfamiliarity with the variety of simple tools available to aid in locating information. While technology and high-speed communication have complicated the information picture, they also have made it possible to find information more easily and quickly.

One way to think about information is to compare it to a broad landscape in front of you. Within this horizon there are many types of information subdivisions, such as databases, periodicals, books, news sources (magazines and newspapers), specialized reference sources, government documents, microfilm, original sources, people, and organizations. Each subdivision offers unique advantages, and so a Master must learn to choose selectively when researching.

We will examine each subdivision in detail, but first it is useful to discuss two major tools that can be used in any research project: indexes and directories. These are the equivalent of telescopes in that both can give you a focused picture of where to look when you are trying to find information. In a sense, the telescope allows you to define your information target zone, just as previewing allows you to do so when you are reading print materials.

TWO KEYS: INDEXES AND DIRECTORIES

Each type of information subdivision has literally hundreds of indexes and directories that you can use to find the information you are seeking. Most indexes and directories are available in either electronic or in printed form. There are even indexes to indexes and directories to directories to help you find the appropriate key for your information needs.

The word *index* is a derivative from the Latin meaning "one who points out." There are countless indexes covering every conceivable information category. An index may be bibliographic, meaning that it simply lists the title, author, name, and date of publication. Other indexes contain more detail ranging from abstracts to the full text of the information source. The index to indexes is *Chicorel Index to Abstracts and Indexing Services*, which lists nearly all of the thousands of indexes available. The following are a few examples of the variety of indexes available in database or printed form.

Applied Science and Technology Index
Art Index
Biography Index
Business Index
Chemical Abstracts
Education Index
Hospital Literature Index
Humanities Index
Music Index
Philosopher's Index
Population Index
Resources in Education Index
Woman's Studies Abstracts

Not having the information you need when *you need it leaves you wanting. Not knowing where to look for that information leaves you powerless. In a society where information is king, none of us can afford that.*

Lois Horowitz

With so much information now online, it is exceptionally easy to simply dive in and drown.

Alfred Glossbrenner

Directories are the second tool to help you find information on a specific subject. Like indexes, they point you to a specific part of the information landscape. Directories exist for almost every subject, from *Directory of Information Sources on Arthritis* to the *Directory of Zoos* and every imaginable category in between. A complete list of directories can be found in the *Directories in Print* (formerly *Directory of Directories*) in book or database form. Over 10,000 directories are listed in this two-volume source. Here are a few examples:

Where to Find Business Information
Directory of Foreign Manufacturers in the United States
International Directory of Importers
Directory of Conventions
Directory for Grants for Graduate Study Abroad
International Directory of Little Magazines and Small Presses

You will become more familiar with the multitude of indexing and directory systems as you continue. For now, it is enough to understand that regardless of the information you are seeking, there is a tool to help you find it.

DATABASES: ENTRYWAYS TO THE INFORMATION LANDSCAPE

The vast and ever-growing field of computers and online databases is to the Information Age what the internal combustion engine was to the Industrial Age. Each technological advance, when coupled with the ingenuity of the human mind, has generated far-reaching consequences for every area of life.

A database is simply a collection of knowledge related to a specific topic. It is the computer equivalent of a neuronal network system in your brain that stores knowledge about a particular subject. For instance, from the experience you have had in your life either traveling or hearing about vacations, you have stored in your brain a "database" of information relating to that topic. If another person were to ask you for advice on where to go for a vacation, you could easily locate a piece of information from all that you remember. This is analogous to the storage and retrieval of information in a database. Suppose that a database producer consulted all of the information available on vacation spots. He then sorted out this information according to categories: location, names of hotels, type of food served, shopping availability, quality of handicrafts, and so on. Then, a user simply has to request that the database spill out the names of every hotel in a certain area; or only those hotels that serve seafood, that offer British imported goods, and so on. (There is a database called *Travel Scan* that performs just these functions.)

Computer-accessed databases began to appear in the early 1960s, primarily in mainframe computers that stored government and scientific information. The space required to bank data was greatly reduced with the advent of disc storage. The proliferation of affordable personal computers further increased the capabilities of databases and vastly enlarged the potential market.

Today there are approximately 5,000 databases available. Of these, 50 percent are business and industry related; 20 percent refer to science and technology; 7 percent social science and humanities; 12 percent multidisciplinary; 6 percent government and law; and 5 percent general public interest.

Databases are generally of two kinds: reference or source. A reference database, similar to an index, can include bibliographic citations to printed information, or it can be a directory that points you to nonprint information such as organizations or individuals. Reference databases can also include abstracts of the original material. Source databases contain the complete original sources and can be numeric (statistics or surveys, for example), full text (newspapers, magazines, or court opinions, for example) or a combination of numeric and text.

The number and diversity of databases is steadily growing. It is estimated that an average of three new ones come to market each day, and the pace of new databases will surely increase. In the future we will likely see a commercial application of a marriage between the field of cybernetics (artificial intelligence) and online database systems. At that point, finding the answer could be as easy as turning on your computer and saying, ''Hello, Hal, I've got a question.''

Imagine being able to sit at your desk and with a few keystrokes on your computer—being able to access almost any information you need from a storehouse of the world's published knowledge.

DIALOG brochure

Failing to take advantage of the easy access to information through computers is like failing to take advantage of fire or electricity. Most libraries have some kind of computer-accessed database systems. Most businesses have computer systems that are or could be hooked up to an online database system. These connections can allow you to interface with virtually any sector of the information landscape and connect you with the answers to your research needs.

To simplify matters, there are directories that list all of the available databases with a brief description of the scope of the particular service: *Directory of Online Databases*, *North American Online Directory*, and *Knowledge Industry Publication Directory*. Each of these directories can be found in either database or book form.

Databases, like any product, vary according to quality and quantity of information. There are differences in the length of the coverage period, frequency of update, information covered, type and complexity of search required to locate the information (vocabulary of keywords used), search aids, user support systems, and, of course, cost.

There are also databanks that include several individual databases in a single package. Instead of needing to have an online connection with each database, a user can subscribe to one databank and thus have access to a multiplicity of databases. The largest databank system is DIALOG, containing over 350 databases in the area of general knowledge and business. The next-largest is BRS with about 200 individual databases, followed by Orbit with about 120. Most of the individual databases mentioned in this chapter are available through one or more of these databank systems. Sometimes the databanks overlap databases; at other times they have exclusive rights to specific databases.

There is yet another larger box called gateway systems. These give you access to all of the previously mentioned databanks plus others. Examples of this type of packaged service are Easynet and the Regional Bell Operating Companies (RBOCs) being developed by the local telephone companies. The gateway systems aim not only to consolidate but also to simplify the searching procedure. The gateway approach is new and its viability will depend upon its acceptance in the home computer market.

In the balance of this chapter you will become familiar with many databases that serve specific information subdivisions.

Connecting Into a Database

Now that you have an idea of what is out there, let's take a brief look at how you can get to it. The connection to an online database or databank is made directly from your computer, through a piece of equipment called a modem that allows you to use a standard telephone to access an intermediary telecommunications link between you and the database or databank service. This link can be provided by your telephone carrier or a network like Telenet or Tymnet that allows the user to access facilities across the country without the cost of a long-distance call.

The major online databanks price their service based on the amount of "connect time" you have to their system, and this cost varies with the particular database you are using within their system. For example, the 1990 DIALOG price sheet indicates costs from $0.25 to $5.00 per minute, depending on which database you connect with. In addition to the databank charges, you must also pay for the telephone or network connection to the databank and a charge for the gateway provider if you are using one. Since you pay for the time you are online, it is worth knowing in advance what you are looking for.

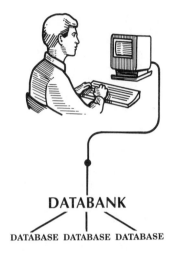

DATABANK

DATABASE DATABASE DATABASE

CD-ROM Technology

The picture of the information landscape would be incomplete without mentioning CD-ROM (CD-Read Only Memory) database technology, often used in libraries and large institutions. Because of the expense of online database connections, database producers and databanks have recently begun utilizing compact disc technology to store the information. A single compact disc can store the equivalent of 1,500 floppy discs, 275,000 pages of paper, or 100 million words.

Once the information from a particular database is transferred to one or more compact discs, they are then leased and the user can enjoy unlimited access to the information without incurring telephone connect time charges. Some of the databases mentioned in this chapter are also available in CD-ROM form. *CD-ROMS in Print*, an annually updated directory of existing CD-ROM packages, is available online or in print.

A library is the delivery room for the birth of ideas, a place where history comes to life.

Norman Cousins

LIBRARIES: YOUR WAREHOUSE CENTRAL

Many people fail to consider the capabilities and scope of library systems. For some, just mentioning the word "library" conjures up images of tedious research projects or a place to take naps. However, libraries not only serve as a repository for the information generated by humankind up to the present; the modern library, with its database and print media access, has become a service organization with the capability to search, retrieve, analyze, format, and deliver information inexpensively. A Master of the Information Age therefore needs to take advantage of all that libraries have to offer.

There are many different types of libraries:

PUBLIC. Public libraries vary in size depending on the region they cover. The breadth of a public library collection is obviously related to its size. The reference departments of nearly all libraries have access to interlibrary loans or other interlibrary computer connections to locate a source of information beyond their own collections.

ACADEMIC LIBRARIES. University and college libraries specialize in research and reference categories and are designed to cover the informational needs of scholars, researchers, students, and professionals. Specialized libraries within the university/college setting cover specific informational areas like law, medicine, education, business, engineering, or nursing. Community college libraries may also carry in-depth lists of trade and vocational information on areas such as cosmetology, real estate, carpentry, and bookkeeping.

HISTORICAL SOCIETY LIBRARIES. In these, you can locate specific and thorough historical information about local events and people.

MUSEUM LIBRARIES. The scope of a museum library is determined by the specific focus of the museum.

RESEARCH CENTER LIBRARIES. These are typically part of in-house research centers, research groups, companies, foundations, and associations like herbariums and botanical or zoological societies.

CORPORATE LIBRARIES. Many corporations, large or small, have libraries focused on their particular business interests. These libraries can include access to numerous online databases as well as printed resource material. Unfortunately, many are not open to the public.

NEWSPAPER LIBRARIES. These libraries are an excellent source of both local and general information. Many are not open to the public but they may collaborate with local public libraries. The following standard reference guides can help you find a library that fits your needs.

There are times when I think that the ideal library is composed solely of reference books. They are like understanding friends —always ready to change the subject when you have had enough of this or that.

J. Donald Adams

1. *American Library Directory.* An alphabetical listing by state of approximately 30,000 libraries in the United States and Canada. It includes all of the types of libraries listed above.
2. *Research Library Directory.* An alphabetical directory of research libraries by subject.
3. *Directory of Historical Societies and Agencies.* A geographical list of historical and genealogical societies in the United States and Canada.
4. *Subject Collections.* Arranged by subject, this directory identifies subject collections in 7,000 public, academic, museum, and historical society libraries in the United States.
5. *Writer's Resource Guide.* A research guide for writers that covers 30 subject categories and lists some 1,600 foundations, associations, government agencies, companies, museums, historical societies, and special collections that carry information in one or more of those categories.

BEYOND THE ENTRYWAYS: EXPLORING THE INFORMATION LANDSCAPE

I have divided the information landscape into six basic sub-divisions.

1. Periodicals: popular, scholarly, trade, and professional magazines, and newsletters
2. Newsmedia sources: newspapers and television
3. Books: popular, scholarly, trade, and professional
4. Specialized reference sources: encyclopedias, almanacs, dictionaries, and other secondary sources
5. Data on people and organizations, including companies, marketing research, and statistics
6. Government documents

All of these categories are available both in libraries and in online databases; some are available in CD-ROM. In addition, many libraries have an information specialist who can assist you in your research. This service may be complimentary or for a fee.

In a typical research project, regardless of size, your information target zone lies somewhere within one or more of the basic categories mentioned. Let's look at each of these subdivisions individually and discuss the possible "telescopes" each offers that you can use to pinpoint the specific information you need.

Periodicals
This category includes magazine and newsletter articles.

MAGAZINE ARTICLES. Since magazines are such a familiar part of the information landscape, many people tend to overlook them as a research source. Because of their diversity and currentness, however, they can be an invaluable place to begin looking for your information target zone. Once you begin to explore the variety of information found in magazine format, you will find that there are magazines in nearly every field.

Besides the more popular, widely distributed magazines you are undoubtedly familiar with, there are thousands of specialized magazines you have probably never seen. A good place to begin your search through popular magazines is the *Reader's Guide to Periodical Literature*, a bibliographic index of nearly 200 magazines, arranged by subject. This guide contains basic information about millions of articles: title, date of publication, and volume and page numbers. By checking this guide you can locate articles of interest to your research. You must then proceed to find the complete article in the magazine, on microfilm, or via database. The *Reader's Guide* is available in printed form in every library and also on database on the Wilsonline system. Additional bibliographic magazine databases available are *Ulrich's International Periodicals Directory* and *Magazine Index*.

Numerous other magazine indexes cover additional popular magazine sources, and they should be consulted if your information target zone falls within a category of magazines not covered by *Reader's Guide*. Examples include:

Access. Covers approximately 150 popular magazines that are not covered by *Reader's Guide*, including *Bicycling*, *Family Circle*, *Modern Maturity*, *TV Guide*, and over 75 city and regional magazines.

Alternative Press Index. As the name suggests, this index covers many magazines that contain "alternative" and at times more left-wing oriented articles.

Index on How-To-Do-It Information. Covers 55 magazines that deal with arts and crafts.

Index to Periodical Articles about Blacks. Indexes articles in numerous magazines.

You may find that you need to look for your information target zone in magazines that treat subjects in more depth or in a more scholarly fashion than popular magazines, such as trade publications, professional publications, and other scholarly journals. You can locate indexes and abstracts that cover these more scholarly periodicals in indexes like *Abstracts and Indexes in the Sciences and Technologies* or *Periodical Indexes in the Social Sciences and Humanities*.

The database industry is extremely thorough in its coverage of business. Examples of databases that cover business-related magazine articles are:

Trade and Industry Index. Covers over 1,500 national and local publications plus the *Wall Street Journal* and the business section of the *New York Times*. The index is bibliographic and many of the entries include abstracts.

Trade and Industry ASAP. Includes the full text of articles from leading trade journals plus major magazines like *Forbes, Fortune*, and *Women's Wear Daily*.

Management Contents. Abstracts and bibliographic citations to over 750 business journals, newsletters, proceedings, books, research reports, and self-study courses.

The Computer Database. Abstracts and bibliographic citations to computer-related publications.

Harvard Business Review Online. Full text of articles from the prestigious business review of the same name.

Abstracts of recent articles are available in Newsearch, a database that contains information from over 2,000 publications, including some newspapers. Full text coverage on a current basis is available through the database *Magazines ASAP*.

You can also consult the index to indexes, *Chicorel Index to Abstracting and Indexing Services*, as well as the database *Directory of Online Periodicals*, to find out where particular magazines are indexed.

NEWSLETTERS. There are thousands of newsletters in circulation that provide information on current developments in almost every area of human endeavor. Newsletters are an excellent source of current and condensed information in a particular field, usually offering much more than broad-based popular magazines. Most newsletters are available by paid subscription, although some are free of charge.

For a complete listing of newsletters consult *Newsletters In Print* covering 10,000 newsletters by commercial and noncommercial publishers; *Oxbridge Directory of Newsletters* listing 17,500 newsletters arranged according to 180 different subjects; or the *Newsletter on Newsletters* listing the publication of all new newsletters. Another valuable source is *News Net*, an online database containing the full text of 320 newsletters in 35 categories.

Following is a brief list of some newsletters, which can give you an idea of what is available.

AARP News Bulletin. News, legislation, and feature coverage of items of interest to older people.

American Right to Read Newsletter. Articles on domestic censorship issues.

Brain-Mind Bulletin. Information on neuroscience discoveries that affect human potential.

Business Opportunities Digest. Business, money-making, and investment opportunities worldwide.

Celebrations. Update articles for parents, teachers, and students who see a cooperative future in humanistic education.

Cottage Connections. Updates, legislation, and other information on home businesses.

DiscList. Information about audio compact disc new releases.

Human Intelligence International Newsletter. Research and application of ideas on human intelligence.

INFOCUS. Products, services, and people in the information resources management industry.

Kiplinger Washington Letter. Briefings for business people on trends and developments affecting their jobs, finances, and business.

Netline. Insider reports on online computer networks, discussing vendors, products, strategies, solutions, and available networks.

Psychic Research Newsletter. Articles on research and discoveries in psychic phenomena.

Think and Grow Rich Newsletter. Articles based on the principles of Napoleon Hill's classic best-seller of the same name.

Newsmedia Sources

Newspaper articles are an excellent source of information for many subjects. Not only are they are extremely current, but as with radio and television, they are on the front of the information delivery chain.

You can find an index to your local newspaper at the publisher's headquarters, and usually through your library. If you need national newspaper information, the following will be helpful:

National Newspaper Index. Covers five major newspapers and is updated weekly.

NewsBank. A microfilm collection of articles from national newspapers arranged by subject.

Business Dateline. Collects business news.

For international news, consult *Facts on File* or a number of other indexes, such as *McCarthy Press Clippings*, *Info South* (South America), *Asian Recorder*, and *Current Digest of the Soviet Press*, all of which digest and index newspaper articles from various international locations.

There are also many online database newspaper sources available, such as *The New York Times Online Database*, *The Information Bank* (which abstracts the *New York Times* and approximately 90 other newspapers), and Nexis or Vu-Text, which provide the full text of various newspapers. All of the information provided by the news wires AP and UPI are available online.

There are also many "clipping service" companies available. For a fee, such companies scout a variety of newspaper and magazine sources for you, looking for any mention of whatever topic you hire them to check. You can also find historical clipping files that provide articles digested from old newspaper articles. Examples of this type of service, which arranges the news by subject from past decades, are *Great Contemporary Issues Series*, *Education USA*, *Crime and Justice*, and *Labor Management*.

Many television news broadcasts are similarly available either in transcript, microfilm, or online database. Examples of this resource are *CBS News Television Broadcasts* (1975–present), *Face the Nation*, *MacNeil-Lehrer Report*, and *Summary of World Broadcasts*.

Books

Nearly 50,000 books are published each year in the United States. The authoritative index for books is the annual *Books in Print*, available in print or database form. This listing of all books in print is compiled in three ways: by author, subject, and title. Other book indexes include *Paperback Books in Print*, *Books Out of Print*, and *Forthcoming Books*.

There are also specialized *Books in Print* editions, such as *Business and Economics Books and Serials in Print*, *Children's Books in Print*, *El-Hi Books in Print*, *Medical Books and Serials in Print*, *Religious Books in Print*, *Scientific and Technical Books and Serials in Print*, and *Law Books in Print*.

You can also locate book reviews of books that interest you through the *Book Review Index* database. *Soundview Executive Book Summaries* publishes a service that abstracts business-related books for subscribers.

Specialized Reference Sources

This category includes almanacs, encyclopedias, dictionaries, and other general reference sources. In many minor research projects, your search can begin and end in this category.

ENCYCLOPEDIAS. Most people immediately think of the standards like *World Book*, *Encyclopedia Britannica*, or *Colliers*, but the modern world of encyclopedias extends far beyond such familiar collections. The increase in specialized knowledge has created a need for encyclopedic collections with specific areas of focus. Today you can find encyclopedias covering specialized areas, such as *Afro American Encyclopedia*, *Encyclopedia for Education*, *Jewish Encyclopedia*, *New Catholic Encyclopedia*, *Encyclo-*

263

pedia for World Art, and *New International Wildlife Encyclopedia*, to list a few. Some encyclopedias are also available in online database.

ALMANACS. Almanacs are perhaps the best information resources for the money. Almanacs are available covering a variety of topics; some, like *The World Almanac and Book of Facts* and *The Information Please Almanac*, can give you a lot of data for under $10. Examples of subject-oriented almanacs are *Almanac of American Politics*, *Dow Jones-Irwin Business and Investment Almanac*, *The Irish-American Almanac*, *The Herbalist Almanac*, and *Places Rated Almanac*.

YEARBOOKS. Yearbooks chronicle the events of a year by subject category. Besides the annual yearbook published by encyclopedia publishers, there are numerous yearbooks that cover more specialized subjects. Examples of those are: *The Statesman's Yearbook*, *Yearbook of Astronomy*, *Yearbook of Drug Therapy*, *International Film and TV Yearbook*, *Yearbook of International Communist Affairs*, *The Annual Register of World Events*, and so forth. You can locate other yearbooks by name in the title volume of *Books in Print*.

DICTIONARIES. Dictionaries extend in scope beyond the normal usage of checking the spelling or meaning of a word. They come in many sizes, are illustrated to varying degrees, and cover all areas of word usage. Some of the larger dictionaries, such as *Webster's Third New International Dictionary*, contain many reference sections that include encyclopedic detail. The *Oxford English Dictionary* is unparalleled for checking the etymological history of a word.

Examples of dictionaries and word and phrase books include: *Dictionary of Afro-American Slang*, *Dictionary of American Slang*, *Dictionary of Symbols*, *Language of the Underworld*, *The Language of the Mosshorn* (cowboy slang), *Soldier and Sailor Words and Phrases*, mathematics dictionaries (over 30 in print), law dictionaries (over 70 in print), and medical dictionaries (over 100 in print).

Quotations. Some of the many books available to help you locate quotations are: *Dictionary of Quotations, Familiar Quotations, Home Book of Quotations, Harvest of a Quiet Eye: A Selection of Scientific Quotes,* and *Manual of Forensic Quotations.* The subject index of *Books in Print* can lead you to many more.

Data on People and Organizations

Finding information about people is equally easy today. Biographical information is readily available through the numerous *Who's Who* publications, ranging from *Who's Who in America* to *Who's Who in California. Marquis Who's Who* is a database source for *Who's Who in America* and *Who's Who in Science and Technology.* There are numerous other biographical sources that don't begin with "Who's Who." The *Biography Master Index,* in book or database form, can lead you to indexes available for various fields, such as *Author Biographies Master Index* and *Journalist Biographies Master Index.*

Additional sources in printed and database form that deal with biographical information include:

Standard and Poor's Register. Personal and professional data on more than 80,000 executives in private and public companies.

Forensic Services Directory. Biographical data and capabilities and requirements of expert witnesses in many areas of expertise.

Geneva Series I, II, and III. Biographies of over 27,000 consultants by industry and service.

You can also obtain information about organizations through The *Thomas Register,* in print or database form, which contains profiles of U.S. companies and their products. If you want to know what companies make a product you need, this is the place to start.

The *Encyclopedia of Associations* contains information about associations covering specific areas of interest.

Financial information about public companies can be procured through Disclosure II, a database that lists all financial reports required to be filed with the Securities & Exchange Commission (SEC) by public companies. *Moody's Corporate Profiles*, in print or database form, consists of descriptive profiles and financial overviews of 3,600 publicly held companies. The information comes from SEC filings, news releases, newspaper and trade journal articles, and other public agencies. *Standard and Poor's Corporate Descriptions* database, corresponding to the printed volumes known as *Standard and Poor's Corporation Records*, is another source for information on public companies.

For privately held companies, Dun & Bradstreet credit reports are available on Dunsprint. Other Dun & Bradstreet databases provide company information as well. The Company Intelligence database lists newsmedia references to various companies.

INFORMATION ON SALES AND MARKETING DECISIONS. Sometimes your information needs call for additional data in order to make a sales- or marketing-related decision. The many database and printed sources in this area include:

Find/SVP. This database, corresponding to the *Findex Directory of Market Research*, references market research reports, studies, and surveys worldwide.

Investext. Provides the full text of research reports prepared by the world's leading investment banking firms.

Company Intelligence. Combines general company information with news media references to each company.

Trademarkscan. Lists all active and pending trademarks.

Corptech. Contains a directory of over 30,000 high-tech companies.

Commercial Business Daily. Summarizes most of the procurements planned by the U.S. government.

Datasearch Inc. National service based in Sacramento, California, that includes searching and reporting information from public records such as secured transactions, motor vehicle registration, and corporate data.

STATISTICAL INFORMATION. There are many statistics directories in print, indexed in *American Statistics Index, Index to International Statistics and Statistical Reference Index*. The Consumer Price Index and the Producer Price Index are also available in print and database form.

Government Documents

The U.S. government is the largest publisher in the world. There are publications for taxpayers, consumers, government employees, children, parents, teachers—just about everyone. Publications originate from every department of the federal government and include pamphlets, brochures, directories, guidebooks, posters, handbooks, manuals, dictionaries, glossaries, magazines, and—luckily—abstracts and indexes.

Several indexes will help you find what you want in this sea of information. The first is the *Monthly Catalog* issued by the Superintendent of Documents. This monthly listing is then indexed in the *Cumulative Index to the Monthly Catalog, Sales Publication Reference Guide* (serves as a *Books in Print* for government publications), and is also available in online databases entitled *GPO Publications Reference File* and *Index to Government Periodicals*.

Congressional Information Service (CIS) indexes, abstracts, and makes available the reports, documents, speeches, and other working papers of the U.S. House and Senate. *Federal Register Abstracts* provides basically the same service for the executive branch. The *National Technical Information Service* (NTIS) is a valuable source of government documents on nearly every technical subject and is online on several systems.

You can get free index sources from the Government Printing Office, such as *The Consumer's Guide to Federal Publications*, a quarterly publication listing the diverse booklets generated by public agencies; *Government Periodicals and Subscription Lists*, which notes all available subscriptions; *The New Catalog*, which represents the most popular books issued by federal agencies; and *New Books*, a bimonthly listing of new publications.

Many embassies have information officers to whom you can write for specific information about that country and its products, services, and business opportunities.

INFORMATION BROKERS

The Information Age has elevated information to the status of a commodity, as sought-after as gold. It is therefore not surprising that the importance and proliferation of this commodity has given rise to the information broker, a breed of hunter-gatherer of the Information Age who, for a fee, helps individuals or businesses find specific information.

Since 80 percent of the time required for information compilation is finding it and 20 percent processing it into a form that best suits the researcher's purpose, having someone else find it is one potential solution to the time constraints imposed by the Information Age.

Information brokerage services are available through private companies and many libraries. Many of the services specialize in areas like business, law, medicine, news, social science, agriculture, bibliographic data, government, and general information. The information brokerage business has proliferated alongside the increase in database sources. Much of the work of an information-gathering specialist is done on computer via the numerous online databases.

There are many large international companies in the information brokering business, such as *Find/SVP* and *Info on Demand*, but numerous small independent companies and individuals also perform this service. The *Directory of Fee-Based Information Services*, by Helen Burwell, provides a list of information brokers, but the field is expanding so rapidly that this directory is always outdated by the time of its publication.

APPLYING WHAT YOU HAVE LEARNED

Now that you are familiar with the diversity of sources on the information landscape, you are ready to apply all you have learned in this book to the process of information research. As you read through this section, you will recognize that finding information utilizes the same basic techniques and concepts you have already learned in managing information. That is, the basic steps in any research project, regardless of its scope, are:

1. Define your information target zone; know your purpose.

2. Ascertain which subdivisions of the information land-scape are the most likely prospects for your target zone.
3. Pick the telescopes (indexes, directories, etc.) that are most likely to serve your information target zone.
4. Apply the Active Reading preparation skills you have learned in this book.
5. Locate the potential sources (magazine articles, books, treatises, etc.) and apply the Active Reading techniques to find the specific information target zone in an efficient period of time.
6. Utilize the information to fulfill your purpose.

In the balance of this chapter we will explore each of these steps and then apply them to a research project.

Define Your Information Target Zone

No matter how small or large, how detailed or general your research project is, *you must start by knowing where you want to end up*. Any information-gathering task begins with defining your target. Research is no exception.

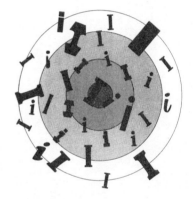

To get an experience of defining your information target zone, take a moment to identify a real or hypothetical research project you would like to complete. If you have something in your life now that you need to research, select that. This might be a need for additional data to support a decision, solve a problem, complete a paper, memorandum, or other project, or it might simply be something you would like to know more about for your own enjoyment. If you don't have a research project readily available, then go into the "act-as-if mode" and choose a topic that you might be interested in.

■ ■ ■ ■

LEARNING ACTIVATOR #34
IDENTIFY YOUR PURPOSE IN A RESEARCH PROJECT

The goal of this research project is:

■ ■ ■ ■

This general description of the information target zone is about as far as most people go in preparing to research a topic. However, a Master of the Information Age strives to refine this general goal, for two reasons. First, the more specific you can be with your goal, the more quickly and inexpensively you can locate what you need. Whether you are searching in a library, using an online database, or hiring an information broker, you hit your target more expeditiously if you can define it with precision. Time is already valuable to you, but it becomes even more precious when you are paying for online time or information broker fees.

Secondly, as you develop your information target zone according to Active Reading principles, you will generate keywords that will be valuable in the research process. Keywords, as the name suggests, are the words that most strongly relate to your information target zone. For example, if you wanted to find out about business opportunities in the food industry in the Soviet Union, the keywords would be "business opportunities," "restaurants," and "Russia." These keywords become the arrows you shoot out aiming for a bull's-eye in the middle of your target zone. One or all of these would help you find the answer in a database or library.

■ ■ ■ ■

LEARNING ACTIVATOR #35
MAKING YOUR PURPOSE STATEMENT MORE SPECIFIC

Using the research goal you generated above, answer the following questions as specifically as you can. Use the mind map form below to indicate your answers.

1. What is your specific purpose in this project? What do you want to accomplish? What do you want to know? How will the information help you?
2. What questions do you have about the project?
3. What keywords embody the essence of your information target zone?
4. What level of detail is needed to satisfy your purpose? (Can your purpose be satisfied with a quick answer from a single

source, or does it necessitate an in-depth analysis from
several different subdivisions?)

The answers to these questions influence your subsequent choice
of subdivisions of the information landscape. For example, you may
be able to locate your information target zone and satisfy your purpose
in an almanac. If your purpose was to find out what is the highest
point in the United States, you could quickly find the answer (the top
of Mount McKinley: 20,320 feet) in the *Information Please Almanac*.
Or you may need to consult several different sources for a more in-
depth analysis of a topic in order to satisfy your purpose.

■ ■ ■ ■

You have just completed the first stage for locating information. Follow this procedure every time you begin a research
project and you will more easily achieve your desired results.
Remember, however, that your mind map should not be static.
It can change as your understanding grows. As you proceed
with a research project, continue to update your mind map.

Also, be flexible. One of the most important assets for successful research is a willingness to modify your approach as
need dictates. Don't get attached to the keywords with which
you began. If your initial approach doesn't produce results,
change it. Continue to expand your keyword base as new ideas
develop, and add them to your mind map.

Ascertain Prospective Subdivisions

One of my students once referred to research as a process of "cornering, like a cat-and-mouse game." The analogy is apt: You need to take a large target and narrow it down until you have a small target. The concept of your mind working like a magnet becomes especially relevant here. You need to find an answer, not spin your wheels considering nonanswers. Rather than eliminating one by one the solutions that don't work, you will be more direct and efficient when you can quickly locate the sources that will work.

The next step, therefore, is to identify the subdivisions within the vast information landscape that are likely prospects for your information target zone: periodicals, newsletters, newsmedia sources, books, specialized reference sources, government documents, people, and organizations.

Sometimes it will be easy to ascertain the most likely sources. Other times, the answer is not clear until you are well into the project. The important thing is to *get started*. Many people get stuck in a trap at this stage, becoming mentally frozen by the "paralysis of analysis." This occurs when you spend too much time pondering the sources and too little time getting on with the project.

Therefore, engage your whole brain and let it operate at its full potential. Allow your peak intelligence to jump into operation. Quickly go through the subdivision list and begin with the one that "jumps out" at you. This is your mind working like a magnet. Trust your brain, and this trust will be justified by the results you achieve.

Pick the Telescopes

If you wanted to look at the bottom of the Grand Canyon you wouldn't use a telescope located on top of the Empire State Building. Each one of the information subdivisions has its own telescopes that allow you to peer more closely into it in search of your target.

In the previous sections of this chapter you learned about many of those telescopes. Now that you have picked a subdivision, the next step is to choose the most likely scope to use for the search, be it an index, directory, or other reference source in print or database form.

Apply Your Skills

Many of the techniques you have learned in this book become especially useful in this step. Whether you are using a printed source or a database, you should always begin the research project in a relaxed state that will prepare your whole brain to close in quickly on the information target zone. A session of alpha breathing can bring your brain into the receptive state quickly. Similarly, in order to clarify your goal, visualize yourself engaged in each step of the research process from beginning to end. With your eyes closed, quickly visualize making the mind map, beginning the search, locating potential sources, finding your information target zone, mind-mapping the results, utilizing the information, and achieving your purpose.

As you begin to explore the subject headings in the print reference source or enter commands for an online database search, you should also utilize one of the levels of grokking to move through the potential sources until something jumps out at you. This means you have "Hit your Information Target" (HIT). Use your intuition as well; it can often tell you whether you are on target. You may get a feeling, a sound, or a visual cue, but you will know you have found the right source.

Moving at this faster rate may be a step outside of your comfort zone. You may still hear your left brain warning that you will miss something if you go too fast. Until you begin to trust the accuracy of the new methods, try an experiment to verify the results. Compare your conclusions with what you come up with employing your former method of analyzing the list word by word. I am sure you will find your new method is more effective than the old.

Locate the Material and Apply Active Reading

Let's assume that you have hit your information target zone. You may have located, for example, a magazine article that satisfies your purpose. This is the stage where your brain needs to digest the information quickly and produce ideas, solutions, and alternatives that can help you achieve your initial research goal.

If you have the choice of reading an abstract or the entire article (depending on the level of detail required by your particular information needs), remember that at your present level

273

of proficiency in Active Reading, you could probably read the entire article in the time it takes most people to read an abstract. Your new skill may allow you the luxury of reading the original in light of your own specific information target zone, rather than relying on an abstract prepared by someone else.

If you are online, you would have several options available at this stage. You could read from the screen, print it out on your printer, or you might request that it be printed offline or photocopied at the source and mailed to you. (Document delivery services can locate, photocopy, and deliver documents overnight if necessary. The amount of detail and the speed required determine the cost.)

Once you have the magazine (complete text or abstract), microfilm, on-screen text, book, or other written source in front of you, apply the steps of Active Reading. Begin by quickly previewing the source material with one of the levels of grokking. This will tell you if your information target zone is truly there or if you need to go to another source. Many times, particularly if it is a research project of small scale, you can achieve your purpose at this stage: you determine whether the article will be of use. In more complex projects, previewing is valuable because it can familiarize you with the written piece. You will understand how it is organized and get a sense for where your target is most likely located in the article.

Once you have completed this stage, take a moment to define your purpose, ask questions, and anticipate answers. If your purpose is complex, it is wise to make a mind map. Then proceed through the source using Active Reading principles. Move quickly through the articles using one of the stages of grokking and stop when you get a HIT.

As you read through the article, begin a mind map of the content that hit your information target zone. This will aid you in encoding the information in your brain and will be a valuable resource if you need to use the information later.

Utilize the Information to Fulfill Your Purpose

Just locating the information is usually not your purpose. You have probably undertaken the research in order to complete a report or a paper, prepare a speech, or make a decision. The value of information resides in the action that results, converting it into knowledge.

TRY THIS: A PRACTICAL EXAMPLE

Let's try a practical example of a specific research project and apply all that you have learned.

Imagine you are on the board of directors of a large and prosperous company. The board wants to hear suggestions for a new project that can benefit the community and increase productivity of future employees. You believe that one of the biggest drains on productivity is the failure of the local education system to properly prepare young people for the working world. You want to suggest some ways in which your company might become involved in a project to improve the quality of education in the local schools. You only have three hours to prepare your suggestions in time for the board meeting.

Let's go through one possible approach.

Begin by making your information target zone mind map. Make certain you note the purpose, questions, anticipated answers, and any keywords you think might apply. After you have completed the mind map, evaluate the level of detail required to achieve the purpose.

Then decide which subdivision of the information landscape would contain the most current, relevant, and easily accessible source for hitting your information target zone: periodicals? newsletters? books? specialized reference sources? government documents? database sources? people and organizations? In this case, the level of detail required is minimal and your time is short. You might therefore select a current magazine article as the most likely source for your needs.

The next step is to see whether there are any magazine articles on this topic. What would be the most likely telescope to help you look into the subdivision of magazine articles? Would you want an index that would lead you into education magazines, business magazines, or general magazines? What keywords would guide you in the search?

There are numerous ways to get a bibliographic record of potential sources. If you are a subscriber to a databank, you could access a periodical index for either business or educational magazines. One databank, DIALOG, has a feature that allows you to search large groups of their databases with a single command. If you had access only to a library, you could begin with *Reader's Guide to Periodical Literature* or a CD-ROM database if the library has one.

The following search comes from Wilsondisc, a CD-ROM version of the *Business Periodicals Index* from the H. W. Wilson Company. I started with the keywords "business/schools." The following data came up on the screen. As you go through this list, which keyword heading do you think would be the most likely to use as your next clue to pursue your goal?

RECORDS	SUBJECT
*	BUSINESS/STATISTICS
*	BUSINESS/STUDY AND TEACHING
*	BUSINESS/TAXATION
6	BUSINESS/ TERMINOLOGY
*	BUSINESS, INTERNATIONAL
*	BUSINESS, SALE AND PURCHASE OF
16	BUSINESSLAND, INC.
30	BUSINESSMEN
13	BUSINESSMEN AS TEACHERS
15	BUSINESSMEN IN GOVERNMENT
*	BUSINESSMEN IN POLITICS
1	BUSINESSMEN/BAHRAIN
6	BUSINESSMEN/CANADA

It seems likely that "Businessmen as Teachers" is the closest, yet it still may not feel like a HIT to you. The next step would be to have the computer supply any related keywords in order to get you closer to your information target zone. By requesting related terms, you would find the following. Which one would you pursue next?

RECORDS	TERM
13	BUSINESSMEN AS TEACHERS
See also: 33	EDUCATION
351	EDUCATION AND INDUSTRY
17	TEACHERS

From this list, "Education and Industry" feels like a stronger HIT, and it offers 351 magazine articles that might have information to satisfy your purpose. With so many possible sources within your general target area, your chances of quickly finding what you need are greatly increased.

You can then instruct the database to display the bibliographic citations for all these articles. The next step would be to go through the citations and locate the magazines that appear to be HITS. If you get enough HITS that you feel can satisfy your purpose, you can then move on to the next stage: looking at some magazine articles themselves.

There is not enough space here to list all 351 citations, but here are some representative references to complete this exercise. Go through the list quickly and note each citation that seems to be a HIT. Select the ones that you want to pursue further. Use your mind like a magnet. Remember, your aim is not to eliminate the ones you don't want; a quicker method is to find the ones you do want.

SUBJECT IS EDUCATION AND INDUSTRY

Iacocca, Lee A.
A challenge to teachers (speech excerpt; National Education Association conference)
Across the Board v26 p43–8 June '89

Freundlich, Naomi J.
Business goes to college (backing university labs)
Business Week vsp issue p50+ '89 Innovation in America

Dawes, Joseph
The business-education link (employers encourage parental involvement in education)
Nation's Business v77 p27 June '89

William Woodside
Ignorance threatens companies (public education reform)
Fortune v120 p69–70 July 3 '89

McGuire, E. Patrick
Education: Business goes back to school (1989 forecast)
Across the Board v26 p36 January–February '89

Horton, Thomas R.
Children and the corporation
Management Review v78 p5–6 January '89

Salkind, Michael
University-industry cooperation is key to bolstering technology base
Aviation Week & Space Technology v129 p95+
December 5 '88

Muller, Helen J.; Porter, James L.; Rehdner, Robert R.
Have the business schools let down U.S. corporations?
Management Review v77 p24–31 October '88

Hallett, Jeffrey
Training and education: the competitive edge
Personnel Administrator v33 p24+ September '88

McGill, Michael E.
Attack of the biz kids (MBAs and American industry)
Business Month v132 p75–8 December '88

Perry, Nancy J.
Saving the schools: how business can help (special report)
Fortune v118 p42–6+ November 7 '88

Murray, Michael L.
Investing in excellence (insurance industry support of university insurance education)
Best's Review (Property/Casualty Insurance Edition) v89 p50–1 July '88

Galagan, Patricia A.
Joining forces: business and education take on
competitiveness
Training and Development Journal v42 p26–9 July '88

Halcrow, Allan
Invest in the future work force (college-entry assistance
program)
Personnel Journal v67 p14–15 May '88

Anderson, David
The crisis in business management: is technology outpacing
the development of good managers?
Research & Development v30 p25 March '88

Altany, David R.
Campus cooperation: links with academia foster forward
thinking
Industry Week v236 p21 February 1 '88

Business Periodicals Index, Data Coverage: July 1982 through September
1989. Copyright the H. W. Wilson Company.

From this sample list, one seems to hit right on the information target zone: the article by Nancy J. Perry, "Saving the schools: how business can help" (special report), *Fortune*, November 7, 1988. Given that it is fairly current (at the time this search was made) and from a credible source, you might surmise that it would be worth your effort to explore.

The next step would be to locate the article and read it to see if it contains what you need. As you do this, you can apply all you know as a Master of the Information Age. You would begin by previewing it to verify that it contains what you need. Keeping your purpose in mind, you would then use the Active Reading techniques to go through the article.

When I originally performed this search in the library, I made a photocopy of the article and went through it making notes with colored pens and underlining specific portions. I then used these notations to prepare a mind map of the article. While this is only an exercise, if I had had to give a report to the board of directors, the entire project would have taken less than one hour to complete.

I encourage you to locate this article yourself and give this exercise a try.

THE MASTER'S SEARCH

This chapter has provided you with a broad overview of the information landscape. With it, you should now feel comfortable any time you need to seek out information. If you have any questions about the various subdivisions or about how you would go through the steps of a research project, review the relevant pages of this chapter. You are now well on your way to being a true Master of the Information Age.

RESOURCES

Research

Glossbrenner, Alfred. *How to Look It up Online*. (New York: St. Martin's Press, 1987). Outlines numerous search options available including a comprehensive resource guide.

Horowitz, Lois. *Knowing Where to Look*. (Cincinnati: Writer's Digest Books, 1988). This book covers all aspects of research possibilities designed to make finding information easier.

McCormick, Mona. *The New York Times Guide to Reference Materials*. (New York: Signet, 1986). This updated version covers the many subdivisions of the information landscape.

Roszak, Theodore. *The Cult of Information*. (New York: Pantheon, 1986). A provocative book on the implications of the computer revolution on thinking skills.

Services

DIALOG Information Services (1-800-334-2564), 3460 Hillview Avenue, Palo Alto, CA 94304.

BRS Information Technologies (1-800-468-0908), 1200 Route 7, Latham, NY 12110.

CHAPTER 11

SHARE INFORMATION EFFECTIVELY

This chapter will help you increase your skills in both writing and speaking. We will explore a six-step program, useful in any situation, to plan and develop your communication abilities in a complete and effective manner. We will then examine practical tips on how to improve your writing and speaking skills in one-to-one, large-group, and small-group presentations.

The topic of communication skills is enormous. This chapter, therefore, is intended to be an overview rather than an indepth analysis of the subject. It will provide you with basic skills and show you how to apply them. Many people simply do not practice effective communication; they know what they should do, they just don't do it. These suggestions, if followed, will help you maximize your talents as a good communicator.

■ ■ ■ ■

The higher you go, the wider spreads the network of communication that will make or break you. It extends not only to more people below, but to new levels above. And it extends all around, to endless other departments and interests interacting with yours.

Donald Walton

A true master of the Information Age is skilled not only in gathering, accessing, and processing information, but also in sharing information effectively with others. Whether it is writing a memo or term paper, conducting a small group meeting with several colleagues about a work problem, or presenting a lecture to an audience, a master knows how to transmit his message clearly, succinctly, and purposefully.

Whatever the situation, the effectiveness of any communication is measured in terms of the results obtained. Whether you want to convince someone to take an action or make a decision, or you simply want to convey to others the knowledge you possess, your goal is to achieve *a purpose*. In terms of the skills you have learned in this book, it might be said that your goal is to make it as easy as possible for the receiver to locate his Information Target Zone within your communication.

THE SIX-STEP PREPARATION

Regardless of the nature of your communication, there are six fundamental steps that can lead you to effective presentations. The speed with which you can complete each of these steps may differ according to the situation. For example, the preparation for writing a letter or making a phone call may take only a minute, while writing a complex report may require weeks. However, if you use this six-step preparation for either of these situations, you will increase your chances of success. As you become more accustomed to using these steps, they will naturally become part of your communication habits. The six steps include the following:

1. Identify your desired results.
2. Identify the information necessary to achieve the desired results.
3. Identify the most efficient form and style of communication.
4. Prepare a mind map of your communication.
5. Visualize your communication.
6. *Cook* the communication by letting it stew in your unconscious.

In examining these steps, note that the first four require a logical and conscious analysis of the communication. The last two encourage your creative unconscious to assist you in the planning phase. The benefits of this six-step preparation are numerous. Taken together, they will help you:

- clarify your thinking
- crystallize your purpose for sharing the information
- engage your whole brain
- deepen your understanding of the subject matter
- plan in advance for contingencies
- get your conscious and unconscious mind involved in the information-gathering process
- organize your written or spoken presentation
- enhance your creativity
- ascertain the most effective means of communication
- consider the needs of your receivers
- produce results-oriented planning
- prepare to communicate simply, efficiently, and clearly

■ ■ ■ ■

LEARNING ACTIVATOR #36
IDENTIFYING A CURRENT COMMUNICATION TASK

Before we begin the six-step preparation, take a moment to identify a need you have now to communicate information to others. Perhaps you need to write a memo within the next few days, or you are working on a report. You may have a speech to give or a one-to-one meeting with a colleague or supervisor. The nature of your communication is not important, but think of a situation now so that you can use it to learn the process. Write out your communication task in the space below.

■ ■ ■ ■

As you proceed through each of the six steps, answer the questions posed or perform the tasks requested. An example is provided to help you with this process.

STEP ONE: IDENTIFYING YOUR PURPOSE. As in Active Reading, you begin any communication task by defining your purpose. This includes two aspects:

- identifying what *you* want to get from the communication, such as a decision, an action, or the sharing of a point of view
- identifying what you want *the other person* to get from the communication, such as general information or specific data upon which to make a decision or take an action

Begin every communication preparation with the question *What do I want to be the result of my sharing this information, both for me and for the recipient?* Then, don't just think of the answer to that question, *write it down*. The process of writing helps you bring in more of your "whole brain" as your kinesthetic and visual senses become involved in the process.

The palest ink lasts longer than the most retentive memory.

A Chinese proverb

Example: My purpose is to communicate to my supervisor that Project X is now running two weeks behind schedule. My goal is to obtain a decision about whether or not I should hire a temporary assistant to help get the job done. I want him to feel assured that I have done all that is within my power, and that hiring this help will bring the project to a close.

STEP TWO: IDENTIFY THE NECESSARY INFORMATION. This step is intended to help you determine what information is necessary to accomplish your purpose. Initially, it is best to approach this step in a free-thinking, brainstorming session designed to generate ideas. Following this session, you must refine your ideas by identifying more specifically the various particular pieces of information that must be communicated in order to achieve your desired result.

The ultimate question to be answered in step two is *In order to achieve the results I desire, what specific information will the recipient need?* Will he or she need facts or financial data or opinions from friends, colleagues, or experts? Will he or she need a well-thought-out strategy and a step-by-step plan? Use your critical and active thinking processes in this stage. It is useful, in fact, to mind map your conclusions to this step before moving on to the next step.

Example: I will show my superior the history of Projects so that he will understand what remains to be done. I will also need to show him a projected cost of hiring temporary help.

STEP THREE: IDENTIFY THE MOST EFFECTIVE TYPE OF COMMUNICATION. In this step, your goal is to determine the most effective way to communicate in order to get your desired result. In some instances, your choice will be predetermined for you. However, many people seldom consider that they have different options. The following are typical questions you might ask yourself in this step.

- Should the communication be made in a phone call or face-to-face with the person?
- Does my communication absolutely require a written form and, if so, should it be long or short?
- If there are a number of people involved, what is the best way to insure that my purpose is achieved?
- What can make my communication have the highest degree of clarity?
- What supporting material, such as graphs, charts, and tables, is necessary to accomplish my purpose?
- How does the learning style of the recipient fit in and how can I tailor my presentation to fit that style?

The discipline of writing something down is the first step toward making it happen.

Lee Iaccoca

This step can be fun and creative because it allows you to explore the many media that exist to carry your message.

Example: I know my supervisor prefers to hear about problems in person. This is clearly not a situation for a phone call or a memo, so I should schedule an appointment to see him. It would be useful to present a visual flow chart of the project history along with a financial analysis of the costs involved.

STEP FOUR: PREPARE A MIND MAP. At this stage you are ready to organize the information you have generated during the previous phases of the six-step preparation. It may be that your communication is simple and you will already have all of the

After all, most writing is done away from the typewriter, away from the desk. I'd say it occurs in the quiet, silent moments, while you're walking or shaving or playing a game, or whatever, or even talking to someone you're not vitally interested in.

Henry Miller

information you need. If you require additional refinement, however, the most effective way is to prepare a mind map.

Use large sheets of paper for your mind map, especially if you have a complex project. This gives your creativity room to work. Your mind map is a whole-brain representation of your communication task and will form the basis for what you are going to say or write. Gabriele Lusser Rico, author of *Writing the Natural Way*, calls the mind-map technique *clustering* and Henriette Anne Klauser, author of *Writing on Both Sides of the Brain*, calls it *branching*. Both authors recommend the technique as the starting place for all writing.

STEP FIVE: VISUALIZE YOUR COMMUNICATION. By this point you have utilized the full power of your conscious mind to plan steps one through four. In this step, however, you will activate your unconscious creativity using the following visualization technique. As you do this or any other results-oriented visualization, assume success, and act as if you cannot fail. Read the following directions and apply the visualization technique to your purpose.

1. Close your eyes and relax. Use alpha breathing or one of the other relaxation techniques you have learned.
2. Imagine that your written or spoken communication is producing the result you desire. Imagine the recipient taking the action you desire as the outcome of your communication, such as making a decision, agreeing with you, or returning your memo with notes.
3. Run your visualized *movie* backwards and forwards in your mind's eye several times. Allow the image of what you desire to refine itself. Imagine as clearly as you can what information you need in order to achieve your intended result. You are the producer and director of the visualization. Allow the images to unfold and add anything that is necessary to ensure success.

As you are imagining this, note any questions that the recipient might raise, either vocally or in his mind. Clarify what additional information you need to communicate. Imagine what visual aids you could use that would help your communication to succeed.

Example: I realized that my supervisor might even ask me if I should hire two people, because my *movie* re-emphasized how important this project is to him. Knowing this now, perhaps I should prepare a flow chart that compares the effects that one or two additional workers would have on the project.

STEP SIX: COOK YOUR COMMUNICATION.   In many instances, you will be ready for effective communication after the completion of step five. Using your mind map as your guide, you can now prepare your talk or write an effective letter, memorandum, or report. In complex situations, however, it can be advantageous to mull over your preparatory work for a few hours or days if you have the time. This allows the unconscious to generate suggestions for improvement.

This *cooking* period can be useful in creating new ideas and approaches. I am sure that you have already experienced a situation in which your best ideas came when you were not even thinking consciously about a situation. How many times have you solved a difficult problem while shaving, taking a bath, exercising, taking a stroll, or any number of unrelated activities?

In chapter 4, we examined the power of your intuition. Many successful business people and leaders recognize that their intuition, springing from the depths of their minds, is often more right than wrong. Give yourself the luxury of not thinking about the particular communication need and you probably will be surprised at the new ideas that can result.

Dreams too can prove to be creative and important sources of ideas. Significant evidence suggests that you can even program your dreams to help you find answers to problems in your life. This last step completes the preparation stage and you are ready to take action.

WRITING WITH A PURPOSE

Effective writing skills are a necessity for a master of the Information Age. An ability to write clearly, sharply, and persuasively is a key to success and can be developed by anyone

The ultimate creative capacity of the brain may be, for all practical purposes, infinite.

George Leonard

who can think clearly. Many corporate CEOs I have spoken with single out the lack of good writing skills as one of the major barriers to advancement on the corporate ladder.

Many texts and teachers divide the writing process into two stages. In the first stage, you creatively generate the basic flow of ideas and information. In the second stage, you edit this flow into a logical, clear, and concise written piece. As we saw in chapter 7 when looking at how writers write, there are clear patterns to good writing that are worth following.

The Creative Phase

In some cases, you will not find it necessary to tarry in this creative phase before writing. You feel certain about your purpose, and the six-step preparation will easily lead you to the writing stage. Other times, however, you may feel an enormous obstacle standing between you and getting started. Commonly called writer's block or cramp, an overarching term signifying a vast number of problems, it may feel as if all your preparation was for naught. One explanation of how and why this happens is that your logical left brain is stifling the creative, free-flowing idea process occurring in your right brain.

However, there is a simple way to allow your right-brain creativity to come forth. In this method you begin writing without consciously paying attention to what you are writing. This technique has been variously called rapid writing, free writing, stream of consciousness, or right-brain writing, and its purpose is to separate the creative-writing phase from the editing phase, the right-brain functions from the left-brain functions. Two steps in this approach are:

1. Look at your mind map and allow your whole brain to soak in the images and feelings expressed therein.
2. Begin writing anything and continue to write without looking at what you are writing. To do this you can turn the screen off on your word processor, flip pages over once you have written them, or even close your eyes.

Keep any analysis out of the way and just write without *paying conscious attention to your writing*. Trust the power of your mind and keep writing without judgment about your words or your thought process. This stage is a personal brainstorming session in which you allow your ideas to come forth, saving your critical evaluation until later. This step can help pull you through the "writers wall" by just getting whatever words come to mind on paper.

Once you have completed writing in this style and read what you have produced, you can begin the more left-brain critical task of fine tuning your thoughts and paring them down to their essence.

Creativity involves breaking out of established patterns in order to look at things in a different way.

Edward de Bono

The Revising and Editing Phase

This second stage of writing involves working with your initial creative draft to develop it into clear, logical, and powerful writing. In this stage, your left brain's sequential and critical attributes come into play. Your goal at this point is to edit and rewrite so that your freewriting will communicate the essence of what you want to say.

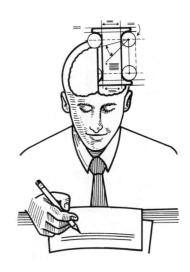

The most important criterion now is to examine the writing from the point of view of the reader. Look again at your mind map. Have you fulfilled your purpose? What is the relationship between the points you wish to make? Is there a logical sequence in which they should be presented? Are some points major ideas while others are secondary themes branching from the former?

Once you determine the logic of your presentation, you can focus on your choice of words. It is helpful to organize your writing first, paragraph by paragraph, and then go back to each one to perfect your style. Consider the following aspects of good writing.

Brevity. There are many excellent books on writing but one of the most helpful and concise is the *The Elements of Style* by William Strunk, Jr. and E.B. White. In this classic book, the suggested elements of style are set forth in numbered rules. For a master of the Information Age, I believe the most relevant and noteworthy of these is Rule 17: *omit needless words.* Your writing will be most powerful if it gets to the point as briefly as possible.

Every writer has the responsibility to edit his own work. Once you have completed writing anything, apply the following tests.

- Are there extra words or paragraphs that don't add to the meaning of my message?
- Can I say this in a simpler way and still achieve my objectives?
- Is my work redundant or overwritten? Have I said the same thing more than once?
- Have I been direct? Are there too many qualifying adverbs or adjectives that weaken my argument or make it sound vague? Have I used strong verbs rather than strings of nouns? (For example, rather than write "In his explanation, he told me the following information," you can write simply: "He explained this point to me.")

CLARITY IS THE KEY TO GOOD WRITING. In addition to brevity, clarity is equally important. There is only one test for the success of any communication: the response you receive. As you write consider the following guidelines for clarity.

Who is my audience? How much do they already understand about this topic? Is there anything about the learning style of my audience that I should take into consideration? Should I modify the writing to meet their learning style, that is, do they need to get a feel for it, picture the idea, or hear what is being said?

Would my audience benefit from the use of graphics or illustrations to understand my message? Most word-processing software now includes a graphic component that allows you to insert drawings, charts, tables, and pictures into your text.

Can I make my message more powerful by presenting an aspect of it in the form of a metaphor? For example, you will recall that in chapter 2 of this book, I used the metaphor of running your brain like a business to convey the concept of actively taking control of your beliefs in order to succeed rather than letting yourself succumb to any habitual negative thought processes. The unconscious mind and the right brain can gain tremendous insight through the use of metaphor representing an underlying message in your communication.

Have I anticipated the questions my reader might have, and have I answered them? During the preparatory stage in which you visualized the recipient reading your written piece, you may have imagined the reader questioning certain portions of your text. Use this to your advantage by structuring your content to include answers to questions the reader might have.

Have I clarified what my reader's purpose is for reading the written piece? Do I want a decision? Do I want an action taken? Do I want the reader to learn something new? By taking such questions into account, you can structure your writing to "prime their mental radar" so that you can achieve your desired results.

One of the most direct ways to acheive this is to include a clear and concise statement of the results you want to achieve. For example, in this book, I have used a statement of objectives to begin each chapter.

Do I have a clear progression in my argument for logical consistency? Have I explained the relationship between the parts? Am I trying to prove a cause-effect argument, and if so, have I clearly demonstrated the linkage? Am I explaining a sequential process, and if so, have I left out any of the steps? Are there other ways I could organize my writing to make it more sound? Review your mind map and see if you have incorporated all of the components you listed while doing the six-step preparation.

Writing Letters and Memos

Of all the complaints senior managers make about what they read, the most frequent is: "Most of the letters and memos I receive are a waste of my time." Consider the following tips when writing a letter or memo.

LETTERS.

- Keep them short, less than one page if possible. With so much information floating across everyone's desk, your point will be more appreciated when it is made quickly.

We do not write in order to be understood; we write in order to understand.

C. Day Lewis

Clutter is the disease of American writing. We are a society strangling in unnecessary words, circular constructions, pompous frills and meaningless jargon.

William Zinsser

Two Ways to Stimulate Creative Thinking and Generate New Ideas

▪ The goal is to produce the greatest *quantity* of ideas. The assumption is that a larger total number of ideas will produce a larger number of useful ones.

▪ Save all evaluations for later. Judgment is to be suspended during the brainstorming session, and all ideas accepted equally.

- Leave a wide margin so that the reader can make notes.
- Break up long paragraphs.
- Give an immediate explanation (in the first sentence, for example, or using a separate reference in the upper right hand corner) of the subject matter and purpose of the letter.
- Use a conversational tone; write to communicate, not impress.
- Use typographic style changes: underline, capitalize. Use headings and sub-headings.
- Use graphics. If you have a graphics program on your word processor, add a relevant chart or table. Be creative. Step outside of your letter-writing comfort zone.
- Ask directly for what you want. Let the reader know exactly what results you desire.
- Use a postscript (P.S.). Studies show that the postcript in any letter receives the highest level of attention.

MEMORANDUMS. Many of the tips from the foregoing list are equally applicable to memo writing. In addition, the following will help you achieve your desired results in writing memos.

- Begin with a concise summary of the reader's purpose for receiving the memo. If it is a long memo, this can take the form of an executive summary.
- Note your *purpose* for writing the memo.
- List the *reasons* you desire those results, including examples and facts that support the purpose.
- Note the possible alternatives that exist and the specific action you are requesting.
- Keep memo simple and to the point.
- Indicate the date or time you expect to receive a response, a decision, or to have action taken.

SPOKEN COMMUNICATION: ONE-TO-ONE INTERACTIONS

Most spoken communication happens in a one-on-one forum via a phone call or a face-to-face meeting. As a result, good interpersonal communication skills are an essential tool for a master of the Information Age. It is therefore vital that you understand how to present information in a way that takes into consideration the individual with whom you are speaking.

Understanding the learning style of your recipient is a major element in accomplishing this. Some people learn best by *seeing*, others by *feeling*, and still others by *hearing*. Consider the following paradigms of three personality types.

1. *Doers* are oriented toward action and want to know and achieve immediately the desired results. This kind of person tends to rely most heavily on the *visual* sense.
2. *Feelers* are oriented toward touch. This kind of person tends to rely on the *kinesthetic* sense.
3. *Thinkers* are methodical, deliberate, and critical. This person tends to process information using the *auditory* sense.

Whenever you deal with any system that tends to categorize people into niches, bear in mind that we all are a combination of the various types. However, most people will tend to have one mode of learning more dominant than others. You have no doubt experienced this before. For example, imagine that you are trying to explain how to use a computer to hook into a database. The visual person would prefer to see an explanation using photos and illustrations, the feeling person would prefer to sit at the machine and actually try the equipment, and the thinking person would tend to prefer receiving a verbal overview. Whatever the case, you need to consider the style of the recipient and construct your language and presentation techniques to match his or her individual needs.

If you know a person beforehand, you can sometimes pick up clues about their learning style by listening to them. Since people tend to speak in terms associated with their primary learning sense, you can let their language direct you toward the proper approach. The following list of words gives you a general guide for expressions to notice.

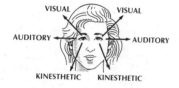

Visual	Auditory	Kinesthetic
an eyeful	tune in	boils down to
view of	sound/noise	feeling for
looks like	clear as a bell	a handle on
image/picture	an earful	grasp/feeling
paint a picture	divulge	in touch with
glimpse of	enunciate	come to grips
appear	mention	catch on
focus	speak about	feel
illustrate	tell	share
show	rings a bell	tap into
watch	loud	hands on
perspective on	talk about	feels right
hazy/clear	grant an audience	soft/hard
examine	inquire into	fondle

If you speak in a language that carries the information in a learning mode that is compatible for your listener, your communication will be more successful. Using the above clues, what would you expect to be the most efficient way to communicate information to a person who says, "I would like to speak with you tomorrow and listen to your opinion on the matter." Or if they said, "See me tomorrow and give me your view," or "Get ahold of me sometime tomorrow and give me your feelings."

Other clues besides language can help too. One is the rate and tone of speech. Visual learners tend to talk rapidly and in a high pitch as they are trying to keep up with images running through their mind. Auditory learners tend to talk in a steady, precise, sometimes monotonous manner, as though they are repeating the words they are hearing. Kinesthetic learners are slower talkers, using low tones since they need the extra time to translate feelings into words.

By observing eye movements too, you can get additional information on how a person processes information. As a general rule, the pupils of the eye tend to dilate when a person is deeply interested in the subject of the communication. Also, a person who is processing information visually tends to look up (toward the visual cortex) when thinking, an auditory processor tends to move the eyes in lateral movements (toward the auditory cortex) and a kinesthetic-oriented learner tends to look downward (into the body).

Monitor the Listener's Level of Understanding

In chapter 4, we discussed the elements of good listening that you can implement. But the other side of this issue, equally important to effective one-to-one communication, is to consider how well your listener is listening to you. Many people do not listen actively, and without even knowing it, they can completely miss the information *you* want to convey.

It is therefore useful to remember in your communication to get feedback from your listener. Don't *assume* that your message has been heard as you intended it; verify by asking direct questions throughout the conversation. Even a request as simple as "Would you explain to me your understanding of what I just said" can go a long way in assuring that your communications are effective.

Don't be hesitant to monitor the response you are getting. If another person reacts unfavorably to your request for feedback, chances are understanding is not taking place. Creating this feedback loop is essential to enable you to obtain the results you desire.

Another important factor to consider when talking to people is nonverbal communication. Studies have shown that as little as 7 percent of understanding comes from the actual words used, whereas the primary carriers of the message are the tone of voice (40 percent) and the posture, gestures, and facial expressions (53 percent). This suggests that no matter how carefully you choose your words or how brilliantly you craft your argument, your communication can be ineffective because of the tone of voice you use or body movements you make.

Following are some tips to consider to ensure that tone and body language do not interfere with your communication.

- Find out how your voice is received by others. The most direct way to do this is to ask your friends or coworkers for feedback. You can also record a sample conversation and then listen objectively to your manner of speaking.

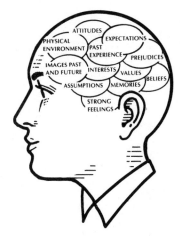

First learn the meaning of what you say, and then speak.

Epictetus

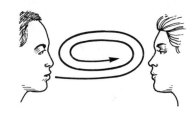

295

- Talk *with*, not *to*, another person. Recognize that communication is a two-way street and be aware of the other person's needs.
- Be mentally present during the conversation. Keep your attention focused on the conversation. Practice the steps to active listening as presented in Chapter 4.
- Maintain eye contact with the other person.
- Smile and stay relaxed.
- Use touch if appropriate to reassure your listener that you have heard their message.
- Actively listen to the response you are getting.
- Listen to what you are saying and how you are saying it. Would you like to be talked to in that way?
- Continually express your points in terms of value to the listener—what is in it for him?
- Keep your body posture open.

According to Madelyn Burley-Allen, a communications-seminar leader and author of *Listening: The Forgotten Skill*, the following physical behaviors are common and tend to exert a negative influence on the effectiveness of communication.

- raising an eyebrow
- frowning
- looking away from the listener
- rolling your eyes
- stiff posture
- behaving restlessly
- sighing
- rotating your head from side to side
- slumping in your chair
- having a critical expression
- drumming your fingers
- puffing your cheeks
- pulling back the corners of your mouth
- swishing your foot
- bouncing your leg

Monitor yourself the next time you are talking with someone and see if any of these traits are part of your communication style.

LARGE-GROUP PRESENTATIONS

Getting ready for a group presentation begins with the same six-step preparation you learned earlier. In some cases, you may be able to make the presentation directly from the mind map you created in the preparation stage. For other presentations, however, you may need to refine your content and method of delivery. The following tips will help you get the results you desire in any group presentation.

Define Your Audience

You may already have a clear understanding of your audience as a result of the six-step preparation. If not, you will need to consider the following in order to prepare and deliver your presentation effectively.

- How many people will be there?
- What is their age range?
- What are their interests?
- What about the local political and economic climate should be taken into consideration?
- What level of education do they have and how much do they understand about the topic you will address?
- What action will they have to take in order for you to achieve your purpose?
- What benefits can they expect to gain from your talk?
- How can the talk be tailored to meet their needs?

Practice

The first place to practice your presentation is in the auditorium of your own mind. Once you have made your mind map and have determined your approach, you should try a mental rehearsal. Visualizing the entire talk in a multisensory way can help you refine your content and delivery. Many great speakers acknowledge that they visualize every presentation before giving it. In their mind, they see their audience, hear themselves speaking, and feel themselves going through the presentation.

Learn from others. Although each of us has a unique speaking style, we can improve it by watching the experts speak. Next time you are enjoying a speech or seminar, take a moment to focus your attention and study the speaker's style and de-

297

livery. How does the person move on the stage? How does the speaker keep the audience interested and involved? How are questions handled? Take the masters as models and you will become one.

In addition to mental rehearsal the following practice tips will be helpful.

- Videotape your presentation or practice in front of a mirror so that you will have the opportunity to observe your body language and gestures.
- Give your talk in front of some friends or associates and listen to their feedback.
- Taperecord your speech and listen to the tone and inflections you are using.

Using Visual Aids

Don't try to communicate by words alone. Most people require and appreciate a visual component to accelerate their learning curve. Today, the accessibility and affordability of computer-generated graphics that can be converted to slides, overheads, or other projected forms has added great latitude to the scope of visual aids you can use to perk up your presentation and clarify your message.

If you don't have the time to prepare a graphic presentation or the scope of your presentation doesn't merit it, you can use flip charts to illustrate your main points. In some cases, if you create the flip chart illustrations *during* your presentation instead of ahead of time, you can generate more audience participation and help people assimilate the information faster. One special trick that helps in this is to place a small note on the flip chart sheets ahead of your talk. That way, when you are ready to write the points to illustrate your talk, you will not forget what you wanted to include.

It can also be useful for your audience if you tape the sheets of paper from the flip chart around the room as a subtle reminder of your message. Here are some tips on the use of graphics.

- Use color as much as possible in your graphics and keep them simple in content and form. Use different colored pens on flip charts to separate the points you write.

- Don't rush showing the visual aid. Leave it visible long enough that the slowest member of the audience can take in the information.
- Maintain contact with the audience while you are demonstrating with the visual aid. Don't talk to the screen or flip chart; they aren't listening.
- Always test your visual-aid equipment ahead of time. There is hardly a speaker in the world who cannot tell you a tragic story of arriving at their presentation only to discover that the equipment does not work.
- Make sure that the visual aid is visible from all parts of the room.

Arranging the Environment

Controlling the environment in which you make your presentation is an important factor in ensuring success. In this regard, use the information you have learned throughout this book to create a peak-learning ambience for your audience.

If appropriate, arrange to have music as background to the presentation. Make the setting as comfortable as possible and ensure that it is arranged for optimal learning. You can set up the room in several different arrangements, including theatre style, classroom style, and U-shape.

If you are going to use flip charts, I recommend using two of them, so that you can move back and forth between them to put some kinetic energy into the presentation. Movement keeps attention as long as it is not frenetic and contrived.

Always arrive at least thirty minutes before your presentation begins to make certain that the room is set up the way you want. Check the amplification and visual-aid systems to make certain they work properly. This advance monitoring can save you frustrating and distracting delays during your talk.

During the Presentation

Almost universally, people rank public speaking as high on their list of stressors as divorce and losing a job. If you are

The human brain is a wonderful organ. It starts to work as soon as you are born and doesn't stop until you get up to deliver a speech.

George Jessel

nervous before you begin, it is normal. Even if you have practiced your talk many times in mental rehearsal or actual rehearsal in front of a mirror, or have been coached by friends, the moment of truth comes when you actually step up to the front of the room. This event can be anxiety-provoking even for the person who does public speaking for a living.

If you have not done public speaking before, it will probably take a few presentations before you have the confidence to get beyond a memorized speech or three-by-five cards, but be easy on yourself. Eventually, you will be able to use a mind map to speak from, since it reflects the whole-brain thinking you have already put into preparation. Here are some additional tips on making a presentation:

1. Practice Alpha Breathing and the Quick-Change technique before you speak to relax you and give you positive messages about your success.
2. Deliver your talk in simple, direct, and unpretentious language. This means to *be yourself*. Many people take on a verbose or superficial personality when they speak in front of a group, thinking they must impress the audience with a formal speaking style. Keeping your language simple and direct is almost always more effective and more appreciated by your audience.
3. Develop a rapport with your audience in the first few minutes. Use humor, honesty, and sincerity to get the audience on your side.
4. Focus on and talk to different people in the audience. Make short visual contact with people in all sections of the audience as a way of developing a bond between you and the crowd. It also helps to keep your presentation personal and gives you the internal feeling of carrying on a conversation.
5. Don't let a negative reaction engage your focus. Concentrate on the positive reactions from the audience.
6. Control the room. Maintain your confidence and presence that gives you the control even if you aren't

actually feeling it. Act as if you are in charge and the audience will believe it.

7. Monitor the pitch, tone, and pace of your speech. Conciously allow yourself to increase or decrease those factors depending on the need.

8. As with writing, the most important rule in presenting information to a group is Strunk's Rule 17: *Omit needless words*. This admonition to keep it simple benefits both you and the audience.

There are many excellent books devoted to public speaking, as well as organizations you can join to learn and practice, such as ToastMasters. Many companies also sponsor public speaking groups. If your business does not, you may be able to initiate such a group.

SMALL GROUP PRESENTATIONS

You can make small group presentations more effective through the application of many of the principles in this book. By completing the six-step preparation, you will eliminate the most common error in small-group presentations—a lack of vision of desired outcome. Knowing what you want to accomplish and what information is necessary to accomplish it will significantly enhance your chances of success. The basic steps to an effective small-group presentation are:

1. Prepare an agenda. Make an outline or agenda that clearly sets forth the specific purpose of the presentation. Distribute the agenda to all participants *before the presentation*. This step will get their whole brain involved toward understanding the goal that has been set.

2. Encourage a feedback loop during the presentation. In a small group setting, it is particularly important to know if the recipients understand the information in order to save time and generate a close-knit group feeling. If you are the presenter, it is your job to make certain that the communication has been received and understood. One effective way of handling this is to

have the participants pair up or form groups and explain to each other what they understand to be the purpose and the meaning of the information you have presented.

3. Summarize. Either you or one of the participants should present a summary at the conclusion of the meeting that articulates the *essence* of the purpose and information. This summary should be written down immediately after the meeting and circulated to all of the partipants. If there are specific actions to take or decisions to make, write them down for all of the participants.

At this point, review the statement of purpose at the beginning of this chapter. Do you feel you have understood the six-step preparation program? If not, you may wish to take a moment to review the steps. Use this chapter as a succinct reference guide the next time you have a written or spoken communication to perform.

RESOURCES

Communication

Bolton, Robert. *People Skills.* (New York: Simon & Schuster, 1979). The author, originator of a number of seminars on communication, has included many tips on how to improve your own skills.

Carnegie, Dale. *Quick & Easy Ways to Effective Speaking.* (New York: Pocket Books, 1983). A short course by one of the masters.

Detz, Joan. *How to Write and Give a Speech.* (New York: St. Martin's Press, 1984). An excellent guide for both professionals and students.

Writing

Klausner, Henriette Anne. *Writing on Both Sides of the Brain.* (San Francisco: Harper & Row, 1986).

Rico, Gabriele Lusser. *Writing the Natural Way.* (Los Angeles: Jeremy P. Tarcher, 1983).

Zinsser, William. *Writing to Learn.* (New York: Harper & Row, 1988). An inspirational book on writing.

EPILOGUE

By reading this book, you have stretched yourself outside of your cocoon. As your intelligence continues to increase, new horizons will open up and you will no longer be able to live within your old confines. Congratulations on your willingness to move out beyond your comfort zone.

Throughout this book our emphasis has been on the practical and pragmatic. I have suggested many ways you can sharpen your thinking and sort out the information you obtain in your reading and conversations. You have learned about the importance of beliefs and how you have the power to control them; how to use your whole brain to achieve peak intelligence; how to improve your memory; how to use relaxation techniques to become a better learner; and how to enlist the subconscious as an ally. You have become familiar with how to find what you need in the information landscape and how to effectively share information with someone else. The techniques you have learned will give you a strong basis for more effective understanding and action.

But the true mastery of the Information Age means more than becoming adept in practical affairs. It also means becoming a broader, deeper, more fulfilled human being. Before we part company, I would like to share with you a few higher-level ideas to help round out the meaning of being a true master.

LIVE YOUR LIFE ON A HIGHER PLANE

I'm sure you have heard the expression, "You are what you eat." But have you ever thought of applying it not only to food, but to all the impressions that your senses take in? I believe that in a real sense we take in and metabolize thoughts, feelings, sounds, colors, smells, and so on, and turn them into *us*. As I pointed out in Chapter 3, we are the product of all the information that comes our way.

Thus if we want to live our life on a higher level, if we want to be a person of some depth and breadth and not be caught up in petty details and endless uninspiring activities and responsibilities, we have to take in a more elevated intellectual food. We have to learn to habitually direct our minds toward higher thoughts.

These two goals are closely connected. Putting any of the suggestions in this book into practice will make you realize that it *is* possible to affect the channels in which the mind flows. It may not be easy, particularly at first, but it is possible. Just as we can decide what company to keep, what books to read, and what shoes to put on, we can also exercise control over our thoughts, inviting higher and purer thoughts and turning away less lofty ones. As Edward Dimnet writes in *The Art of Thinking*:

> Certainly we cannot help thinking any more than we can help breathing, but, just as we can choose to breathe pure air in a pine wood on a high hill, we can place our mind where the images it will work upon will be of a higher nature.
>
> One of the places to find such images is in the study of great books and great lives. Great books deal with the issues the best minds and hearts of humanity have considered over the centuries. Great lives exemplify how the finest people have come to terms with the same issues of life that you confront every day. Our serious hours cannot be devoted to a more useful occupation than studying the lives or ideas of great men.

If you feed your body junk food, it will respond with less than optimum functioning. The same is true for your mind. Whenever you get a chance, feed it thoughts saturated with

So in all these little ways we spin a web, a cocoon, around ourselves. The cocoon becomes nice and snug and comfortable because it is very familiar. We know every little corner of our life; we can even write poetry about it. We may also have ideas about the "great mystery" which religions speak of, which gives our cocoon an especial sense of security: we can worship the great mystery outside of it and feel good about that. The cocoon is safe, bounded, claustrophobic, and a little stale. We settle into it and live our lives.

Jeremy W. Hayward
Perceiving Ordinary Magic

intelligence, beauty, and high ideals. Treat yourself to fresh air, beautiful scenery, great art, literature, and music—to whatever uplifts your spirit.

THINK LIFE-ENHANCING THOUGHTS

You can use your mind for selfish ends or to make a better world. In your daily life, you can be a source of negativity, criticism, complaints, and worse; or you can be a source of positivity, appreciation, truthfulness, and other life-supporting qualities.

Learn to appreciate others. In every situation, try to find what is positive, good, and uplifting. If you look, you will always find something. In every encounter, find something in the other person to appreciate, and tell the person about it.

> I appreciate your insight.
>
> I appreciate your candor.
>
> I appreciate your willingness to compromise.
>
> I appreciate your integrity in not being willing to compromise.

This is a subtle and challenging skill, but well worth learning.

Decide what is right and *do* it. Many public-opinion polls indicate that ethics—the study of right and wrong—will be a major concern of the nineties. Examine the way you live your life, congratulate yourself for your successes, and change the areas you are not proud of. Economic and material comfort are important aspects of life, but it is counterproductive to get so caught up in the quest for money and possessions that you blind yourself to higher-valued information.

SEE THE BIG PICTURE

Develop a mind that sees the big picture of life. Most of the problems in the world, both personal and social, come from narrow thinking and looking for expediency in the moment.

We need to think about implications and ramifications, about how the words we speak and the actions we perform affect the people we are close to and expand outwardly from

I will act as if what I do makes a difference.

William James

The danger of the past was that men became slaves. The danger of the future is that man may become robots.

Erich Fromm

Read the best books first, for you may not have the chance to read them all.

Thoreau

them to affect others. It is good to act not only on our own behalf, but for the greater whole. In this era when the balance is so delicate, we need to clarify and change our self-interest to comply with the interest of the planet, our fellow humans, and future generations.

The latest understanding of life, being expressed by environmentalists, ecologists, physicists, and by explorers of the inner realms of consciousness, is that the world is a *wholeness* in which all things and beings are interconnected. Peter Russell, in his book *The Global Brain* advances the theory that the human race is like the brain for the planet—each one of us a neuron in that brain. How we think and act, then, influences how effectively the global brain works. Any action (or thought) that harms any part ultimately harms the whole. Any action (or thought) that supports life in any part is life-supporting for the whole. Train your mind to see a larger picture of life. Some ways to do this:

- Read articles and books by people who have a broader view.
- Practice meditation to expand your conscious awareness.
- Practice the brain-stimulating exercises in the Learning Activators of this book.
- Develop a habit of thought that refuses to be tied into narrow boundaries of private interests and mental biases.

The world is changing. New economic, environmental, social, political, and interpersonal realities are being born throughout the world. Information in its many forms is the delivery room for this birth. Somewhere within the vast information landscape lie the technologies and ideas that you can convert into knowledge and use to benefit yourself, your career, your family, and the planet. Use the tools you have gained from this book to quickly find, extract, and process the information that supports you in this quest. Establish this goal as your information target zone. Trust your aim and shoot straight. Be a Master.

Read everyday something no one else is reading. Think everyday something no one else is thinking. It is bad for the mind to be always a part of unanimity.

Christopher Morley

And, most important, we have to shift our understanding of ourselves as separate individuals, each seeking our own welfare, to an understanding of how we fit into social, biological, and physical environments.

Robert Ornstein
Paul Ehrlich